BIOETHICS:
A CASEBOOK

BIOETHICS:
A CASEBOOK

MARK COPPENGER

Prentice-Hall, Inc., Englewood Cliffs, New Jersey 07632

Library of Congress Cataloging in Publication Data

Coppenger, Mark T.

  Bioethics: a casebook

  1. Medical laws and legislation—United States—Cases. 2. Bioethics—United States. I. Title.
KF3821.A7C67   1985   174'.95   84-17718
ISBN 0-13-078239-4

© 1985 by Prentice-Hall, Inc., Englewood Cliffs, New Jersey 07632

Printed in the United States of America

10 9 8 7 6 5 4 3 2 1

Editorial/production supervision
  and interior design: Virginia Cavanagh Neri
Cover Design: Lundgren Graphics, Ltd.
Manufacturing buyer: Harry Baisley

ISBN   0-13-078239-4   01

Prentice-Hall International, Inc., *London*
Prentice-Hall of Australia Pty. Limited, *Sydney*
Editora Prentice-Hall do Brasil, Ltda., *Rio de Janeiro*
Prentice-Hall Canada Inc., *Toronto*
Prentice-Hall of India Private Limited, *New Delhi*
Prentice-Hall of Japan, Inc., *Tokyo*
Prentice-Hall of Southeast Asia Pte. Ltd., *Singapore*
Whitehall Books Limited, *Wellington, New Zealand*

To Sharon, My Wife

CONTENTS

2

RIGHT TO CARE
AND TREATMENT 29

3

INFORMED CONSENT
TO TREATMENT 44

4

EXPERIMENTATION 92

5

PRIVACY 112

6

PROFESSIONAL STANDARDS 124

7

PUBLIC HEALTH AND SAFETY 138

8
GENETICS 155

9
BIOLOGY AND ETHICS:
OTHER ISSUES   172

GLOSSARY   205

PREFACE

A bioethical decision is an ethical decision that should be made in light of biological understanding. Failure to consult the life sciences here is failure to decide responsibly. So we must inquire of genetics, ecology, histology, or another of the allied sciences.

This is not to say that the bioethicist always or usually develops his own puzzles and then turns to the scientist for information. Indeed, life and medical scientists are often the very ones who raise the questions in their pioneering work. But whoever identifies the issues, the perspectives and special insights of the biologists are crucial to ethical choice. That has been my working principle for case selection.

These cases have proven to be good vehicles for teaching bioethics at Wheaton College. In this introduction to the text, I offer suggestions for their use in the classroom.

SOCRATIC TEACHING

The cases in this book provide excellent springboards for Socratic teaching. This is not to say that all Socratic teaching which springs from them will be excellent, or that all teaching which springs from them must or will be Socratic.

Socratic dialogue is not, first of all, jumbled discussion or an exercise in mutual ventilation. It is a cooperative pursuit of truth. This cooperation does not entail agreement on the various points at issue or a chummy spirit. The cooperation comes at the point of serious commitment to discovery and the elimination of confusion and error. It asks that the parties involved stick to the issue until it is resolved or a genuine impasse occurs.

Most people are incapable of sustaining pointed discussion. They drift and shift to something they've wanted to say in some context or other for some time. As the various hobby horses are mounted, the dialogue disintegrates. A strong leader, one not afraid to exercise authority, is virtually indispensable. Otherwise, the participants will avert their gaze on the question, declining to study it with care.

In settling an issue, one is, of course, free to range throughout the universe of ideas. A discussion of doctor/patient confidentiality need not stay fixed on doctors. It can easily extend to attorneys, the clergy, and beyond. Yet the links with the original matter should be made clear.

One simple method of control is to write the base question on the black-board, for example: "Is it ever morally permissible to let a radically defective newborn die when its life could be sustained?" or "Is it always wrong to sterilize retarded persons?" As the discussion strays into accounts of an uncle's retarded child who enjoyed painting and televised basketball or to sermons on the sexual irresponsibility of today's youth, you can point to the board and ask how that helps them get closer to an answer.

All this talk of control is not meant to suggest that you must have your answer in mind and that you will deflect any comments that do not clearly move toward your position. This is pseudo-Socratic teaching. If you insist upon ending with forceful advocacy of your own theory, then you might as well lecture and skip the preliminaries. The students will recognize the dialogue as nothing more than an exercise meant to create merely the appearance of give and take.

For the teaching to be truly Socratic, you must at least play the role of an honest inquirer. Whether or not you are settled in your own mind, you must give students' suggestions a fair hearing. Your impatience should come not at the fact that the discussion is moving toward the wrong answer, but that it is not moving toward any answer whatsoever. If you cannot, by pointed questioning, turn their thoughts where you will, you should not scuttle the whole enterprise, but continue to press whatever analysis you can. If your own view is correct, perhaps they will arrive at it on their own by means of their freshly honed analytic skills.

Among the sorts of questions you might ask are these:

What general rule then lies behind your decision?
Can you think of a situation where this rule might not work?
Have you thought how your rule might apply to this other case?
How does what you just said square with your earlier claim?
What exactly are you saying the doctor needs to do?
Are you saying that this would just be nice to do or that it should be demanded by law?
Here's a common criticism of your position. How do you answer it?

You've told us what in fact occurs. Now tell us whether it should occur and why.
Assuming that what you say is true, how would you convince the doctor that it is?
You didn't really answer the question. Let me put it another way.
Can you see any connection between these two decisions?
Is your rule so vague that anybody could embrace it?
Would you give us an example of the sort of thing you have in mind?

Each chapter begins with brief introductions to the cases. Those introductions suggest questions for both reading and class discussion. You will find as you read the cases that any number of profitable questions can be drawn from them. Because this is so, it's very difficult to categorize the cases. The Quinlan case, for example, could easily fit into a number of possible chapters. If there were a chapter on death and dying, it would suit since the judge takes note of the Harvard criteria for determining death. It could also fit within the chapter, "Right to Care and Treatment," since we might ask whether one in Karen's condition is due continued care, or whether she is no longer sufficiently human to enjoy human rights. In this book, the case is assigned to "Informed Consent to Treatment" because it prompts us to ask what one does when the patient is unable to give informed consent.

You should not, then, feel bound to handle a case in just one way. Extract or pose the questions which suit your teaching purposes. Perhaps you will find the introductory questions useful. If not, the great body of current literature, the words of the court opinions themselves, and your own imagination should well equip you with pointed questions.

TEAM TEACHING

When philosophers engage in ethical deliberation, they often employ imaginary "what if?" questions. Many of these questions are not only contrary to fact, but also contrary to reasonable expectation. For instance, one may ask what we should do if, by pressing a button which would annihilate a hermit Tibetan monk, we could save the world from war and disease forever. This is a good question for forcing a decision on end-justifies-means or lesser-of-two-evils thinking. But, of course, in the real world there simply is no such button, no such strategic opportunity.

This book's cases are, however, not only possible, but actual. And so they enjoy an immediacy the others do not. They provide an opportunity for testimony from a variety of disciplines. We would not call in a theologian, electrician, or sociologist to discuss the feasibility of wiring that monk. The practicality of the dilemma is beside the point. It is just a conceptual ploy. But in these legal opinions, there is good reason to scrutinize the data. Has the court gotten the facts right? Were the doctors laboring under a medical misconception?

Because the biologist or the medical scientist has something important to say in each of the book's areas, the text is also well suited for both team teaching and cross-disciplinary enrollments. Scientists and philosophers need each other in addressing these issues. Each specialty informs and sharpens its wits against the other. The science teacher or student can prepare to speak to the scientific aspects of the case, the philosophers to the philosophical. Of the scientists, we may ask such questions as the following:

In artificial insemination, are some fertilized eggs wasted or destroyed? (*Adoption of Anonymous*)

How reliable is amniocentesis? (*Gleitman* v. *Cosgrove*)

Where do things stand now with laetrile research? (*People* v. *Privitera*)

Is the medical theory behind acupuncture bogus? (*People* v. *Amber*)

What are the common guidelines for the treatment of lab animals? (*New Jersey SPCA* v. *Board of Education*)

What's happened to the snail darter? (*TVA* v. *Hill*)

How dangerous is it for nonsmokers in a smoke-filled room? (*Gasper* v. *Louisiana Stadium*)

What safeguards has the government imposed upon genetic research? (*Diamond* v. *Chakrabarty*)

The philosophers in turn can speak of duty and reprehensibility, of the Categorical Imperative and the Hedonistic Calculus.

This is not to suggest that the philosophers and scientists must keep silent on the other's discipline. Philosophers can profitably pick at the scientist's use of evidence while a morally sensitive scientist can expose a philosopher's ethical contortions. They can check each other at every point. But there is a natural division of basic contribution to the discussion.

There is a tendency in the literature to equate bioethics with medical ethics. This book does not ignore that practice, for most of these cases involve the work of physicians. But the field is properly as broad as the interface between biology and ethics. And so there are, for example, cases concerning endangered species and oil-spill-eating bacteria. I hope that such inclusions will help to attract science students who are not preparing for health professions.

A DISCLAIMER

The cases in this collection were chosen to arouse interest and provoke pointed discussion, not to equip you for litigation. Please do not think that reading them will make you legally informed. Consult an attorney or law librarian before you swing into action in the operating room, court room, or political caucus. A warning example should suffice: the U.S. Supreme Court ruling in *Rochin* v. *California* represents fresh law on the question of stomach pumping to acquire criminal evidence, but I chose the earlier *People* v. *One 1941 Mercury Sedan* because it included a survey of ways in which the bodies of suspects are scrutinized and invaded.

If we were attorneys at work with one of these cases, we would be most interested in the holding of the court (*ratio decidendi*); the court's rationale, commentary, or discussion (*obiter dictum*) would be of secondary importance. But we are bioethicists and the discussion is of most importance for our purposes. We do not plan to use the case in a legal argument from precedent, so the precise holding of the court is irrelevant. It's not where the court arrived but how it got there (or how one might get there) that concerns us.

If you find the court system or the structure of these opinions puzzling, there are some good books to help you. You might begin with Morris Cohen's venerable *Legal Research in a Nutshell*, particularly chapters 2 and 3 on judicial reports and case finding.

The cases should read smoothly. Thickets of legal jargon, jurisdictional dispute, and citation have been cleared. A short glossary at the end will cover the legal expressions which remain.

Let me offer one other word of warning. Don't confuse law with morality. There is properly a good deal of overlap; laws can and should be moral and moral behaviour can be permitted and encouraged by law. But the two spheres are not identical. For instance, the U.S. Supreme Court legitimized and enforced slavery in their 1850s Dred Scott Decision. This was law lacking moral rectitude. On the other hand, it is immoral but not illegal to make bigoted comments. Law neither can nor should prohibit all evil or demand all good. These cases are chosen not to establish moral truth but to provide lively occasions for the search for moral truth.

ACKNOWLEDGEMENTS

I'm indebted to both individuals and institutions. Wheaton College's bioethics course, and so my research, was supported by Philosophy Chairman Arthur Holmes and Academic Vice-Presidents Donald Mitchell and Ward Kriegbaum. Biology Professor Albert Smith was my congenial and effective teaching partner; he encouraged my search for cases from the start.

I've enjoyed access to and assistance in the law libraries of Northern Illinois University, The University of Chicago, Texas Tech University, The University of Missouri, Fort Sheridan, the Tarrant County (Texas) Civil Courts, the Missouri Supreme Court, University of Arkansas at Little Rock–Pulaski County, Murphy Oil Company, and U.S. Senior District Judge Oren Harris. And special thanks are due to Colorado attorney, Robert H. Sonheim, for locating the Lovato case, to Marna Howarth of the Hastings Center, to my secretary, Betty Monzingo, and to Doris Michaels, Barbara Bernstein, and Virginia Neri of Prentice-Hall.

My in-laws, the R. L. Souths, provided me a haven for the completion of this book. My wife and sons have graciously tolerated my research forays and the clutter with which I've returned.

BIOETHICS:
A CASEBOOK

1

REPRODUCTION

Pregnancy is, for some couples, the fulfillment of a dream. For others, it is seen as a curse. Bearing a child is momentous, and our emotions reflect our understanding that it is so.

Some of those who long for a child but who are unable to have one turn to alternatives of questionable moral status. Two of this chapter's cases concern the use of controversial reproductive options.

In *Adoption of Anonymous,* a woman's second husband wants to adopt her daughter. The first husband blocks the adoption. But is he indeed the father? For the sperm by which she was conceived was not his. The child is a product of artificial insemination using an anonymous donor. We see a division of courts here. *People* v. *Sorensen* says that he is the father. *Gursky* v. *Gursky* says that he isn't. What do you say?

Should the practice of artificial insemination be encouraged, tolerated but discouraged, or prohibited? Should infertile parents seek the latest technology or should they accept their infertility and move toward traditional adoption?

This case can serve to open discussion on such reproductive techniques as "test tube" (*in vitro*) fertilization and embyro transplants. At what point, if any, do we go too far in our efforts to have children?

Might there be a responsibility to seek or supply the most promising sperm for artificial insemination? Once we accept the practice, are we bound to think eugenically? Should society encourage gifted men to make their sperm available for the production of champion offspring? Or is this morally grotesque?

In *Doe* v. *Kelley*, we find a wife incapable of artificial insemination. In the couple's efforts to have a child anyway, they run afoul of a Michigan law forbidding a market in babies. While the judge does not rule out the possibility of surrogate motherhood, he does block this particular agreement because it involves the exchange of money.

Is the Doe's plan perverse? And even if it is, should it be declared illegal? Contrast this case with *Adoption of Anonymous*. There a third party donated semen. Here a third party donates ovum and womb. Are they on equal moral footing?

Would and should a defective baby or a surge of motherly attachment in Mary Roe disrupt the arrangement? Are the parties involved just flirting with disaster?

Turning now from those who welcome pregnancy to those who object to it, we find two similar concepts at work. When a defective child sues the doctor whose error made his miserable life possible, he employs the expression, "wrongful life." When the parents sue the doctor because of the burden the doctor's error imposed upon them, they speak of "wrongful birth." In the latter instance, the child may well be healthy. Such is the situation in *Terrell* v. *Garcia*.

Justice Barrow finds little merit in the parents' complaint. Justice Cadena is both sympathetic with the parents and convinced that the doctor should be penalized for his blunder. With which Justice do you side? Can you strengthen his argument?

"Wrongful life" gets a hearing in the next case, *Gleitman* v. *Cosgrove*. In the first month of her pregnancy Sandra Gleitman contracted German measles. Dr. Cosgrove did not emphasize the connection between this illness and birth defects. When Jeffrey was born, he suffered a variety of problems, and the Gleitmans sued Cosgrove.

They maintain that Jeffrey's life was wrongful and that it should have been aborted. Both Dr. Cosgrove and Judge Proctor take a dim view of this theory. Examine the judge's reasoning.

Do you think Judge Proctor would soften his position on abortion if the pregnant woman were a rape victim? Should he?

The next case *Roe* v. *Wade* comes at the abortion question squarely. The young woman represented by the fictitious name, Jane Roe, claims that the Texas antiabortion laws are unconstitutional. In this landmark decision, Justice Blackmun consults the history of ideas and current professional codes for direction and then charts the Court's course.

The decision contains the following curious passage: "We need not resolve the difficult question of when life begins. When those trained in the respective disciplines of medicine, philosophy, and theology are unable to arrive at any consensus, the judiciary, at this point in the development of man's knowledge, is not in a position to speculate as to the answer." Blackmun then proceeds to hand down a decision in which just such an answer is implicit.

There are both philosophical and scientific concepts at play regarding contraception. And so we must hear from both sides.

Some forms of "contraception" are actually methods of abortion. The intrauterine device and proposed morning-after pills cause the conceptus to die. Is there a morally relevant difference between the hours-old conceptus and the eight-month-old fetus?

Woods v. *Lancet* provides a different sort of occasion for considering the status of the fetus. During the ninth month of his development, Woods was injured. Since he was in the womb at the time, his right to recover for damages is contested. However, Judge Desmond declares that he has money coming. He reasons that a viable fetus has separate existence. Does this square with *Roe* v. *Wade*?

One might consider whether fetal damage from the mother is equivalent to fetal damage from a third party. For example, should her alcohol abuse be viewed in the same way as an attacker's blows to her abdomen or a doctor's malpractice?

Roe v. *Wade* spoke of a shift of policy from trimester to trimester. In *Jefferson* v. *Griffin Spalding County Hospital Authority*, we find a standoff late in the third trimester. If Jesse Mae Jefferson does not have a caesarean section, the child will die and her own life will be in peril. She asks that the court order requiring the section be put on hold. The Georgia Supreme Court refuses.

Do they have any right to force major abdominal surgery upon her? Is there indeed a duty to secure the life of this unborn child? And if so, is it so great as to warrant this bodily intrusion with its attendant discomforts?

What if the doctors wished to correct a life-threatening defect in a seven-month-old fetus and, to do so, they had to involve the mother in surgery? Should she be forced to face the knife for the fetus' sake? Where should we draw the line on such treatment?

Our final two cases concern financial support, one for abortion, one for procreation. It is one thing to permit a form of behavior, another to support or fund it. This would seem to be true whether the topic is hang-gliding, worship of Allah, or abortion. In *Maher* v. *Roe* the justices must decide whether the Constitution requires financial support for the activity judged permissible in *Roe* v. *Wade*.

The majority say it doesn't. The minority reason that the permission granted in *Roe* v. *Wade* is meaningless for a great many people unless they're given the money to enjoy it—what appears to be a right is not a right at all. Does their argument hold up?

Dandridge v. *Williams* examines the other side of the coin. The State of Maryland does not forbid welfare families to grow. It merely imposes a ceiling on the financial support a family may receive. So those families with many children find themselves in a bind. There is no fresh funding for newborns beyond a certain point. This, of course, tends to limit procreation without actually prohibiting it.

Some argue that procreation is a strictly personal matter, but there is clear public impact. In the case of welfare recipients, fellow citizens must assist if the new child is to survive. Are they obliged to do so? If they are, are there limits to this obligation?

IN THE MATTER OF THE ADOPTION OF ANONYMOUS*

Surrogates' Court, Kings County, N.Y. (1973)

NATHAN R. SOBEL, Surrogate. . . .

As a preliminary, there are two types of artificial insemination. Homologous insemination is the process by which the wife is artificially impregnated with the semen of her husband. This procedure is referred to as AIH (Artificial Insemination Husband) and creates no legal problems since the child is considered the natural child of the husband and wife. Heterologous insemination is the artificial insemination of the wife by the semen of a third party donor. This procedure is referred to as AID (Artificial Insemination Donor). AID may be "consensual" i.e. with the consent of the husband or "nonconsensual" i.e. without his consent. As will be observed in later discussion there are very few reported decisions concerning consensual AID and none at all with respect to nonconsensual AID. . . .

Predictably issues involving AID children will multiply. The medical technique of artificial insemination is of relatively recent origin—about 30 years old. The parents of these children will die and create for the courts problems of intestate succession and will construction. The utilization of AID procedures is bound to increase because of the unavailability—no doubt due to the "pill" and liberalized abortion laws—of adoptive children. Relatively recent too is the practice of AID where the husband's family has a history of hereditary disease or where RH incompatibility has led to repeated stillbirths. As yet the legislatures and the courts have been unresponsive in declaring the status and rights of AID children.

The facts in this proceeding are briefly stated. During the marriage the child was born of consensual AID. The husband was listed as the father on the birth certificate. Later the couple separated and the separation was followed by a divorce. Both the separation agreement and the divorce decree declare the child to be the "daughter" and "child" of the couple. The wife was granted support and the husband visitation rights. He has faithfully visited and performed all the support conditions of the decree. The wife later remarried and her new husband is petitioning to adopt the child. The first husband has refused his consent. Confronted with that legal impediment, the petitioner has suggested that the first husband's consent is not required since he is not the "parent" of the child. . . .

*345 N.Y.S. 2d 430

The leading case in the Nation is *People* v. *Sorensen* ([1968]. . . . *Sorensen* was a criminal prosecution on complaint of the welfare authorities against the husband for failure to support a minor child born during the marriage of consensual AID. The California Supreme Court without dissent held: the defendant is the lawful father of a dependent child born of consensual AID; that the term "father" as used in the penal statute is not limited to a biologic or natural father; the determinative factor is whether the *legal* relationship of father and child exists. The Court reasoned that a child conceived through AID does not have a "natural" father; that the anonymous donor is not the "natural" father; that he does have a "lawful" father and the intent of the legislature was to include a lawful father in the penal sanctions; further . . . that

> In light of these principles of statutory construction, a reasonable man who, because of his inability to procreate, actively participates and consents to his wife's artificial insemination in the hope that a child will be produced whom they will treat as their own, knows that such behavior carries with it the legal responsibilities of fatherhood and criminal responsibility for nonsupport. One who consents to the production of a child cannot create a temporary relation to be assumed and disclaimed at will, but the arrangement must be of such character as to impose an obligation of supporting those for whose existence he is directly responsible. . . .

The leading case in New York and the only one which discusses the issue, is *Gursky* v. *Gursky* [1963]. . . . The husband sued the wife for separation and despite the birth of a child to them by consensual AID, he alleged that there were no issue of the marriage. . . .

The basic finding . . . was that "the child . . . which was indisputably the offspring of artificial insemination by a third-party donor with the consent of the mother's husband, is not the legitimate issue of the husband." . . .

At the outset, it is observed that *Gursky* is not persuasive. It is the only published decision which flatly holds that AID children are illegitimate. . . . The "historical concept" and the statutory definition of "a child born out of wedlock" upon which it relies were developed and enacted long before the advent of the practice of artificial insemination. The birth of AID children was not then contemplated. An AID child is not "begotten" by a father who is not the husband; the donor is anonymous; the wife does not have sexual intercourse or commit adultery with him; if there is any "begetting" it is by the doctor who in this specialty is often a woman. The suggestion that the husband might not regard the child as his own has been dispelled by our gratifying experience with adoptive parents. Since there is consent by the husband, there is no marital infidelity. The child is not born "out of wedlock" but in and during wedlock. . . .

New York has a strong policy in favor of legitimacy. This is evidenced by the recent enactment of section 24 of the Domestic Relations Law. . . . Under that statute a child born of a void . . . or voidable . . . marriage, even if the marriage is deliberately and knowingly bigamous, incestuous or adulterous, is legitimate and entitled to all the rights (inheritance, support, etc.) of a child born during a perfectly valid marriage. In the face of the liberal policy expressed by such a statute, it would seem absurd to hold illegitimate a child born during a valid marriage, of parents desiring but unable to conceive a child, and both consenting and agreeing to the impregnation of the mother by a carefully and medically selected anonymous donor.

It must be recognized that there exist moral and religious objections to artificial insemination. . . . But these are stronger against bigamous, incestuous and adulterous relationships. That such objections have not prevented as a matter of state policy the legitimation of the children of such marriages, establishes that our liberal policy is for the protection of the child, not the parents. It serves no purpose whatsoever to stigmatize the AID child; or to compel the parents formally to adopt in order to confer upon the AID child the status and rights of a naturally conceived child.

. . . It is determined that a child born of consensual AID during a valid marriage is a legitimate child entitled to the rights and privileges of a naturally conceived child of the same marriage. The father of such child is therefore the "parent" . . . whose consent is required to the adoption of such child by another. . . .

DOE V. KELLEY*

Court of Appeals of Michigan (1981)

KELLY, Judge.

In this case, we are asked to declare unconstitutional those sections of the Michigan Adoption Code . . . which prohibit the exchange of money or other consideration in connection with adoption and related proceedings. . . .

Jane Doe and John Doe are pseudonyms for a married couple residing in Wayne County. In response to interrogatories posed by the Attorney General concerning the Does' marriage and whether any children were born of the marriage, the Does filed virtually identical affidavits stating the following information:

2. That he [she] was married in the City of Farmington, Michigan, on August 20, 1965.

3. That he [she] is the father [mother] of two sons, ages eleven and seven years.

From the nonresponsive answer to question #3, we are unable to say whether the two children were born of the Does' marriage or are adopted.

It is alleged that Jane Doe has undergone a tubal ligation, rendering her biologically incapable of bearing children and that the Does "wish to have a child biologically related to JOHN DOE." Mary Roe is employed as a secretary by

*307 N.W. 2d. 438

John Doe and also resides in Wayne County. The complaint alleges that these parties contemplate and intend to enter into the following agreement:

(a) That JANE DOE and JOHN DOE will pay MARY ROE a sum of money in consideration for her promise to bear and deliver JOHN DOE's child by means of artificial insemination.

(b) That a licensed physician will conduct the artificial insemination process.

(c) That prior to the delivery of said child, JOHN DOE will file a notice of intent to claim paternity.

(d) That at the time the child is born, JOHN DOE will formally acknowledge the paternity of said child.

(e) That MARY ROE will acknowledge that JOHN DOE is the father of said child.

(f) That MARY ROE will consent to the adoption of said child by JOHN DOE and JANE DOE.

The agreement also provided that plaintiffs would pay to Mary Roe the sum of $5,000 plus medical expenses. In addition, Mary Roe would be covered by sick leave, pregnancy disability insurance, and medical insurance from her employment while she is off work having the child and recuperating from the delivery.

The plaintiffs allege that the disputed statutory provisions impermissibly infringe upon their constitutional right to privacy. . . .

. . . The statute in question does not directly prohibit John Doe and Mary Roe from having the child as planned. It acts instead to preclude plaintiffs from paying consideration in conjunction with their use of the state's adoption procedures. In effect, the plaintiffs' contractual agreement discloses a desire to use the adoption code to change the legal status of the child—*i.e.,* its right to support, intestate succession, etc. We do not perceive this goal as within the realm of fundamental interests protected by the right to privacy from reasonable governmental regulation. . . .

TERRELL V. GARCIA*

Court of Civil Appeals of Texas (1973)

BARROW, Chief Justice.

The sole question presented by this appeal . . . is whether the parents of an unwanted, but normal, healthy child conceived after an unsuccessful sterilization operation on the mother, may recover from the negligent doctor for the financial expenses of the care and maintenance of said child. . . .

*496 S.W. 2d. 124

It was alleged that in November, 1970, Mrs. Terrell entered the Robert B. Green Hospital for the dual purpose of delivery of the couple's third child, and for the performance of a bilateral tubal ligation to insure her future sterility. Mrs. Terrell was assured that such operation, which was performed by Dr. Garcia, would prevent her from ever having children in the future. Nevertheless, she subsequently became pregnant and on January 17, 1972, a normal, healthy son was born and is living with Mrs. Terrell, who is now separated from her husband. It is alleged that the fourth child, in addition to the other three children imposes a heavy financial strain upon the couple, and that she sought the sterilization operation to avoid such strain. . . .

. . . Who can place a price tag on a child's smile or the parental pride in a child's achievement? Even if we consider only the economic point of view, a child is some security for the parents' old age. Rather than attempt to value these intangible benefits, our courts have simply determined that public sentiment recognizes that these benefits to the parents outweigh their economic loss in rearing and educating a healthy, normal child. We see no compelling reason to change such rule at this time. . . .

CADENA, Justice (dissenting). . . .

It may, indeed, be difficult to "place a price tag on a child's smile." But there is no support for the conclusion that the task cannot be performed. The courts of other states have undertaken the difficult task of assigning a value on a child's smile in cases involving the wrongful killing of children, and have awarded the bereaved parents damages for the loss of companionship and comfort. . . .

I see no reason for departing from the rule that a negligent person is liable for the foreseeable consequences of his negligence. There is no justification for holding, as a matter of law, that the birth of an "unwanted" child is a "blessing." The birth of such a child may be a catastrophe not only for the parents and the child itself, but also for previously born siblings. The doctor whose negligence brings about such an undesired birth should not be allowed to say, "I did you a favor," secure in the knowledge that the courts will give to this claim the effect of an irrebuttable presumption. . . .

GLEITMAN V. COSGROVE*

Supreme Court of New Jersey (1967)

PROCTOR, J.

This is a malpractice suit for money damages. . . .

The first count of the complaint is on behalf of Jeffrey Gleitman, an infant, for his birth defects. The second count is by his mother, Sandra Gleitman, for the

*227 A. 2d 689

effects on her emotional state caused by her son's condition. And the third count is by his father, Irwin Gleitman, for the costs incurred in caring for Jeffrey. Defendants, Robert Cosgrove, Jr. and Jerome Dolan, are physicians specializing in obstetrics and gynecology engaged together in the practice of medicine in Jersey City.

Sandra Gleitman consulted defendants on April 20, 1959. She was examined by Dr. Robert Cosgrove, Jr., and found by him to be two months pregnant. She informed him that on or about March 20, 1959 she had had an illness diagnosed as German measles. Mrs. Gleitman testified that Dr. Cosgrove, on receipt of this information and on inquiry by her, told her that the German measles would have no effect at all on her child.

For the next three months Mrs. Gleitman received her prenatal medical care from the army doctors at Fort Gordon, Georgia where her husband was stationed. She informed the army doctors about the German measles she had had in her early pregnancy, and they instructed her to ask her regular physician about this when she returned home. . . .

She next consulted defendants in July at which time she saw Dr. Dolan. Mrs. Gleitman testified that she repeated her inquiry about the effects of German measles and again received a reassuring answer. These inquiries and answers occurred on each of her subsequent monthly visits.

On November 25, 1959 Mrs. Gleitman was delivered of a boy, Jeffrey, at the Margaret Hague Maternity Hospital in Jersey City. Although at first the baby seemed normal, a few weeks later the substantial defects which Jeffrey has in sight, hearing, and speech began to become apparent. He has had several operations which have given him some visual capacity, and he attends a special correctional institute for blind and deaf children. His physical condition, which is seriously impaired, is not in dispute on this appeal.

Plaintiffs' medical expert, Dr. Louis Fraulo, gave his opinion that Jeffrey's condition was causally related to the viral disease of German measles which Mrs. Gleitman had in March. Dr. Fraulo testified that women who have German measles in the first trimester of their pregnancy will produce infants with birth defects in 20 to 50 per cent of the cases. Dr. Fraulo further stated that a physician who finds pregnancy and is given a history of German measles occurring during the term of pregnancy should inform his female patient of the likelihood of birth defects. In answer to a hypothetical question based on Mrs. Gleitman's testimony, Dr. Fraulo stated that defendants had deviated from generally accepted medical standards by not informing their pregnant patient of the likelihood of birth defects. A patient so informed, Dr. Fraulo testified, could then decide whether to bear the baby or have the pregnancy terminated by an abortion.

Dr. Robert Cosgrove, Jr. agreed that Mrs. Gleitman had consulted him for her pregnancy on April 20, 1959 and had thereafter been the patient of Dr. Dolan and himself until November 25, 1959 when Jeffrey was born. He further agreed that the history given him had included the illness of German measles in March, and acknowledged that his duty as a physician required him to inform his patient of the possibility of birth defects. He testified, however, that in the presence of Dr. Samuel Cosgrove, since deceased, and a woman who appeared to be the mother of Mrs. Gleitman, he told his patient of a 20 per cent chance her baby would have some defect. He also stated that he informed her that some doctors would recommend and perform an abortion for this reason, but that he did not think it proper to destroy four healthy babies because the fifth one would have some defect.

Dr. Dolan testified that Mrs. Gleitman, whom he first saw in July when in any event it was too far along in the pregnancy for a medically safe abortion, had never asked him about the effects of German measles, and that he had never mentioned these effects to her. Dr. Dolan, as well as Dr. Edward C. Waters, who was called as an expert for defendants, agreed that a physician had the duty of informing his patient as to the likelihood of birth defects which they both estimated would occur in some 20 to 25 per cent of the cases where a female has German measles in the first trimester of her pregnancy.

The theory of plaintiffs' suit is that defendants negligently failed to inform Mrs. Gleitman, their patient, of the effects which German measles might have upon the infant then in gestation. Had the mother been so informed, plaintiffs assert, she might have obtained other medical advice with a view to the obtaining of an abortion. Plaintiffs do not assert that Mrs. Gleitman's life or health was in jeopardy during the term of her pregnancy. . . .

. . . In the present case there is no contention that anything the defendants could have done would have decreased the likelihood that the infant would be born with defects. The conduct of defendants was not the cause of infant plaintiff's condition.

The infant plaintiff is therefore required to say not that he should have been born without defects but that he should not have been born at all. In the language of tort law he says: but for the negligence of defendants, he would not have been born to suffer with an impaired body. In other words, he claims that the conduct of defendants prevented his mother from obtaining an abortion which would have terminated his existence, and that his very life is "wrongful."

. . . The normal measure of damages in tort actions is compensatory. Damages are measured by comparing the condition plaintiff would have been in, had the defendants not been negligent, with plaintiff's impaired condition as a result of the negligence. The infant plaintiff would have us measure the difference between his life with defects against the utter void of nonexistence, but it is impossible to make such a determination. This Court cannot weigh the value of life with impairments against the nonexistence of life itself. By asserting that he should not have been born, the infant plaintiff makes it logically impossible for a court to measure his alleged damages because of the impossibility of making the comparison required by compensatory remedies. As a recent commentator put the matter:

[N]o comparison is possible since were it not for the act of birth the infant would not exist. By his cause of action, the plaintiff cuts from under himself the ground upon which he needs to rely in order to prove his damage. Tedeschi, "On Tort Liability for 'Wrongful Life,' " . . .

Israel L.Rev. . . .

. . . We hold that the first count of the complaint on behalf of Jeffrey Gleitman is not actionable because the conduct complained of, even if true, does not give rise to damages cognizable at law.

The mother and father stand in a somewhat different position from the infant. They are equally subject to the factual circumstance that no act by the defendants could have decreased the likelihood that the infant would be defective. However, Mrs. Gleitman can say that an abortion would have freed her of the emotional problems caused by the raising of a child with birth defects; and Mr. Gleitman can assert that it would have been less expensive for him to abort rather than raise the child.

A considerable problem is raised by the claim of injury to the parents. In order to determine their compensatory damages a court would have to evaluate the denial to them of the intangible, unmeasurable, and complex human benefits of motherhood and fatherhood and weigh these against the alleged emotional and money injuries. Such a proposed weighing is similar to that which we have found impossible to perform for the infant plaintiff. When the parents say their child should not have been born, they make it impossible for a court to measure their damages in being the mother and father of a defective child.

Denial of the claim for damages by adult plaintiffs is also required by a close look at exactly what it is they are here seeking. The thrust of their complaint is that they were denied the opportunity to terminate the life of their child while he was an embryo. Even under our assumption that an abortion could have been obtained without making its participants liable to criminal sanctions, substantial policy reasons prevent this Court from allowing tort damages for the denial of the opportunity to take an embryonic life.

It is basic to the human condition to seek life and hold on to it however heavily burdened. If Jeffrey could have been asked as to whether his life should be snuffed out before his full term of gestation could run its course, our felt intuition of human nature tells us he would almost surely choose life with defects as against no life at all. "For the living there is hope, but for the dead there is none." Theocritus. . . .

The right to life is inalienable in our society. A court cannot say what defects should prevent an embryo from being allowed life such that denial of the opportunity to terminate the existence of a defective child in embryo can support a cause for action. Examples of famous persons who have had great achievement despite physical defects come readily to mind, and many of us can think of examples close to home. A child need not be perfect to have a worthwhile life.

We are not faced here with the necessity of balancing the mother's life against that of her child. The sanctity of the single human life is the decisive factor in this suit in tort. Eugenic considerations are not controlling. We are not talking here about the breeding of prize cattle. It may have been easier for the mother and less expensive for the father to have terminated the life of their child while he was an embryo, but these alleged detriments cannot stand against the preciousness of the single human life to support a remedy in tort. Cf. Jonathan Swift, "A Modest Proposal." . . .

. . . Though we sympathize with the unfortunate situation in which these parents find themselves, we firmly believe the right of their child to live is greater than and precludes their right not to endure emotional and financial injury. We hold therefore that the second and third counts of the complaint are not actionable because the conduct complained of, even if true, does not give rise to damages cognizable at law; and even if such alleged damages were cognizable, a claim for them would be precluded by the countervailing public policy supporting the preciousness of human life. . . .

ROE V. *WADE**

U.S. Supreme Court (1973)

Mr. Justice BLACKMUN delivered the opinion of the Court. . . .

We forthwith acknowledge our awareness of the sensitive and emotional nature of the abortion controversy, of the vigorous opposing views, even among physicians, and of the deep and seemingly absolute convictions that the subject inspires. One's philosophy, one's experiences, one's exposure to the raw edges of human existence, one's religious training, one's attitudes toward life and family and their values, and the moral standards one establishes and seeks to observe, are all likely to influence and to color one's thinking and conclusions about abortion.

In addition, population growth, pollution, poverty, and racial overtones tend to complicate and not to simplify the problem.

Our task, of course, is to resolve the issue by constitutional measurement, free of emotion and of predilection. We seek earnestly to do this, and, because we do, we have inquired into, and in this opinion place some emphasis upon, medical and medical-legal history and what that history reveals about man's attitudes toward the abortion procedure over the centuries. . . .

Jane Roe . . . a single woman who was residing in Dallas County, Texas, instituted this federal action in March 1970 against the District Attorney of the county. She sought a declaratory judgment that the Texas criminal abortion statutes were unconstitutional on their face, and an injunction restraining the defendant from enforcing the statutes.

*410 U.S. 113

Roe alleged that she was unmarried and pregnant; that she wished to terminate her pregnancy by an abortion "performed by a competent, licensed physician, under safe, clinical conditions"; that she was unable to get a "legal" abortion in Texas because her life did not appear to be threatened by the continuation of her pregnancy; and that she could not afford to travel to another jurisdiction in order to secure a legal abortion under safe conditions. She claimed that the Texas statutes were unconstitutionally vague and that they abridged her right of personal privacy, protected by the First, Fourth, Fifth, Ninth, and Fourteenth Amendments. By an amendment to her complaint Roe purported to sue "on behalf of herself and all other women" similarly situated. . . .

It perhaps is not generally appreciated that the restrictive criminal abortion laws in effect in a majority of States today are of relatively recent vintage. Those laws, generally proscribing abortion or its attempt at any time during pregnancy except when necessary to preserve the pregnant woman's life, are not of ancient or even of common-law origin. Instead, they derive from statutory changes effected, for the most part, in the latter half of the 19th century.

. . . *Ancient attitudes.*   These are not capable of precise determination. We are told that at the time of the Persian Empire abortifacients were known and that criminal abortions were severely punished. . . . We are also told, however, that abortion was practiced in Greek times as well as in the Roman Era . . . and that "it was resorted to without scruple." . . . The Ephesian, Soranos, often described as the greatest of the ancient gynecologists, appears to have been generally opposed to Rome's prevailing free-abortion practices. He found it necessary to think first of the life of the mother, and he resorted to abortion when, upon this standard, he felt the procedure advisable. . . . Greek and Roman law afforded little protection to the unborn. If abortion was prosecuted in some places, it seems to have been based on a concept of a violation of the father's right to his offspring. Ancient religion did not bar abortion. . . .

. . . *The Hippocratic Oath.*   What then of the famous Oath that has stood so long as the ethical guide of the medical profession and that bears the name of the great Greek (460(?)–377(?) B.C.), who has been described as the Father of Medicine, the "wisest and the greatest practitioner of his art," and the "most important and most complete medical personality of antiquity," who dominated the medical schools of his time, and who typified the sum of the medical knowledge of the past? . . . The Oath varies somewhat according to the particular translation, but in any translation the content is clear: "I will give no deadly medicine to anyone if asked, nor suggest any such counsel; and in like manner I will not give to a woman a pessary to produce abortion," . . . or "I will neither give a deadly drug to anybody if asked for it, nor will I make a suggestion to this effect. Similarly, I will not give to a woman an abortive remedy." . . .

Although the Oath is not mentioned in any of the principal briefs in this case . . . it represents the apex of the development of strict ethical concepts in medicine, and its influence endures to this day. Why did not the authority of Hippocrates dissuade abortion practice in his time and that of Rome? The late Dr. Edelstein provides us with a theory: . . . The Oath was not uncontested even in Hippocrates' day; only the Pythagorean school of philosophers frowned upon the related act of suicide. Most Greek thinkers, on the other hand, commended abortion, at least prior to viability. See Plato, Republic, V, 461; Aristotle, Politics, VII, 1335b 25. For the Pythagoreans, however, it was a matter of dogma. For them the embryo was animate from the moment of conception, and abortion meant destruction of a living being. The abortion clause of the Oath, therefore, "echoes Pythagorean doctrines," and "[i]n no other stratum of Greek opinion were such views held or proposed in the same spirit of uncompromising austerity." . . .

Dr. Edelstein then concludes that the Oath originated in a group representing only a small segment of Greek opinion and that it certainly was not accepted by all ancient physicians. He points out that medical writings down to Galen (A.D. 130–200) "give evidence of the violation of almost every one of its injunctions." . . . But with the end of antiquity a decided change took place. Resistance against suicide and against abortion became common. The Oath came to be popular. The emerging teachings of Christianity were in agreement with the Pythagorean ethic. The Oath "became the nucleus of all medical ethics" and "was applauded as the embodiment of truth." Thus, suggests Dr. Edelstein, it is "a Pythagorean manifesto and not the expression of an absolute standard of medical conduct." . . .

This, it seems to us, is a satisfactory and acceptable explanation of the Hippocractic Oath's apparent rigidity. It enables us to understand, in historical context, a long-accepted and revered statement of medical ethics. . . .

. . . The common law. It is undisputed that at common law, abortion performed *before* "quickening"—the first recognizable movement of the fetus *in utero*, appearing usually from the 16th to the 18th week of pregnancy . . .—was not an indictable offense. . . . The absence of a common-law crime for pre-quickening abortion appears to have developed from a confluence of earlier philosophical, theological, and civil and canon law concepts of when life begins. These disciplines variously approached the question in terms of the point at which the embryo or fetus became "formed" or recognizably human, or in terms of when a "person" came into being, that is, infused with a "soul" or "animated." A loose concensus evolved in early English law that these events occurred at some point between conception and live birth.[1] This was "mediate animation." Although Christian theology and the canon law came to fix the point of animation at 40 days for a

---

[1] Early philosophers believed that the embryo or fetus did not become formed and begin to live until at least 40 days after conception for a male, and 80 to 90 days for a female. See, for example, Aristotle, Hist. Anim. 7.3.583b; Gen. Anim. 2.3.736, 2.5.741; Hippocrates, Lib. de Nat.Puer., No. 10. Aristotle's thinking derived from his three-stage theory of life: vegetable, animal, rational. The vegetable stage was reached at conception, the animal at "animation," and the rational soon after live birth. This theory, together with the 40/80 day view, came to be accepted by early Christian thinkers.

male and 80 days for a female, a view that persisted until the 19th century, there was otherwise little agreement about the precise time of formation or animation. There was agreement, however, that prior to this point the fetus was to be regarded as part of the mother, and its destruction, therefore, was not homicide. Due to continued uncertainty about the precise time when animation occurred, to the lack of any empirical basis for the 40–80-day view, and perhaps to Aquinas' definition of movement as one of the two first principles of life, Bracton focused upon quickening as the critical point. The significance of quickening was echoed by later common-law scholars and found its way into the received common law in this country. . . .

   . . . *The American law.*   . . . Gradually, in the middle and late 19th century the quickening distinction disappeared from the statutory law of most States and the degree of the offense and the penalties were increased. By the end of the 1950's a large majority of the jurisdictions banned abortion, however and whenever performed, unless done to save or preserve the life of the mother. The exceptions, Alabama and the District of Columbia, permitted abortion to preserve the mother's health. . . . Three States permitted abortions that were not "unlawfully" performed or that were not "without lawful justification," leaving interpretation of those standards to the courts. . . . In the past several years, however, a trend toward liberalization of abortion statutes has resulted in adoption, by about one-third of the States, of less stringent laws, most of them patterned after the ALI Model Penal Code. . . .

   It is thus apparent that at common law, at the time of the adoption of our Constitution, and throughout the major portion of the 19th century, abortion was viewed with less disfavor than under most American statutes currently in effect. Phrasing it another way, a woman enjoyed a substantially broader right to terminate a pregnancy than she does in most States today. At least with respect to the early stage of pregnancy, and very possibly without such a limitation, the opportunity to make this choice was present in this country well into the 19th century.

   The theological debate was reflected in the writings of St. Augustine, who made a distinction between *embryo inanimatus*, not yet endowed with a soul, and *embryo animatus*. He may have drawn upon Exodus 21:22. At one point, however, he expressed the view that human powers cannot determine the point during fetal development at which the critical change occurs. See Augustine, De Origine Animae 4.4 (Pub.Law 44.527). See also W. Reany, The Creation of the Human Soul, c.2 and 83–86 (1932); Huser, The Crime of Abortion in Canon Law 15 (Catholic Univ. of America, Canon Law Studies No. 162, Washington, D. C., 1942).

   Galen, in three treatises related to embryology, accepted the thinking of Aristotle and his followers. Quay 426–427. Later, Augustine on abortion was incorporated by Gratian into the Decretum, published about 1140. Decretum Magistri Gratiani 2.32.2.7 to 2.32.2.10, in 1 Corpus Juris Canonici 1122, 1123 (A. Friedberg, 2d ed. 1879). This Decretal and the Decretals that followed were recognized as the definitive body of canon law until the new Code of 1917.

   For discussions of the canon-law treatment, see Means I, pp. 411–412; Noonan 20–26; Quay 426–430; see also J. Noonan, Contraception: A History of Its Treatment by the Catholic Theologians and Canonists 18–29 (1965).

Even later, the law continued for some time to treat less punitively an abortion procured in early pregnancy. . . .

   . . . *The position of the American Medical Association.* . . .   On June 25, 1970, the House of Delegates adopted preambles and most of the resolutions proposed by the reference committee. The preambles emphasized "the best interests of the patient," "sound clinical judgment," and "informed patient consent," in contrast to "mere acquiescence to the patient's demand." The resolutions asserted that abortion is a medical procedure that should be performed by a licensed physician in an accredited hospital only after consultation with two other physicians and in conformity with state law, and that no party to the procedure should be required to violate personally held moral principles. . . . Proceedings of the AMA House of Delegates 220 (June 1970). The AMA Judicial Council rendered a complementary opinion. . . .

   . . . *The position of the American Public Health Association.*   In October 1970, the Executive Board of the APHA adopted Standards for Abortion Services. These were five in number:

   a. Rapid and simple abortion referral must be readily available through state and local public health departments, medical societies, or other non-profit organizations.
   b. An important function of counseling should be to simplify and expedite the provision of abortion services; it should not delay the obtaining of these services.
   c. Psychiatric consultation should not be mandatory. As in the case of other specialized medical services, psychiatric consultation should be sought for definite indications and not on a routine basis.
   d. A wide range of individuals from appropriately trained, sympathetic volunteers to highly skilled physicians may qualify as abortion counselors.
   e. Contraception and/or sterilization should be discussed with each abortion patient. Recommended Standards for Abortion Services, 61 Am. J. Pub. Health 396 (1971). . . .

   . . . *The position of the American Bar Association.*   At its meeting in February 1972 the ABA House of Delegates approved, with 17 opposing votes, the Uniform Abortion Act that had been drafted and approved the preceding August by the Conference of Commissioners on Uniform State Laws. 58 A.B.A. J. 380 (1972). We set forth the Act in full in the margin.[2] . . .

[2]   "UNIFORM ABORTION ACT
   "Section 1. [*Abortion Defined; When Authorized.*]
   "(a) 'Abortion' means the termination of human pregnancy with an intention other than to produce a live birth or to remove a dead fetus.
   "(b) An abortion may be performed in this state only if it is performed:
   "(1) by a physician licensed to practice medicine [or osteopathy] in this state or by a physician practicing medicine [or osteopathy] in the employ of the government of the United States or of this state, [and the abortion is performed [in the physician's office or in a medical clinic, or] in a hospital

Three reasons have been advanced to explain historically the enactment of criminal abortion laws in the 19th century and to justify their continued existence.

It has been argued occasionally that these laws were the product of a Victorian social concern to discourage illicit sexual conduct. Texas, however, does not advance this justification in the present case, and it appears that no court or commentator has taken the argument seriously. . . .

A second reason is concerned with abortion as a medical procedure. When most criminal abortion laws were first enacted, the procedure was a hazardous one for the woman. . . . This was particularly true prior to the development of antisepsis. Antiseptic techniques, of course, were based on discoveries by Lister, Pasteur, and others first announced in 1867, but were not generally accepted and employed until about the turn of the century. Abortion mortality was high. Even after 1900, and perhaps until as late as the development of antibiotics in the 1940's, standard modern techniques such as dilation and curettage were not nearly so safe as they are today. Thus, it has been argued that a State's real concern in enacting a criminal abortion law was to protect the pregnant woman, that is, to restrain her from submitting to a procedure that placed her life in serious jeopardy. . . .

Modern medical techniques have altered this situation. Appellants and various *amici* refer to medical data indicating that abortion in early pregnancy, that is, prior to the end of the first trimester, although not without its risk, is now relatively safe. Mortality rates for women undergoing early abortions, where the procedure is legal, appear to be as low as or lower than the rates for normal childbirth. . . . Consequently, any interest of the State in protecting the woman from an inherently hazardous procedure, except when it would be equally dangerous for her to forgo it, has largely disappeared. Of course, important state interests in the areas of health and medical standards do remain. The State has a legitimate interest in seeing to it that abortion, like any other medical procedure, is performed under circumstances that insure maximum safety for the patient. This interest obviously extends at least to the performing physician and his staff, to the facilities involved, to the availability of after-care, and to adequate provision for any complication or emergency that might arise. The prevalence of high mortality rates at illegal "abortion mills" strengthens, rather than weakens, the State's interest in regulating the conditions under which abortions are performed. Moreover, the risk to the

approved by the [Department of Health] or operated by the United States, this state, or any department, agency, or political subdivision of either;] or by a female upon herself upon the advice of the physician; and

"(2) within [20] weeks after the commencement of the pregnancy [or after [20] weeks only if the physician has reasonable cause to believe (i) there is a substantial risk that continuance of the pregnancy would endanger the life of the mother or would gravely impair the physical or mental health of the mother, (ii) that the child would be born with grave physical or mental defect, or (iii) that the pregnancy resulted from rape or incest, or illicit intercourse with a girl under the age of 16 years].

"Section 2. [*Penalty.*] Any person who performs or procures an abortion other than authorized by this Act is guilty of a [felony] and, upon conviction thereof, may be sentenced to pay a fine not exceeding [$1,000] or to imprisonment [in the state penitentiary] not exceeding [5 years], or both.

woman increases as her pregnancy continues. Thus, the State retains a definite interest in protecting the woman's own health and safety when an abortion is proposed at a late stage of pregnancy. . . .

The third reason is the State's interest—some phrase it in terms of duty—in protecting prenatal life. Some of the argument for this justification rests on the theory that a new human life is present from the moment of conception. . . . The State's interest and general obligation to protect life then extends, it is argued, to prenatal life. Only when the life of the pregnant mother herself is at stake, balanced against the life she carries within her, should the interest of the embryo or fetus not prevail. Logically, of course, a legitimate state interest in this area need not stand or fall on acceptance of the belief that life begins at conception or at some other point prior to live birth. In assessing the State's interest, recognition may be given to the less rigid claim that as long as at least *potential* life is involved, the State may assert interests beyond the protection of the pregnant woman alone. . . .

. . . This right of privacy, whether it be founded in the Fourteenth Amendment's concept of personal liberty and restrictions upon state action, as we feel it is, or, as the District Court determined, in the Ninth Amendment's reservation of rights to the people, is broad enough to encompass a woman's decision whether or not to terminate her pregnancy. The detriment that the State would impose upon the pregnant woman by denying this choice altogether is apparent. Specific and direct harm medically diagnosable even in early pregnancy may be involved. Maternity, or additional offspring, may force upon the woman a distressful life and future. Psychological harm may be imminent. Mental and physical health may be taxed by child care. There is also distress, for all concerned, associated with the unwanted child, and there is the problem of bringing a child into a family already unable, psychologically and otherwise, to care for it. In other cases, as in this one, the additional difficulties and continuing stigma of unwed motherhood may be involved. All these are factors the woman and her responsible physician necessarily will consider in consultation.

On the basis of elements such as these, appellant and some *amici* argue that the woman's right is absolute and that she is entitled to terminate her pregnancy at whatever time, in whatever way, and for whatever reason she alone chooses. With this we do not agree. Appellant's arguments that Texas either has no valid interest at all in regulating the abortion decision, or no interest strong enough to support any limitation upon the woman's sole determination, are unpersuasive. The Court's decisions recognizing a right of privacy also acknowledge that some state regulation in areas protected by that right is appropriate. As noted above, a State may properly assert important interests in safeguarding health, in maintaining medical standards, and in protecting potential life. At some point in pregnancy, these respective interests become sufficiently compelling to sustain regulation of the factors that govern abortion decision. The privacy right involved, therefore, cannot be said to be absolute. In fact, it is not clear to us that the claim asserted by some *amici* that one has an unlimited right to do with one's body as one pleases bears a close relationship to the right of privacy previously articulated in the Court's decisions. The Court has refused to recognize an unlimited right of this kind in the past. . . .

We, therefore, conclude that the right of personal privacy includes the abortion decision, but that this right is not unqualified and must be considered against important state interests in regulation. . . .

. . . The appellee and certain *amici* argue that the fetus is a "person" within the language and meaning of the Fourteenth Amendment. In support of this, they outline at length and in detail the well-known facts of fetal development. If this suggestion of personhood is established, the appellant's case, of course, collapses, for the fetus' right to life would then be guaranteed specifically by the Amendment. The appellant conceded as much on reargument. . . . On the other hand, the appellee conceded on reargument . . . that no case could be cited that holds a fetus is a person within the meaning of the Fourteenth Amendment.

The Constitution does not define "person" in so many words. Section 1 of the Fourteenth Amendment contains three references to "person." The first, in defining "citizens," speaks of "persons born or naturalized in the United States." The word also appears both in the Due Process Clause and in the Equal Protection Clause. "Person" is used in other places in the Constitution: in the listing of qualifications for Representatives and Senators, Art. I, § 2, cl. 2, and § 3, cl. 3; in the Apportionment Clause, Art. I, § 2, cl. 3; . . . in the Migration and Importation provision, Art. I, § 9, cl. 1; in the Emolument Clause, Art. I, § 9, cl. 8; in the Electors provisions, Art. II, § 1, cl. 2, and the superseded cl. 3; in the provision outlining qualifications for the office of President, Art. II, § 1, cl. 5; in the Extradition provisions, Art. IV, § 2, cl. 2, and the superseded Fugitive Slave Clause 3; and in the Fifth, Twelfth, and Twenty-second Amendments, as well as in §§ 2 and 3 of the Fourteenth Amendment. But in nearly all these instances, the use of the word is such that it has application only postnatally. None indicates, with any assurance, that it has any possible prenatal application. . . .

. . . All this, together with our observation, *supra*, that throughout the major portion of the 19th century prevailing legal abortion practices were far freer than they are today, persuades us that the word "person," as used in the Fourteenth Amendment, does not include the unborn. . . .

Texas urges that, apart from the Fourteenth Amendment, life begins at conception and is present throughout pregnancy, and that, therefore, the State has a compelling interest in protecting that life from and after conception. We need not resolve the difficult question of when life begins. When those trained in the respective disciplines of medicine, philosophy, and theology are unable to arrive at any consensus, the judiciary, at this point in the development of man's knowledge, is not in a position to speculate as to the answer.

It should be sufficient to note briefly the wide divergence of thinking on this most sensitive and difficult question. There has always been strong support for the view that life does not begin until live birth. This was the belief of the Stoics. . . . It appears to be the predominant, though not the unanimous, attitude of the Jewish faith. . . . It may be taken to represent also the position of a large segment of the Protestant community, insofar as that can be ascertained; organized groups that have taken a formal position on the abortion issue have generally regarded abortion as a matter for the conscience of the individual and her family. . . . As we have noted, the common law found greater significance in quickening. Physicians and their scientific colleagues have regarded that event with less interest and have tended to focus either upon conception, upon live birth, or upon the interim point at which the fetus becomes "viable," that is, potentially able to live outside the mother's womb, albeit with artificial aid. . . . Viability is usually placed at about seven months (28 weeks) but may occur earlier, even at 24 weeks. . . . The Aristotelian theory of "mediate animation," that held sway throughout the Middle Ages and the Renaissance in Europe, continued to be official Roman Catholic dogma until the 19th century, despite opposition to this "ensoulment" theory from those in the Church who would recognize the existence of life from the moment of conception. . . . The latter is now, of course, the official belief of the Catholic Church. As one brief *amicus* discloses, this is a view strongly held by many non-Catholics as well, and by many physicians. Substantial problems for precise definition of this view are posed, however, by new embryological data that purport to indicate that conception is a "process" over time, rather than an event and by new medical techniques such as menstrual extraction, the "morning-after" pill, implantation of embryos, artificial insemination, and even artificial wombs.

In areas other than criminal abortion, the law has been reluctant to endorse any theory that life, as we recognize it, begins before live birth or to accord legal rights to the unborn except in narrowly defined situations and except when the rights are contingent upon live birth. For example, the traditional rule of tort law denied recovery for prenatal injuries even though the child was born alive. . . . That rule has been changed in almost every jurisdiction. In most States, recovery is said to be permitted only if the fetus was viable, or at least quick, when the injuries were sustained, though few courts have squarely so held. . . . In a recent development, generally opposed by the commentators, some States permit the parents of a stillborn child to maintain an action for wrongful death because of prenatal injuries. . . . Such an action, however, would appear to be one to vindicate the parents' interest and is thus consistent with the view that the fetus, at most, represents only the potentiality of life. Similarly, unborn children have been recognized as acquiring rights or interests by way of inheritance or other devolution of property, and have been represented by guardians *ad litem*. . . . Perfection of the interests involved, again, has generally been contingent upon live birth. In short, the unborn have never been recognized in the law as persons in the whole sense. . . .

In view of all this, we do not agree that, by adopting one theory of life, Texas may override the rights of the pregnant woman that are at stake. We repeat, however, that the State does have an important and legitimate interest in preserving and protecting the health of the pregnant woman, whether she be a resident of the State or a nonresident who seeks medical consultation and treatment there, and that it has still *another* important and legitimate interest in protecting the potentiality of human life. These interests are separate and distinct. Each grows in substantiality as the woman approaches term and, at a point during pregnancy, each becomes "compelling." . . .

. . . With respect to the State's important and legitimate interest in the health of the mother, the "compelling" point, in the light of present medical knowledge, is at approximately the end of the first trimester. This is so because of the now-established medical fact, referred to above . . . , that until the end of the first trimester mortality in abortion may be less than mortality in normal childbirth. It follows that, from and after this point, a State may regulate the abortion procedure to the extent that the regulation reasonably relates to the preservation and protection of maternal health. Examples of permissible state regulation in this area are requirements as to the qualifications of the person who is to perform the abortion; as to the licensure of that person; as to the facility in which the procedure is to be performed, that is, whether it must be a hospital or may be a clinic or some other place of less-than-hospital status; as the the licensing of the facility; and the like.

This means, on the other hand, that, for the period of pregnancy prior to this "compelling" point, the attending physician, in consultation with his patient, is free to determine, without regulation by the State, that, in his medical judgment, the patient's pregnancy should be terminated. If that decision is reached, the judgment may be effectuated by an abortion free of interference by the State. . . .

. . . With respect to the State's important and legitimate interest in potential life, the "compelling" point is at viability. This is so because the fetus then presumably has the capability of meaningful life outside the mother's womb. State regulation protective of fetal life after viability thus has both logical and biological justifications. If the State is interested in protecting fetal life after viability, it may go so far as to proscribe abortion during that period, except when it is necessary to preserve the life or health of the mother.

. . . Measured against these standards, Art. 1196 of the Texas Penal Code, in restricting legal abortions to those "procured or attempted by medical advice for the purpose of saving the life of the mother" sweeps too broadly. The statute makes no distinction between abortions performed early in pregnancy and those performed later, and it limits to a single reason, "saving" the mother's life, the legal justification for the procedure. The statute, therefore, cannot survive the constitutional attack made upon it here. . . .

To summarize and to repeat:

. . . A state criminal abortion statute of the current Texas type, that excepts from criminality only a *life-saving* procedure on behalf of the mother, without regard to pregnancy stage and without recognition of the other interests involved, is violative of the Due Process Clause of the Fourteenth Amendment.

... For the stage prior to approximately the end of the first trimester, the abortion decision and its effectuation must be left to the medical judgment of the pregnant woman's attending physician.

... For the stage subsequent to approximately the end of the first trimester, the State, in promoting its interest in the health of the mother, may, if it chooses, regulate the abortion procedure in ways that are reasonably related to maternal health.

... For the stage subsequent to viability, the State in promoting its interest in the potentiality of human life may, if it chooses, regulate, and even proscribe, abortion except where it is necessary, in appropriate medical judgment, for the preservation of the life or health of the mother. . . .

This holding, we feel, is consistent with the relative weights of the respective interests involved, with the lessons and examples of medical and legal history, with the lenity of the common law, and with the demands of the profound problems of the present day. The decision leaves the State free to place increasing restrictions on abortion as the period of pregnancy lengthens, so long as those restrictions are tailored to the recognized state interests. The decision vindicates the right of the physician to administer medical treatment according to his professional judgment up to the points where important state interests provide compelling justifications for intervention. Up to these points, the abortion decision in all its aspects is inherently, and primarily, a medical decision, and basic responsibility for it must rest with the physician. If an individual practitioner abuses the privilege of exercising proper medical judgment, the usual remedies, judicial and intra-professional, are available. . . .

WOODS V. LANCET*

Court of Appeals of New York (1951)

DESMOND, J. The complaint served on behalf of this infant plaintiff alleges that, while the infant was in his mother's womb during the ninth month of her pregnancy, he sustained, through the negligence of defendant, such serious injuries that he came into this world permanently maimed and disabled. . . .

Two ... reasons for dismissal (besides lack of precedent) are given in Drobner v. Peters. . . . The first of those . . . has to do with the supposed difficulty of proving or disproving that certain injuries befell the unborn child, or that they produced the defects discovered at birth, or later. Such difficulties there are, of course, and, indeed, it seems to be commonly accepted that only a blow of tremendous force will ordinarily injure a foetus, so carefully does nature insulate it. But

*102 N.E. 2d 691

such difficulty of proof or finding is not special to this particular kind of lawsuit (and it is beside the point anyhow, in determining sufficiency of a pleading). Every day in all our trial courts (and before administrative tribunals, particularly the Workmen's Compensation Board), such issues are disposed of, and it is an inadmissible concept that uncertainty of proof can ever destroy a legal right. The questions of causation, reasonable certainty, etc., which will arise in these cases are no different, in kind, from the ones which have arisen in thousands of other negligence cases decided in this State, in the past.

The other objection to recovery here is the purely theoretical one that a foetus *in utero* has no existence of its own separate from that of its mother, that is, that it is not "a being *in esse*." We need not deal here with so large a subject. It is to be remembered that we are passing on the sufficiency of a complaint which alleges that this injury occurred during the ninth month of the mother's pregnancy, in other words, to a viable foetus, later born. Therefore, we confine our holding in this case to prepartum injuries to such viable children. Of course such a child, still in the womb, is, in one sense, a part of its mother, but no one seems to claim that the mother, in her own name and for herself, could get damages for the injuries to her infant. To hold, as matter of law, that no viable foetus has any separate existence which the law will recognize is for the law to deny a simple and easily demonstrable fact. This child, when injured, was in fact, alive and capable of being delivered and of remaining alive separate from its mother. We agree with the dissenting Justice below that "To deny the infant relief in this case is not only a harsh result, but its effect is to do reverence to an outmoded, timeworn fiction not founded on fact and within common knowledge untrue and unjustified." . . .

*MAHER V. ROE**

U.S. Supreme Court (1977)

MR. JUSTICE POWELL delivered the opinion of the Court. . . .

A regulation of the Connecticut Welfare Department limits state Medicaid benefits for first trimester abortions . . . to those that are "medically necessary," a term defined to include psychiatric necessity. . . . Connecticut enforces this limitation through a system of prior authorization from its Department of Social Services. In order to obtain authorization for a first trimester abortion, the hospital or clinic where the abortion is to be performed must submit, among other things, a certificate from the patient's attending physician stating that the abortion is medically necessary.

*432 U.S. 464

This attack on the validity of the Connecticut regulation was brought against appellant Maher, the Commissioner of Social Services, by appellees Poe and Roe, two indigent women who were unable to obtain a physician's certificate of medical necessity.[1] . . .

The central question in this case is whether the regulation "impinges upon a fundamental right explicitly or implicitly protected by the Constitution." The District Court read our decisions in *Roe* v. *Wade* . . . and the subsequent cases applying it, as establishing a fundamental right to abortion and therefore concluded that nothing less than a compelling state interest would justify Connecticut's different treatment of abortion and childbirth. We think the District Court misconceived the nature and scope of the fundamental right recognized in *Roe*. . . .

. . . *Roe* did not declare an unqualified "constitutional right to an abortion," as the District Court seemed to think. Rather, the right protects the woman from unduly burdensome interference with her freedom to decide whether to terminate her pregnancy. It implies no limitation on the authority of a State to make a value judgment favoring childbirth over abortion, and to implement that judgment by the allocation of public funds.

The Connecticut regulation before us is different in kind from the laws invalidated in our previous abortion decisions. The Connecticut regulation places no obstacles—absolute or otherwise—in the pregnant woman's path to an abortion. An indigent woman who desires an abortion suffers no disadvantage as a consequence of Connecticut's decision to fund childbirth; she continues as before to be dependent on private sources for the service she desires. The State may have made childbirth a more attractive alternative, thereby influencing the woman's decision, but it has imposed no restriction on access to abortions that was not already there. The indigency that may make it difficult—and in some cases, perhaps, impossible—for some women to have abortions is neither created nor in any way affected by the Connecticut regulation. We conclude that the Connecticut regulation does not impinge upon the fundamental right recognized in *Roe*. . . .

Our conclusion signals no retreat from *Roe* or the cases applying it. There is a basic difference between direct state interference with a protected activity and state encouragement of an alternative activity consonant with legislative policy. . . .

. . . ."[i]t is one thing to say that a State may not prohibit the maintenance of private schools and quite another to say that such schools must, as a matter of equal protection, receive state aid." Yet, were we to accept appellees' argument, an indigent parent could challenge the state policy of favoring public rather than private schools, or of preferring instruction in English rather than German, on

---

[1]At the time this action was filed, Mary Poe, a 16-year-old high school junior, had already obtained an abortion at a Connecticut hospital. Apparently because of Poe's inability to obtain a certificate of medical necessity, the hospital was denied reimbursement by the Department of Social Services. As a result, Poe was being pressed to pay the hospital bill of $244. Susan Roe, an unwed mother of three children, was unable to obtain an abortion because of her physician's refusal to certify that the procedure was medically necessary.

grounds identical in principle to those advanced here. We think it abundantly clear that a State is not required to show a compelling interest for its policy choice to favor normal childbirth any more than a State must so justify its election to fund public but not private education. . . . .

. . . . The medical costs associated with childbirth are substantial, and have increased significantly in recent years. As recognized by the District Court in this case, such costs are significantly greater than those normally associated with elective abortions during the first trimester. The subsidizing of costs incident to childbirth is a rational means of encouraging childbirth. . . .

In conclusion, we emphasize that our decision today does not proscribe government funding of nontherapeutic abortions. It is open to Congress to require provision of Medicaid benefits for such abortions as a condition of state participation in the Medicaid program. Also, under Title XIX as construed in *Beal* v. *Doe*. . . . Connecticut is free—through normal democratic processes—to decide that such benefits should be provided. We hold only that the Constitution does not require a judicially imposed resolution of these difficult issues. . . .

MR. JUSTICE BRENNAN, with whom MR. JUSTICE MARSHALL and MR. JUSTICE BLACKMUN join, dissenting. . . . .

. . . a distressing insensitivity to the plight of impoverished pregnant women is inherent in the Court's analysis. The stark reality for too many, not just "some," indigent pregnant women is that indigency makes access to competent licensed physicians not merely "difficult" but "impossible." As a practical matter, many indigent women will feel they have no choice but to carry their pregnancies to term because the State will pay for the associated medical services, even though they would have chosen to have abortions if the State had also provided funds for that procedure, or indeed if the State had provided funds for neither procedure. This disparity in funding by the State clearly operates to coerce indigent pregnant women to bear children they would not otherwise choose to have, and just as clearly, this coercion can only operate upon the poor, who are uniquely the victims of this form of financial pressure. Mr. Justice Frankfurter's words are apt:

> "To sanction such a ruthless consequence, inevitably resulting from a money hurdle erected by the State, would justify a latter-day Anatole France to add one more item to his ironic comments on the 'majestic equality' of the law. 'The law, in its majestic equality, forbids the rich as well as the poor to sleep under bridges, to beg in the streets, and to steal bread'. . . ." *Griffin* v. *Illinois*. . . .

Roe v. *Wade* and cases following it hold that an area of privacy invulnerable to the State's intrusion surrounds the decision of a pregnant woman whether or not to carry her pregnancy to term. The Connecticut scheme clearly impinges upon that area of privacy by bringing financial pressures on indigent women that force them to bear children they would not otherwise have. That is an obvious impairment of the fundamental right established by *Roe* v. *Wade*. . . .

DANDRIDGE, CHAIRMAN, MARYLAND BOARD OF PUBLIC WELFARE V. WILLIAMS*

U.S. Supreme Court (1970)

MR. JUSTICE STEWART delivered the opinion of the Court.

This case involves the validity of a method used by Maryland, in the administration of an aspect of its public welfare program, to reconcile the demands of its needy citizens with the finite resources available to meet those demands. . . .

The operation of the Maryland welfare system is not complex. By statute . . . the State participates in the AFDC program. It computes the standard of need for each eligible family based on the number of children in the family and the circumstances under which the family lives. In general, the standard of need increases with each additional person in the household, but the increments become proportionately smaller. . . . The regulation here in issue imposes upon the grant that any single family may receive an upper limit of $250 per month in certain counties and Baltimore City, and of $240 per month elsewhere in the State. . . . The appellees all have large families, so that their standards of need as computed by the State substantially exceed the maximum grants that they actually receive under the regulation. The appellees urged in the District Court that the maximum grant limitation operates to discriminate against them merely because of the size of their families, in violation of the Equal Protection Clause of the Fourteenth Amendment. . . .

. . . Moreover, it is argued that the regulation, in limiting the amount of money any single household may receive, contravenes a basic purpose of the federal law by encouraging the parents of large families to "farm out" their children to relatives whose grants are not yet subject to the maximum limitation.

It cannot be gainsaid that the effect of the Maryland maximum grant provision is to reduce the per capita benefits to the children in the largest families. Although the appellees argue that the younger and more recently arrived children in such families are totally deprived of aid, a more realistic view is that the lot of the entire family is diminished because of the presence of additional children without any increase in payments. . . .

We do not decide today that the Maryland regulation is wise, that it best fulfills the relevant social and economic objectives that Maryland might ideally espouse, or that a more just and humane system could not be devised. Conflicting claims of morality and intelligence are raised by opponents and proponents of almost every measure, certainly including the one before us. But the intractable economic, social, and even philosophical problems presented by public welfare assistance programs are not the business of this Court. The Constitution may impose certain procedural safeguards upon systems of welfare administration. . . . But the Constitution does not empower this Court to second-guess state officials

*397 U.S. 471

charged with the difficult responsibility of allocating limited public welfare funds among the myriad of potential recipients. . . .

*JEFFERSON V. GRIFFIN SPALDING COUNTY HOSPITAL AUTHORITY**

Supreme Court of Georgia (1981)

PER CURIAM. . . .

. . . After appointing counsel for the parents and for the child, the court conducted a joint hearing in both the superior court and juvenile court cases and entered the following order on the afternoon of January 23: . . . .

Based on the evidence presented, the Court finds that Jessie Mae Jefferson is due to begin labor at any moment. There is a 99 to 100 percent certainty that the unborn child will die if she attempts to have the child by vaginal delivery. There is a 99 to 100 percent chance that the child will live if the baby is delivered by Caesarean section prior to the beginning of labor. There is a 50 percent chance that Mrs. Jefferson herself will die if vaginal delivery is attempted. There is an almost 100 percent chance that Mrs. Jefferson will survive if a delivery by Caesarean section is done prior to the beginning of labor. The Court finds that as a matter of fact the child is a human being fully capable of sustaining life independent of the mother.

Mrs. Jefferson and her husband have refused and continue to refuse to give consent to a Caesarean section. This refusal is based entirely on the religious beliefs of Mr. and Mrs. Jefferson. They are of the view that the Lord has healed her body and that whatever happens to the child will be the Lord's will.

Based on these findings, the Court concludes and finds as a matter of law that this child is a viable human being and entitled to the protection of the Juvenile Court Code of Georgia. The Court concludes that this child is without the proper parental care and subsistence necessary for his or her physical life and health.

Temporary custody of the unborn child is hereby granted to the State of Georgia Department of Human Resources and the Butts County Department of Family and Children Services. The Department shall have full authority to make all decisions, including giving consent to the surgical delivery appertaining to the birth of this child. The temporary custody of the Department shall terminate when the child has been successfully brought from its mother's body into the world or until the child dies, whichever shall happen.

Because of the unique nature of these cases, the powers of the Superior Court of Butts County are invoked and the defendant, Jessie Mae Jefferson, is hereby Ordered to submit to a sonogram (ultrasound) at the Griffin Spalding County Hospital or some other place which may be chosen by her where such procedure can be given. Should said sonogram indicate to the attending physician that the complete placenta privia

*274 S.E. 2d. 457

is still blocking the child's passage into this world, Jessie Mae Jefferson, is Ordered to submit to a Caesarean section and related procedures considered necessary by the attending physician to sustain the life of this child.

The Court finds that the State has an interest in the life of this unborn, living human being. The Court finds that the intrusion involved into the life of Jessie Mae Jefferson and her husband, John W. Jefferson, is outweighed by the duty of the State to protect a living, unborn human being from meeting his or her death before being given the opportunity to live. . . .

Motion for Stay Denied.

2

RIGHT TO CARE
AND TREATMENT

When we reach the point of deciding that a moral society helps its citizens in peril, we still have many questions to answer. How much help must we give? How much peril is necessary to warrant our attention? Are some properly disqualified from care? The cases in this chapter pose and address such questions.

We begin by considering the status of a brand new citizen in *Maine Medical Center* v. *Houle*. Robert Houle wants the hospital to let his terribly malformed son die. Judge Roberts resists him on grounds that young Houle is a human being. In the course of his opinion, he observes that doctors, as doctors, are not competent to judge whether a life is worth preserving. Who, if anyone, is competent to make such a judgment?

What sort of birth defect, if any, would make medical care morally unnecessary? And if it is ever permissible to let a newborn die, how should that death be arranged? Should it come by lethal inattention or by direct lethal action?

Repouille v. *United States* comes at the issue indirectly by way of a citizenship hearing. Repouille faces resistance to his becoming a U.S. citizen because his character is in question. Five years earlier he chloroformed his son who is described as "an idiot and a physical monstrosity." Judge Learned Hand must decide whether this act renders Repouille incapable of satisfying the "good moral character" clause of the Nationality Act. Young Repouille, unlike Houle, was not a newborn. Does this make a difference? Houle's parents asked the hospital to withhold care. Repouille directly killed his son. Is there a morally relevant difference between these actions?

McCabe v. *Nassau County Medical Center* is not a matter of life and death; the stakes are lower. It gives us the occasion to consider how far the right to treatment extends.

Unable to use birth control pills and lacking the money for sterilization, Linda McCabe asked for the operation without charge. The medical center refused since, according to their rules, a woman of her age must have five children before sterilization is performed. McCabe argues that this refusal caused her great suffering over the prospects of another pregnancy. Does she in fact have a right to sterilization when she chooses?

Do people, by virtue of their humanity, deserve basic medical care whether or not they can pay for it? If so, what shall count as basic medical care?

Are we obliged to provide our fellow man with treatments whose absence would cause them anguish? If we were to accept this principle, would we be morally bound to fund cosmetic surgery for indigents? At what point should people foot their own bill for care? And where shall we draw the line in defining elective surgery? Was sterilization necessary or merely desirable for Linda McCabe?

When a person is convicted of a crime, he forfeits certain rights, such as the right to move about freely or the right to use all of his money as he pleases. Could it be that he also forfeits a measure of his right to health care and treatment? *Pugh* v. *Locke* raises the question of a universal standard for such care. Recalling the "Andersonville Trial" of Captain Wirtz, we might also extend the query to prisoners of war.

Convict, Jerry Lee Pugh, sues Judson Locke, Commissioner of the Alabama Board of Corrections, because the prison living conditions are so bad. Judge Johnson sides with the prisoners and issues minimum standards for their care.

Notice that in his efforts to eliminate "cruel and unusual punishment" he relies heavily on the counsel of medical and public health specialists. His directives encompass such factors as crowding, ventilation, lighting, sanitation, nutrition, and exercise. Is he coddling the criminals, or are these the essentials for human living?

We might extend the question beyond prison walls. Are these standards generally applicable to humanity? Should welfare programs be keyed to the minimums for adults? What does it take to live with dignity?

The Queen v. *Dudley and Stephens*, a case of cannibalism on a life raft, seems an odd selection to include here. But in contemporary legal discussions of the allocation of scarce lifesaving resources, it is often cited. For it is an instance of some men's living at the expense of others. The seamen's lives meant the death of a cabin boy, Richard Parker. And so the situation is similar to those in which my access to treatment excludes you from that same scarce treatment.

If we must select some for treatment, and so, in effect, some for death, how shall we do it? If there isn't enough serum or equipment or there's a shortage of transplant organs, who will get what's available? Shall we proceed on a first come, first serve basis? Or shall we hold a lottery? Perhaps we should determine who can best serve society, or whose loss would be most tragic. Such questions were once appropriate to kidney dialysis. And with each new cure, there is the possibility of similar conflict.

There is still another question. If a committee declares that you will receive the lifesaving care, should you accept it? Should you rather turn it down so that another might live in your place? Would this be your duty or would it be beyond the call of duty? Would it even be irresponsible?

This case dramatically presents an issue pertinent to all ethical reasoning: Is every moral rule suspendable in some situation or other, or are there moral rules which may not be suspended? In this instance, we find the rule, "Don't kill innocents," up for grabs. Should the seamen have faced their own deaths rather than violate it? Or were they warranted in weighing costs and benefits so as to set aside the rule?

MAINE MEDICAL CENTER V. HOULE*

Superior Court of Maine (1974)

DAVID ROBERTS, Justice of the Superior Court:
The complaint herein seeks the intervention of the court between the parents of a newborn child and the hospital and attending physician concerning parental decision as to the future course of treatment. . . .

The testimony herein indicates that a male child was born to the defendants on February 9, 1974, at the Maine Medical Center. Medical examination by the hospital staff revealed the absence of a left eye, a rudimentary left ear with no ear canal, a malformed left thumb and a tracheal esophageal fistula. The latter condition prevented the ingestion of nourishment, necessitated intravenous feeding and allowed the entry of fluids into the infant's lungs leading to the development of pneumonia and other complications. The recommended medical treatment was surgical repair of the tracheal esophageal fistula to allow normal feeding and respiration. Prior to February 11, 1974, the child's father directed the attending physician not to conduct surgical repair of the fistula and to cease intravenous feeding.

By Temporary Restraining Order issued . . . on February 11, 1974, this court authorized the continuance of such measures as might be medically dictated to maintain said child in a stable and viable condition and restrained the defendants from issuing any orders, which, in the opinion of the attending physician, would be injurious to the current medical situation of said child.

*Civil Action, Docket No. 74-145

In the interim the child's condition has deteriorated. Periods of apnea have necessitated the use of a bag breathing device to artifically sustain respiration. Several convulsive seizures of unknown cause have occurred. Medications administered include gentimycin for the treatment of pneumonia and phenobarbitol to control convulsive seizures. Further medical evaluation indicates the lack of response of the right eye to light stimuli, the existence of some non-fused vertebrae and the virtual certainty of some brain damage resulting from anoxia. The most recent developments have caused the attending physician to form the opinion that all life-supporting measures should be withdrawn. The doctor is further of the opinion that without surgical correction of the tracheal esophageal fistula the child will certainly die and that with surgical correction the child can survive but with some degree of permanent brain damage.

The court heard further testimony concerning the present posture of the mother's emotional condition and attitude toward the future survival of the child. Without disparaging the seriousness of the emotional impact upon the parents and without ignoring the difficulties which this court's decision may cause in the future, it is the firm opinion of this court that questions of permanent custody, maintenance and further care of the child are for the moment legally irrelevant.

Quite literally the court must make a decision concerning the life or death of a newborn infant. Recent decisions concerning the right of the state to intervene with the medical and moral judgments of a prospective parent and attending physician may have cast doubts upon the legal rights of an unborn child; but at the moment of live birth there does exist a human being entitled to the fullest protection of the law. The most basic right enjoyed by every human being is the right to life itself.

Where the condition of a child does not involve serious risk of life and where treatment involves a considerable risk, parents as the natural guardians have a considerable degree of discretion and the courts ought not intervene. The measures proposed in this case are not in any sense heroic measures except for the doctor's opinion that probable brain damage has rendered life not worth preserving. Were it his opinion that life itself could not be preserved, heroic measures ought not be required. However, the doctor's qualitative evaluation of the value of the life to be preserved is not legally within the scope of his expertise.

In the court's opinion the issue before the court is not the prospective quality of the life to be preserved, but the medical feasibility of the proposed treatment compared with the almost certain risk of death should treatment be withheld. Being satisfied that corrective surgery is medically necessary and medically feasible, the court finds that the defendants herein have no right to withhold such treatment and that to do so constitutes neglect in the legal sense. Therefore, the court will authorize the guardian ad litem to consent to the surgical correction of the tracheal esophageal fistula and such other normal life supportive measures as may be medically required in the immediate future. It is further ordered that Respondents are hereby enjoined until further order of this court from issuing any orders to Petitioners or their employees which, in the opinion of the attending physicians or surgeons would be injurious to the medical condition of the child.

The court will retain jurisdiction for the purpose of determining any further measures that may be required to be taken and eventually for the purpose of determining the future custody of the child should the court determine that it is appropriate to do so.

REPOUILLE V. UNITED STATES*

U.S. Circuit Court of Appeals, Second Circuit (1947)

L. HAND, Circuit Judge.

The District Attorney, on behalf of the Immigration and Naturalization Service, has appealed from an order, naturalizing the appellee, Repouille. The ground of the objection in the district court and here is that he did not show himself to have been a person of "good moral character" for the five years which preceded the filing of his petition. The facts were as follows. The petition was filed on September 22, 1944, and on October 12, 1939, he had deliberately put to death his son, a boy of thirteen, by means of chloroform. His reason for this tragic deed was that the child had "suffered from birth from a brain injury which destined him to be an idiot and a physical monstrosity malformed in all four limbs. The child was blind, mute, and deformed. He had to be fed; the movements of his bladder and bowels were involuntary, and his entire life was spent in a small crib." Repouille had four other children at the time towards whom he has always been a dutiful and responsible parent; it may be assumed that his act was to help him in their nurture, which was being compromised by the burden imposed upon him in the care of the fifth. The family was altogether dependent upon his industry for its support. He was indicted for manslaughter in the first degree; but the jury brought in a verdict of manslaughter in the second degree with a recommendation of the "utmost clemency"; and the judge sentenced him to not less than five years nor more than ten, execution to be stayed, and the defendant to be placed on probation, from which he was discharged in December, 1945. Concededly, except for this act he conducted himself as a person of "good moral character" during the five years before he filed his petition. Indeed, if he had waited before filing his petition from September 22, to October 14, 1944, he would have had a clear record for the necessary period, and would have been admitted without question.

. . . Very recently we had to pass upon the phrase "good moral character" in the Nationality Act; . . . and we said that it set as a test, not those standards

*165 F. 2d 152

which we might ourselves approve, but whether "the moral feelings, now prevalent generally in this country" would "be outraged" by the conduct in question: that is, whether it conformed to "the generally accepted moral conventions current at the time." . . . In the absence of some national inquisition, like a Gallup poll, that is indeed a difficult test to apply; often questions will arise to which the answer is not ascertainable, and where the petitioner must fail only because he has the affirmative. Indeed, in the case at bar itself the answer is not wholly certain; for we all know that there are great numbers of people of the most unimpeachable virtue, who think it morally justifiable to put an end to a life so inexorably destined to be a burden to others, and—so far as any possible interest of its own is concerned—condemned to a brutish existence, lower indeed than all but the lowest forms of sentient life. Nor is it inevitably an answer to say that it must be immoral to do this, until the law provides security against abuses which would inevitably follow, unless the practice were regulated. Many people—probably most people—do not make it a final ethical test of conduct that it shall not violate law; few of us exact of ourselves or of others the unflinching obedience of a Socrates. There being no lawful means of accomplishing an end, which they believe to be righteous in itself, there have always been conscientious persons who feel no scruple in acting in defiance of a law which is repugnant to their personal convictions, and who even regard as martyrs those who suffer by doing so. In our own history it is only necessary to recall the Abolitionists. It is reasonably clear that the jury which tried Repouille did not feel any moral repulsion at his crime. Although it was inescapably murder in the first degree, not only did they bring in a verdict that was flatly in the face of the facts and utterly absurd—for manslaughter in the second degree presupposes that the killing has not been deliberate—but they coupled even that with a recommendation which showed that in substance they wished to exculpate the offender. Moreover, it is also plain, from the sentence which he imposed, that the judge could not have seriously disagreed with their recommendation.

One might be tempted to seize upon all this as a reliable measure of current morals; and no doubt it should have its place in the scale; but we should hesitate to accept it as decisive, when, for example, we compare it with the fate of a similar offender in Massachusetts, who, although he was not executed, was imprisoned for life. Left at large as we are, without means of verifying our conclusion, and without authority to substitute our individual beliefs, the outcome must needs be tentative; and not much is gained by discussion. We can say no more than that, quite independently of what may be the current moral feeling as to legally administered euthanasia, we feel reasonably secure in holding that only a minority of virtuous persons would deem the practice morally justifiable, while it remains in private hands, even when the provocation is as overwhelming as it was in this instance.

. . . However, we wish to make it plain that a new petition would not be open to this objection; and that the pitiable event, now long passed, will not prevent Repouille from taking his place among us as a citizen. . . .

McCABE V. NASSAU COUNTY MEDICAL CENTER*

U.S. Court of Appeals, Second Circuit (1971)

FEINBERG, Circuit Judge:

This case raises grave issues concerning the right of a woman to decide how many children she shall bear. In the summer of 1970, plaintiff Linda McCabe and her husband agreed, for reasons sufficient for them, that she should be sterilized. For that purpose, she went to the Nassau County Medical Center, a public hospital. The Medical Center refused to perform the operation because, according to its rules, Mrs. McCabe had to have five children before she could be sterilized. Mrs. McCabe felt that the rule was arbitrary and violated her right to decide for herself how many children she wanted. . . .

According to the papers before the district judge: Plaintiff was a mature woman of 25 when this action was brought. By that time she had been pregnant six times and had four small children. Because of concern for her health, and for emotional and economic reasons, Mrs. McCabe and her husband decided not to have any more children. But due to a thyroid condition plaintiff could not take birth control pills. The McCabes felt that they could not rely upon other, riskier means of contraception and decided upon sterilization. In early August 1970, plaintiff and her husband visited the Family Planning Clinic of the Medical Center and plaintiff signed various forms consenting to the operation. On August 26, 1970, plaintiff was told orally by a doctor in the Department of Obstetrics and Gynecology that the regulations of the Medical Center forbade the operation unless the applicant already had five children. This advice was confirmed in September in a letter from defendant Dr. Marcus to plaintiff's attorney, which stated in part:

> I have reviewed Mrs. McCabe's medical records and have spoken to the physician whom she consulted here. According to the bylaws, rules, and regulations governing sterilization at the Nassau County Medical Center, Mrs. McCabe is not eligible for voluntary sterilization.
>
> According to our records Mrs. McCabe is 26 years old and has four living children. For a woman between the ages of 25 to 29 years, the regulations of the Nassau County Medical Center permit sterilization if the woman has five living children.
>
> The bylaws and regulations at this center are based upon the guide lines and recommendations of the American College of Obstetricians and Gynecologists. . . .

Because of inability to pay, plaintiff is unable to go to a private hospital and find a doctor who would perform the operation. Plaintiff went to the Medical Center

*453 F. 2d 698

because it is the only public hospital in the community where she lives and has a sliding scale of fees based on ability to pay. The Center is "funded, regulated and controlled fully or in part" by New York State or Nassau County. . . .

. . . In January 1971, as already indicated, the Medical Center changed its mind and gave plaintiff permission to be sterilized. She entered the hospital promptly and the operation was performed within two weeks, under a stipulation preserving various rights of the parties.

Shortly thereafter defendants moved to dismiss the complaint as moot. Plaintiff opposed the motion on the ground that performance of the surgery did not extinguish her claim for damages.. . .

. . . plaintiff claims, among other things, that defendants' refusal to permit her to be sterilized, based upon an age-parity formula, . . . invaded her right to privacy in her marital relationship, imposed upon her the religious beliefs of others, and denied her the equal protection of the laws not only because the age-parity rule discriminates against the poor but also because the distinctions based upon age are irrational. . . .

. . . the claim for damages is not conceded to be nominal, since the complaint sought damages of $250,000. Although that amount may be familiar hyperbole, the complaint and supporting affidavits allege that for the period when defendants refused to perform the operation plaintiff was in constant fear of becoming pregnant, which caused great pain and suffering and increased the likelihood of further irreparable injury. . . .

. . . We need not determine whether plaintiff's contentions are sound, particularly without a full development of the facts, but it is massive understatement to say that they are not frivolous. . . .

PUGH V. LOCKE*

U.S. District Court for the Middle District of Alabama (1976)

JOHNSON, Chief Judge. . . .

The Alabama Board of Corrections (hereinafter the Board) is charged with the responsibility for managing the state's penal institutions. . . . The Board currently operates four large institutions for male inmates—Holman Unit Prison, G. K. Fountain Correctional Center, Draper Correctional Center, and Kilby Corrections Facility. Kilby also contains the hospital facility for all state prisoners and the classification center for male inmates. The Board also maintains Julia Tutwiler Prison for women and the Frank Lee Youth Center for young men. . . . Additionally, there are six road camps, one pre-release center, and eight work-

*406 F. Supp. 318

release centers. Currently the inmate population of these institutions is in excess of 5,000.

The four principal institutions are horrendously overcrowded. At the time of the trial of these cases the prison population in these four institutions was as follows:

	Maximum Number for Which Designed	Number in Custody
Fountain	632	Over 1100
Holman	540	Over 750
Draper	632	Over 1000
Kilby	503	Over 700

The effects of severe overcrowding are heightened by the dormitory living arrangements which prevail in these institutions. Bunks often are packed together so closely that there is no walking space between them. Sanitation and security are impossible to maintain. There was testimony that the quarantine population at Kilby . . . is so crowded that inmates have to sleep on mattresses spread on floors in hallways and next to urinals. As will be noted, overcrowding is primarily responsible for and exacerbates all the other ills of Alabama's penal system.

The dilapidation of the physical facilities contributes to extremely unsanitary living conditions. Testimony demonstrated that windows are broken and unscreened, creating a serious problem with mosquitoes and flies. Old and filthy cotton mattresses lead to the spread of contagious diseases and body lice. Nearly all inmates' living quarters are inadequately heated and ventilated. The electrical systems are totally inadequate, exposed wiring poses a constant danger to the inmates, and insufficient lighting results in eye strain and fatigue.

In general, Alabama's penal institutions are filthy. There was repeated testimony at trial that they are overrun with roaches, flies, mosquitoes, and other vermin. A public health expert testified that he found roaches in all stages of development—a certain indicator of filthy conditions. This gross infestation is due in part to inadequate maintenance and housekeeping procedures, and in part to the physical structure of the buildings themselves. For example, floors in many shower rooms are so porous that it is impossible to keep them clean. Plumbing facilities are in an exceptional state of disrepair. In one area at Draper, housing well over 200 men, there is one functioning toilet. Many toilets will not flush and are overflowing. Some showers cannot be turned off and continually drip or even pour water. Frequently there is no hot running water for substantial periods of time. Witnesses repeatedly commented on the overpowering odor emanating from these facilities.

Personal hygiene is an insurmountable problem in these circumstances. The parties stipulated that the state supplies prisoners only with razor blades and soap. It was further stipulated that the state furnished no toothpaste, toothbrushes, shampoo, shaving cream, razors or combs; but that such items are available for those inmates who can afford them. Further, household cleaning supplies rarely are available for inmates to maintain their living areas.

Food service conditions are equally unsanitary. Food is improperly stored in dirty storage units, and is often infested with insects. Mechanical dishwashers are not adequately maintained and therefore do not even approach the minimum temperature required for proper sanitation. Moreover, food service personnel, many of whom are inmates, are often untrained and do not follow proper sanitation procedures in the handling and preparation of food. Inmates are not supplied with reasonable eating and drinking utensils; some inmates drink from used tin cans, and have to wash and save their own utensils from meal to meal. Garbage sits in large open drums throughout the dining halls. As a general rule, the food is unappetizing and unwholesome. Inmates with some source of funds may supplement their diets from the prison canteen, but the large majority must subsist only on what is supplied by the kitchen. One menu is prepared for all inmates who require a special diet, regardless of whether it meets their particular needs.

One expert witness, a United States public health officer, toured facilities at Draper, Fountain, Holman, and Kilby. He testified at trial that he found these facilities wholly unfit for human habitation according to virtually every criterion used for evaluation by public health inspectors. With very few exceptions, his testimony was that, if such facilities were under his jurisdiction, he would recommend that they be closed and condemned as an imminent danger to the health of the individuals exposed to them. The Court credits this testimony and makes it a part of these findings. . . .

An oral order enjoining the use of isolation and segregation cells which do not meet minimum standards was issued by the Court at the conclusion of the trial in these cases. The indescribable conditions in the isolation cells required immediate action to protect inmates from any further torture by confinement in those cells. As many as six inmates were packed in four foot by eight foot cells with no beds, no lights, no running water, and a hole in the floor for a toilet which could only be flushed from the outside. The infamous Draper "doghouse" is a separate building, locked from the outside, with no guard stationed inside. Inmates in punitive isolation received only one meal per day, frequently without utensils. They were permitted no exercise or reading material and could shower only every 11 days. Punitive isolation has been used to punish inmates for offenses ranging from swearing at guards and failing to report to work on time, to murder.

. . . In light of the foregoing facts, this Court has a clear duty to require the defendants in these cases to remedy the massive constitutional infirmities which plague Alabama's prisons. It is with great reluctance that federal courts intervene in the day-to-day operation of state penal systems. . . .

. . . The living conditions in Alabama prisons constitute cruel and unusual punishment. Specifically, lack of sanitation throughout the institutions—in living areas, infirmaries, and food service—presents an imminent danger to the health of each and every inmate. Prisoners suffer from further physical deterioration because there are no opportunities for exercise and recreation. Treatment for prisoners with physical or emotional problems is totally inadequate. This Court has previously ordered that the penal system provide reasonable medical care for inmates in these institutions on a finding that

> [f]ailure of the Board of Corrections to provide sufficient medical facilities and staff to afford inmates basic elements of adequate medical care constitutes a willful and intentional violation of the rights of prisoners guaranteed under the Eighth and Fourteenth Amendments. . .

Newman v. Alabama. . . .

. . . The evidence in these cases leads to the inescapable conclusion that the gross inadequacies in medical care found in that case have not been remedied. . . .

. . . The Court now acts in these cases with a recognition that prisoners are not to be coddled, and prisons are not to be operated as hotels or country clubs. However, this does not mean that responsible state officials, including the Alabama Legislature, can be allowed to operate prison facilities that are barbaric and inhumane. Let the defendant state officials now be placed on notice that failure to comply with the minimum standards set forth in the order of this Court filed with this opinion will necessitate the closing of those several prison facilities herein found to be unfit for human confinement. . . .

APPENDIX

MINIMUM CONSTITUTIONAL STANDARDS FOR INMATES OF ALABAMA PENAL SYSTEM

. . . Overcrowding

. . . The number of inmates in each institution in the Alabama penal system shall not exceed the design capacity for that institution. . . .

. . . Segregation and Isolation

1. No more than one prisoner shall be confined in a single cell, and each such cell shall be a minimum of 40 square feet. Within six months, the area of each single occupancy isolation cell shall be no less than 60 square feet.

2. Each cell shall be equipped with a toilet which can be flushed from the inside, a sink with hot and cold running water, ventilation and lighting which meet minimum standards of the United States Public Health Service, clean linen, and a bed off the floor.

3. Each inmate confined in isolation shall be

    (a) permitted to bathe at least every other day;

    (b) provided three wholesome and nutritious meals per day, served with eating and drinking utensils;

(c) supplied the same toilet articles and linens as are required to be provided to the general inmate population;

(d) provided reading and writing materials, and allowed any personal legal papers or research materials;

(e) allowed at least 30 minutes outdoor exercise per day; and

(f) afforded adequate medical and mental health care, including examination by a physician and a qualified mental health care professional at least every third day. No inmate shall be deprived of physical aids or prosthetic devices. . . .

. . . Living Conditions

1. Prisoners shall be supplied, without charge, toothbrushes, toothpaste, shaving cream, razors and razor blades, soap, shampoo, and combs. Each prisoner also shall be provided adequate clean clothing and a storage locker with a lock.

2. Each prisoner shall be supplied weekly with clean bed linen and towels.

3. Each inmate shall have access to household cleaning supplies in order to maintain living areas, and sanitary conditions within the institutions shall meet minimum public health standards. The defendants shall be responsible for implementing a regular and effective program of insect and rodent control.

4. All institutions shall be adequately heated, lighted and ventilated. Windows and doors shall be properly screened and otherwise properly maintained. Electrical wiring must be safe.

5. Each prisoner shall have a bed off the floor, a clean mattress, and blankets as needed.

6. Each institution shall maintain in working order one toilet per 15 inmates, one urinal or one foot of urinal trough per 15 inmates, one shower per 20 inmates, and one lavatory per 10 inmates.

7. Each inmate shall have a minimum of 60 square feet of living space. . . .

. . . Food Service

1. Every prisoner is entitled to three wholesome and nutritious meals per day, served with proper eating and drinking utensils.

2. The food served to inmates shall be nutritionally adequate and properly prepared under the direction of a food service supervisor for each institution; each supervisor shall have at least bachelor's level training in dietetics or its equivalent. The defendants shall employ a nutrition consultant for the Board of Corrections, who shall be a registered dietitian, to assist in menu planning, methods of food preparation, purchasing standards, and sanitation.

3. Food shall be stored, prepared and served under sanitary conditions which meet minimum public health standards. Equipment shall be maintained in good working condition. All kitchen employees shall be trained in the handling of food and those who assist in the preparation of food shall receive training in food preparation. Regulations relating to food service will be rigorously enforced.

4. Each inmate who requires a special diet for reasons of health or religion shall be provided a diet to meet his or her individual need. . . .

THE QUEEN V. DUDLEY AND STEPHENS*

Queen's Bench Division (1884)

INDICTMENT for the murder of Richard Parker on the high seas. . . . At the trial before Huddleston, B. . . .

November 7, 1884, the jury, at the suggestion of the learned judge, found the facts of the case in a special verdict which stated "that on July 5, 1884, the prisoners, Thomas Dudley and Edward Stephens, with one Brooks, all able-bodied English seamen, and the deceased also an English boy, between seventeen and eighteen years of age, the crew of an English yacht, a registered English vessel, were cast away in a storm on the high seas 1600 miles from the Cape of Good Hope, and were compelled to put into an open boat belonging to the said yacht. That in this boat they had no supply of water and no supply of food, except two 1 lb. tins of turnips, and for three days they had nothing else to subsist upon. That on the fourth day they caught a small turtle, upon which they subsisted for a few days, and this was the only food they had up to the twentieth day when the act now in question was committed. That on the twelfth day the remains of the turtle were entirely consumed, and for the next eight days they had nothing to eat. That they had no fresh water, except such rain as they from time to time caught in their oilskin capes. That the boat was drifting on the ocean, and was probably more than 1000 miles away from land. That on the eighteenth day, when they had been seven days without food and five without water, the prisoners spoke to Brooks as to what should be done if no succour came, and suggested that some one should be sacrificed to save the rest, but Brooks dissented, and the boy, to whom they were understood to refer, was not consulted. That on the 24th of July, the day before the act now in question, the prisoner Dudley proposed to Stephens and Brooks that lots should be cast who should be put to death to save the rest, but Brooks refused to consent, and it was not put to the boy, and in point of fact there was no drawing of lots. That on that day the prisoners spoke of their having families, and suggested it would be better to kill the boy that their lives should be saved, and Dudley proposed that if there was no vessel in sight by the morrow morning the boy should be killed. That next day, the 25th of July, no vessel appearing, Dudley told Brooks that he had better go and have a sleep, and made signs to Stephens and Brooks that the boy had better be killed. The prisoner Stephens agreed to the act, but Brooks dissented from it. That the boy was then lying at the bottom of the boat quite helpless, and extremely weakened by famine and by drinking sea water, and unable to make any resistance, nor did he ever assent to his being killed. The prisoner Dudley offered a prayer asking forgiveness for them all if either of them should be tempted to commit a rash act, and that their souls might be saved. That Dudley, with the assent of Stephens, went to the boy, and telling him that his time

*XIV Q.B. 273

was come, put a knife into his throat and killed him then and there; that the three men fed upon the body and blood of the boy for four days; that on the fourth day after the act had been committed the boat was picked up by a passing vessel, and the prisoners were rescued, still alive, but in the lowest state of prostration. That they were carried to the port of Falmouth, and committed for trial at Exeter. That if the men had not fed upon the body of the boy they would probably not have survived to be so picked up and rescued, but would within the four days have died of famine. That the boy, being in a much weaker condition, was likely to have died before them. That at the time of the act in question there was no sail in sight, nor any reasonable prospect of relief. That under these circumstances there appeared to the prisoners every probability that unless they then fed or very soon fed upon the boy or one of themselves they would die of starvation. That there was no appreciable chance of saving life except by killing some one for the others to eat. That assuming any necessity to kill anybody, there was no greater necessity for killing the boy than any of the other three men."

LORD COLERIDGE, C.J. . . .

Now, except for the purpose of testing how far the conservation of a man's own life is in all cases and under all circumstances, an absolute, unqualified, and paramount duty, we exclude from our consideration all the incidents of war. We are dealing with a case of private homicide, not one imposed upon men in the service of their Sovereign and in the defence of their country. Now it is admitted that the deliberate killing of this unoffending and unresisting boy was clearly murder, unless the killing can be justified by some well-recognised excuse admitted by the law. It is further admitted that there was in this case no such excuse, unless the killing was justified by what has been called "necessity." But the temptation to the act which existed here was not what the law has ever called necessity. Nor is this to be regretted. Though law and morality are not the same, and many things may be immoral which are not necessarily illegal, yet the absolute divorce of law from morality would be of fatal consequence; and such divorce would follow if the temptation to murder in this case were to be held by law an absolute defence of it. It is not so. To preserve one's life is generally speaking a duty, but it may be the plainest and the highest duty to sacrifice it. War is full of instances in which it is a man's duty not to live, but to die. The duty, in case of shipwreck, of a captain to his crew, of the crew to the passengers, of soldiers to women and children, as in the noble case of the *Birkenhead;* these duties impose on men the moral necessity, not of the preservation, but of the sacrifice of their lives for others, from which in no country, least of all, it is to be hoped, in England, will men ever shrink, as indeed, they have not shrunk. It is not correct, therefore, to say that there is any absolute or unqualified necessity to preserve one's life. "Necesse est ut eam, non ut vivam," is a saying of a Roman officer quoted by Lord Bacon himself with high eulogy in the very chapter on necessity to which so much reference has been made. It would be a very easy and cheap display of commonplace learning to quote from Greek and Latin authors, from

Horace, from Juvenal, from Cicero, from Euripides, passage after passage, in which the duty of dying for others has been laid down in glowing and emphatic language as resulting from the principles of heathen ethics; it is enough in a Christian country to remind ourselves of the Great Example whom we profess to follow. It is not needful to point out the awful danger of admitting the principle which has been contended for. Who is to be the judge of this sort of necessity? By what measure is the comparative value of lives to be measured? Is it to be strength, or intellect, or what? It is plain that the principle leaves to him who is to profit by it to determine the necessity which will justify him in deliberately taking another's life to save his own. In this case the weakest, the youngest, the most unresisting, was chosen. Was it more necessary to kill him than one of the grown men? The answer must be "No"—

"So spake the Fiend, and with necessity,
The tyrant's plea, excused his devilish deeds."

It is not suggested that in this particular case the deeds were "devilish," but it is quite plain that such a principle once admitted might be made the legal cloak for unbridled passion and atrocious crime. There is no safe path for judges to tread but to ascertain the law to the best of their ability and to declare it according to their judgment; and if in any case the law appears to be too severe on individuals, to leave it to the Sovereign to exercise that prerogative of mercy which the Constitution has intrusted to the hands fittest to dispense it.

It must not be supposed that in refusing to admit temptation to be an excuse for crime it is forgotten how terrible the temptation was; how awful the suffering; how hard in such trials to keep the judgment straight and the conduct pure. We are often compelled to set up standards we cannot reach ourselves, and to lay down rules which we could not ourselves satisfy. But a man has no right to declare temptation to be an excuse, though he might himself have yielded to it, nor allow compassion for the criminal to change or weaken in any manner the legal definition of the crime. It is therefore our duty to declare that the prisoners' act in this case was wilful murder, that the facts as stated in the verdict are no legal justification of the homicide; and to say that in our unanimous opinion the prisoners are upon this special verdict guilty of murder. . . .

THE COURT then proceeded to pass sentence of death upon the prisoners.[1]

[1]This sentence was afterwards commuted by the Crown to six months' imprisonment.

3

INFORMED CONSENT
TO TREATMENT

As the name implies, informed consent requires both knowledge and will. When the adult capacity to know and to will is absent, however, interpretation becomes tricky. How do we treat infants, retarded persons, or animals? How much must the subject know? How freely must he or she will? It is difficult to eliminate all misunderstanding and pressure. How much should we tolerate?

These questions, of course, presuppose the value in seeking informed consent from the person to be treated. But should we assume that it is always wrong to treat a person against his or her will, that is, without personal consent? Are there times when we properly override a patient's objections to treatment? Is informed consent always necessary?

We may also ask whether it is always sufficient. Might someone be properly denied a treatment to which he or she has consented with clear understanding of the risks involved?

The judge in *Canterbury* v. *Spence* goes to great lengths to explain his decision to hold Dr. Spence to a new trial. The prose is difficult, but the wide-ranging discussion of informed consent make this case a classic.

In *Truman* v. *Thomas* we are led to consider not the doctor's duty to outline the dangers in a procedure, but the dangers in declining a procedure. Is the doctor responsible for "informed dissent" as well as informed consent?

Are the two essentially the same, or is the latter more compelling than the former? Dissenting Justice Clark is alarmed that the court equates the two. Is his alarm justified?

In *Strunk* v. *Strunk*, we're concerned not with the denial of informed consent, but with its impossibility. Tommy Strunk needs a kidney and his brother Jerry is an ideal donor. But because Jerry is retarded, he cannot grasp the full range of implications and so is poorly equipped to make this big decision. Should the doctors and his parents be allowed to speak for him?

Notice that Jerry's mental age is set at six. What would we say if Jerry were indeed six? Would it make a difference? Should children be allowed to consent to kidney transplant? At what age do their wishes count, either for or against surgery? May parents overrule a child's refusal to donate a kidney, much as they overrule a refusal to go to church or eat vegetables?

Superintendent of Belchertown State School v. *Saikewicz* also concerns a retarded person, but death rather than organ loss is the issue. Sixty-seven-year-old Joseph Saikewicz has contracted leukemia. Taking into account the rigors of treatment, the chances of success, the extremely low IQ of the patient, and the potential quality of prolonged life, the court agrees with the school's decision to withhold chemotherapy.

Judge Liacos observes that while we express our interests, the interests of "incompetents" are a matter of speculation. We must speak for them as if they were standing outside and rationally considering their own situation. And since their retardation would be a factor in their decision, they might well be treated differently.

If they would want treatment, then they will get it. Is this the right way for us to decide for them?

In the Matter of Karen Quinlan presents us with another instance of "proxy" informed consent. Karen has no prospect of regaining cognition. She is only capable of persistent "vegetative" life. Her father argues that she should be removed from the respirator.

May he properly give informed consent to the removal of life support? Is talk of Karen's "presumed will" legitimate? Does the fact that she is unconscious serve to morally distinguish her case from that of Saikewicz?

People v. *Privitera* brings us to the question of the sufficiency of informed consent. Dr. Privitera's use of laetrile is illegal. The substance enjoys neither federal nor state approval, and so he is not free to prescribe it, no matter how anxiously his patients request it. If they wish, they may trek to Mexico for the treatment, since Mexico declines to regulate so closely.

Does California have any business telling dying people what medicine they may or may not try? Would the state do better to publish its findings on the various potions and then let adults make their own selections, their own informed consent?

Consider the arguments pro and con as framed by Judges Stanforth and Cologne. Which judge is right? Would it make a difference if the disease were not fatal or if there were known alternative cures?

In the Matter of Robert Quackenbush is the first of two cases which question the necessity of gaining a rational patient's consent before proceeding. Quackenbush, a seventy-two-year-old semirecluse, needs to have both his legs amputated. Otherwise, he will die from the effects of gangrene. He doesn't want the operation. Should he be allowed to refuse it?

Note the Heston case as well. Jehovah's Witnesses consider the reception of a blood transfusion to be equivalent to eating blood, a practice forbidden in Leviticus 17:10–12. And so time and again they've resisted medical treatment. Should they be allowed, with Quackenbush, to, in effect, commit suicide? May we insist upon life for the person who sets him or herself against the means to preserve it?

The treatment in *Peek* v. *Ciccone* also proceeds without consent. But here, the threat of death is not the issue. Federal convict, Harold Peek, objects to forced dosages of thorazine. Officials argue that without the calming drugs, the life and work of the prison would be disrupted. Peek maintains that the drugs interfere with his power to communicate with those on the outside.

Has the prison acted unjustly? Is there something peculiarly objectionable in pharmaceutically tampering with a man's consciousness? Is this more serious that surgically altering his viscera?

Peek's coercion is clear, but the coercion in *Rockford Clutch* v. *Industrial Commission* is not so plain. If Walter Zabawa does not agree to undergo back surgery, he could find himself without financial support. The court must decide whether this threat may be used against him. If it may, then Zabawa will not, strictly speaking, be forced to have the operation. But the prospects of poverty will likely drive him into surgery. Is this sort of economic pressure compatible with informed consent?

*CANTERBURY V. SPENCE**

U.S. Court of Appeals, District of Columbia Circuit (1972)

SPOTTSWOOD W. ROBINSON, III, Circuit Judge:
The record we review tells a depressing tale. A youth troubled only by back pain submitted to an operation without being informed of a risk of paralysis incidental thereto. A day after the operation he fell from his hospital bed after having been left without assistance while voiding. A few hours after the fall, the lower half of his body was paralyzed, and he had to be operated on again. Despite extensive medical care, he has never been what he was before. Instead of the back pain, even years later, he hobbled about on crutches, a victim of paralysis of the

*464 F. 2d 772

bowels and urinary incontinence. In a very real sense this lawsuit is an understandable search for reasons.

At the time of the events which gave rise to this litigation, appellant was nineteen years of age, a clerk-typist employed by the Federal Bureau of Investigation. In December, 1958, he began to experience severe pain between his shoulder blades. . . . He consulted two general practitioners, but the medications they prescribed failed to eliminate the pain. Thereafter, appellant secured an appointment with Dr. Spence, who is a neurosurgeon.

Dr. Spence examined appellant in his office at some length but found nothing amiss. On Dr. Spence's advice appellant was X-rayed, but the films did not identify any abormality. Dr. Spence then recommended that appellant undergo a myelogram—a procedure in which dye is injected into the spinal column and traced to find evidence of disease or other disorder—at the Washington Hospital Center.

Appellant entered the hospital on February 4, 1959. . . . The myelogram revealed a "filling defect" in the region of the fourth thoracic vertebra. Since a myelogram often does no more than pinpoint the location of an aberration, surgery may be necessary to discover the cause. Dr. Spence told appellant that he would have to undergo a laminectomy—the excision of the posterior arch of the vertebra—to correct what he suspected was a ruptured disc. Appellant did not raise any objection to the proposed operation nor did he probe into its exact nature.

Appellant explained to Dr. Spence that his mother was a widow of slender financial means living in Cyclone, West Virginia, and that she could be reached through a neighbor's telephone. Appellant called his mother the day after the myelogram was performed and, failing to contact her, left Dr. Spence's telephone number with the neighbor. When Mrs. Canterbury returned the call, Dr. Spence told her that the surgery was occasioned by a suspected ruptured disc. Mrs. Canterbury then asked if the recommended operation was serious and Dr. Spence replied "not anymore than any other operation." He added that he knew Mrs. Canterbury was not well off and that her presence in Washington would not be necessary. The testimony is contradictory as to whether during the course of the conversation Mrs. Canterburg expressed her consent to the operation. Appellant himself apparently did not converse again with Dr. Spence prior to the operation.

Dr. Spence performed the laminectomy on February 11 . . . at the Washington Hospital Center. Mrs. Canterbury traveled to Washington, arriving on that date but after the operation was over, and signed a consent form at the hospital. The laminectomy revealed several anomalies: a spinal cord that was swollen and unable to pulsate, an accumulation of large tortuous and dilated veins, and a complete absence of epidural fat which normally surrounds the spine. A thin hypodermic needle was inserted into the spinal cord to aspirate any cysts which might have been present, but no fluid emerged. In suturing the wound, Dr. Spence attempted to relieve the pressure on the spinal cord by enlarging the dura—the outer protective wall of the spinal cord—at the area of swelling.

... For approximately the first day after the operation appellant recuperated normally, but then suffered a fall and an almost immediate setback. Since there is some conflict as to precisely when or why appellant fell, ... we reconstruct the events from the evidence most favorable to him. ... Dr. Spence left orders that appellant was to remain in bed during the process of voiding. These orders were changed to direct that voiding be done out of bed, and the jury could find that the change was made by hospital personnel. Just prior to the fall, appellant summoned a nurse and was given a receptacle for use in voiding, but was then left unattended. Appellant testified that during the course of the endeavor he slipped off the side of the bed, and that there was no one to assist him, or side rails to prevent the fall.

Several hours later, appellant began to complain that he could not move his legs and that he was having trouble breathing; paralysis seems to have been virtually total from the waist down. Dr. Spence was notified on the night of February 12, and he rushed to the hospital. Mrs. Canterbury signed another consent form and appellant was again taken into the operating room. The surgical wound was reopened and Dr. Spence created a gusset to allow the spinal cord greater room in which to pulsate.

Appellant's control over his muscles improved somewhat after the second operation but he was unable to void properly. As a result of this condition, he came under the care of a urologist while still in the hospital. In April, following a cystoscopic examination, appellant was operated on for removal of bladder stones, and in May was released from the hospital. He reentered the hospital the following August for a 10-day period, apparently because of his urologic problems. For several years after his discharge he was under the care of several specialists, and at all times was under the care of a urologist. At the time of the trial in April, 1968, appellant required crutches to walk, still suffered from urinal incontinence and paralysis of the bowels, and wore a penile clamp.

In November, 1959 on Dr. Spence's recommendation, appellant was transferred by the F.B.I. to Miami where he could get more swimming and exercise. Appellant worked three years for the F.B.I. in Miami, Los Angeles and Houston, resigning finally in June, 1962. From then until the time of the trial, he held a number of jobs, but had constant trouble finding work because he needed to remain seated and close to a bathroom. The damages appellant claims include extensive pain and suffering, medical expenses, and loss of earnings. ...

Appellant filed suit in the District Court on March 7, 1963, four years after the laminectomy and approximately two years after he attained his majority. The complaint stated several causes of action against each defendant. Against Dr. Spence it alleged, among other things, negligence in the performance of the laminectomy and failure to inform him beforehand of the risk involved. Against the hospital the complaint charged negligent post-operative care in permitting appellant to remain unattended after the laminectomy, in failing to provide a nurse or orderly to assist him at the time of his fall, and in failing to maintain a side rail on his bed. The answers denied the allegations of negligence. ...

Suits charging failure by a physician . . . adequately to disclose the risks and alternatives of proposed treatment are not innovations in American law. They date back a good half-century, . . . and in the last decade they have multiplied rapidly. . . . There is, nonetheless, disagreement among the courts and the commentators . . . on many major questions, and there is no precedent of our own directly in point. . . . For the tools enabling resolution of the issues on this appeal, we are forced to begin at first principles. . . .

. . . The root premise is the concept, fundamental in American jurisprudence, that "[e]very human being of adult years and sound mind has a right to determine what shall be done with his own body. . . ." . . . True consent to what happens to one's self is the informed exercise of a choice, and that entails an opportunity to evaluate knowledgeably the options available and the risks attendant upon each. . . . The average patient has little or no understanding of the medical arts, and ordinarily has only his physician to whom he can look for enlightenment with which to reach an intelligent decision. . . . From these almost axiomatic considerations springs the need, and in turn the requirement, of a reasonable divulgence by physician to patient to make such a decision possible.[1]

. . . A physician is under a duty to treat his patient skillfully . . . but proficiency in diagnosis and therapy is not the full measure of his responsibility. The cases demonstrate that the physician is under an obligation to communicate specific information to the patient when the exigencies of reasonable care call for it. . . . Due care may require a physician perceiving symptoms of bodily abnormality to alert the patient to the condition. . . . It may call upon the physician confronting an ailment which does not respond to his ministrations to inform the patient thereof. . . . It may command the physician to instruct the patient as to any limitations to be presently observed for his own welfare, . . . and

[1]The doctrine that a consent effective as authority to form therapy can arise only from the patient's understanding of alternatives to and risks of the therapy is commonly denominated "informed consent." . . . The same appellation is frequently assigned to the doctrine requiring physicians, as a matter of duty to patients, to communicate information as to such alternatives and risks. . . . While we recognize the general utility of shorthand phrases in literary expositions, we caution that uncritical use of the "informed consent" label can be misleading. . . .

In duty-to-disclose cases, the focus of attention is more properly upon the nature and content of the physician's divulgence than the patient's understanding or consent. Adequate disclosure and informed consent are, of course, two sides of the same coin—the former a *sine qua non* of the latter. But the vital inquiry on duty to disclose relates to the physician's performance of an obligation, while one of the difficulties with analysis in terms of "informed consent" is its tendency to imply that what is decisive is the degree of the patient's comprehension. As we later emphasize, the physician discharges the duty when he makes a reasonable effort to convey sufficient information although the patient, without fault of the physician, may not fully grasp it. . . .

Even though the factfinder may have occasion to draw an inference on the state of the patient's enlightenment, the factfinding process on performance of the duty ultimately reaches back to what the physician actually said or failed to say. And while the factual conclusion on adequacy of the revelation will vary as between patients—as, for example, between a lay patient and a physician-patient—the fluctuations are attributable to the kind of divulgence which may be reasonable under the circumstances.

as to any precautionary therapy he should seek in the future. . . . It may oblige the physician to advise the patient of the need for or desirability of any alternative treatment promising greater benefit than that being pursued.[2] Just as plainly, due care normally demands that the physician warn the patient of any risks to his well-being which contemplated therapy may involve. . . .

. . . The context in which the duty of risk-disclosure arises is invariably the occasion for decision as to whether a particular treatment procedure is to be undertaken. To the physician, whose training enables a self-satisfying evaluation, the answer may seem clear, but it is the prerogative of the patient, not the physician, to determine for himself the direction in which his interests seem to lie. . . . To enable the patient to chart his course understandably, some familiarity with the therapeutic alternatives and their hazards becomes essential. . . .

. . . A reasonable revelation in these respects is not only a necessity but, as we see it, is as much a matter of the physician's duty. It is a duty to warn of the dangers lurking in the proposed treatment, and that is surely a facet of due care. . . . It is, too, a duty to impart information which the patient has every right to expect.[3] The patient's reliance upon the physician is a trust of the kind which traditionally has exacted obligations beyond those associated with arms-length transactions. . . . His dependence upon the physician for information affecting his well-being, in terms of contemplated treatment, is well-nigh abject. As earlier noted, long before the instant litigation arose, courts had recognized that the physician had the responsibility of satisfying the vital informational needs of the patient. . . . More recently, we ourselves have found "in the fiducial qualities of [the physician-patient] relationship the physician's duty to reveal to the patient that which in his best interests it is important that he should know." . . . We now find, as a part of the physician's overall obligation to the patient, a similar duty of reasonable disclosure of the choices with respect to proposed therapy and the dangers inherently and potentially involved. . . .

. . . This disclosure requirement, on analysis, reflects much more of a change in doctrinal emphasis than a substantive addition to malpractice law. It is well established that the physician must seek and secure his patient's consent before commencing an operation or other course of treatment. . . . It is also clear that the consent, to be efficacious, must be free from imposition upon the patient. . . . It is

---

[2] The typical situation is where a general practitioner discovers that the patient's malady calls for specialized treatment, whereupon the duty generally arises to advise the patient to consult a specialist.

[3] Some doubt has been expressed as to ability of physicians to suitably communicate their evaluations of risks and the advantages of optional treatment, and as to the lay patient's ability to understand what the physician tells him. . . . We do not share these apprehensions. The discussion need not be a disquisition, and surely the physician is not compelled to give his patient a short medical education; the disclosure rule summons the physician only to a reasonable explanation. . . . That means generally informing the patient in non-technical terms as to what is at stake: the therapy alternatives open to him, the goals expectably to be achieved, and the risks that may ensue from particular treatment and no treatment. . . . So informing the patient hardly taxes the physician, and it must be the exceptional patient who cannot comprehend such an explanation at least in a rough way.

the settled rule that therapy not authorized by the patient may amount to a tort—a common law battery—by the physician. . . . And it is evident that it is normally impossible to obtain a consent worthy of the name unless the physician first elucidates the options and the perils for the patient's edification. . . . Thus the physician has long borne a duty, on pain of liability for unauthorized treatment, to make adequate disclosure to the patient.[4] The evolution of the obligation to communicate for the patient's benefit as well as the physician's protection has hardly involved an extraordinary restructuring of the law.

Once the circumstances give rise to a duty on the physician's part to inform his patient, the next inquiry is the scope of the disclosure the physician is legally obliged to make. The courts have frequently confronted this problem but no uniform standard defining the adequacy of the divulgence emerges from the decisions. Some have said "full" disclosure, . . . a norm we are unwilling to adopt literally. It seems obviously prohibitive and unrealistic to expect physicians to discuss with their patients every risk of proposed treatment—no matter how small or remote . . .—and generally unnecessary from the patient's viewpoint as well. Indeed, the cases speaking in terms of "full" disclosure appear to envision something less than total disclosure, . . . leaving unanswered the question of just how much.

The larger number of courts, as might be expected, have applied tests framed with reference to prevailing fashion within the medical profession. . . . Some have measured the disclosure by "good medical practice," . . . others by what a reasonable practitioner would have bared under the circumstances, . . . and still others by what medical custom in the community would demand. . . . We have explored this rather considerable body of law but are unprepared to follow it. The duty to disclose, we have reasoned, arises from phenomena apart from medical custom and practice. . . . The latter, we think, should no more establish the scope of the duty than its existence. Any definition of scope in terms purely of a professional standard is at odds with the patient's prerogative to decide on projected therapy himself. . . . That prerogative, we have said, is at the very foundation of the duty to disclose, . . . and both the patient's right to know and the physician's correlative obligation to tell him are diluted to the extent that its compass is dictated by the medical profession. . . .

. . . In our view, the patient's right of self-decision shapes the boundaries of the duty to reveal. That right can be effectively exercised only if the patient

[4]We discard the thought that the patient should ask for information before the physician is required to disclose. Caveat emptor is not the norm for the consumer of medical services. Duty to disclose is more than a call to speak merely on the patient's request, or merely to answer the patient's questions; it is a duty to volunteer, if necessary, the information the patient needs for intelligent decision. The patient may be ignorant, confused, overawed by the physician or frightened by the hospital, or even ashamed to inquire. . . . Perhaps relatively few patients could in any event identify the relevant questions in the absence of prior explanation by the physician. Physicians and hospitals have patients of widely divergent socio-economic backgrounds, and a rule which presumes a degree of sophistication which many members of society lack is likely to breed gross inequities. . . .

possesses enough information to enable an intelligent choice. The scope of the physician's communications to the patient, then, must be measured by the patient's need, . . . and that need is the information material to the decision. Thus the test for determining whether a particular peril must be divulged is its materiality to the patient's decision: all risks potentially affecting the decision must be unmasked. . . . And to safeguard the patient's interest in achieving his own determination on treatment, the law must itself set the standard for adequate disclosure. . . .

. . . Optimally for the patient, exposure of a risk would be mandatory whenever the patient would deem it significant to his decision, either singly or in combination with other risks. Such a requirement, however, would summon the physician to second-guess the patient, whose ideas on materiality could hardly be known to the physician. That would make an undue demand upon medical practitioners, whose conduct, like that of others, is to be measured in terms of reasonableness. Consonantly with orthodox negligence doctrine, the physician's liability for nondisclosure is to be determined on the basis of foresight, not hindsight; no less than any other aspect of negligence, the issue on nondisclosure must be approached from the viewpoint of the reasonableness of the physician's divulgence in terms of what he knows or should know to be the patient's informational needs. If, but only if, the fact-finder can say that the physician's communication was unreasonably inadequate is an imposition of liability legally or morally justified. . . .

Of necessity, the content of the disclosure rests in the first instance with the physician. Ordinarily it is only he who is in position to identify particular dangers; always he must make a judgment, in terms of materiality, as to whether and to what extent revelation to the patient is called for. He cannot know with complete exactitude what the patient would consider important to his decision, but on the basis of his medical training and experience he can sense how the average, reasonable patient expectably would react. . . . Indeed, with knowledge of, or ability to learn, his patient's background and current condition, he is in a position superior to that of most others—attorneys, for example—who are called upon to make judgments on pain of liability in damages for unreasonable miscalculation. . . .

. . . From these considerations we derive the breadth of the disclosure of risks legally to be required. The scope of the standard is not subjective as to either the physician or the patient; it remains objective with due regard for the patient's informational needs and with suitable leeway for the physician's situation. In broad outline, we agree that "[a] risk is thus material when a reasonable person, in what the physician knows or should know to be the patient's position, would be likely to attach significance to the risk or cluster of risks in deciding whether or not to forego the proposed therapy." . . .

. . . The topics importantly demanding a communication of information are the inherent and potential hazards of the proposed treatment, the alternatives to that treatment, if any, and the results likely if the patient remains untreated. The factors contributing significance to the dangerousness of a medical technique are, of course, the incidence of injury and the degree of the harm threatened. . . . A very small chance of death or serious disablement may well be significant; a potential disability which dramatically outweighs the potential benefit of the therapy or the detriments of the existing malady may summon discussion with the patient. . . .

. . . There is no bright line separating the significant from the insignificant; the answer in any case must abide a rule of reason. Some dangers—infection, for example—are inherent in any operation; there is no obligation to communicate those of which persons of average sophistication are aware. . . . Even more clearly, the physician bears no responsibility for discussion of hazards the patient has already discovered, . . . or those having no apparent materiality to patients' decision on therapy. . . . The disclosure doctrine, like others marking lines between permissible and impermissible behavior in medical practice, is in essence a requirement of conduct prudent under the circumstances. . . .

. . . Two exceptions to the general rule of disclosure have been noted by the courts. Each is in the nature of a physician's privilege not to disclose, and the reasoning underlying them is appealing. Each, indeed, is but a recognition that, as important as is the patient's right to know, it is greatly outweighed by the magnitudinous circumstances giving rise to the privilege. The first comes into play when the patient is unconscious or otherwise incapable of consenting, and harm from a failure to treat is imminent and outweighs any harm threatened by the proposed treatment. When a genuine emergency of that sort arises, it is settled that the impracticality of conferring with the patient dispenses with need for it. . . . Even in situations of that character the physician should, as current law requires, attempt to secure a relative's consent if possible. . . . But if time is too short to accommodate discussion, obviously the physician should proceed with the treatment. . . .

. . . The second exception obtains when risk-disclosure poses such a threat of detriment to the patient as to become unfeasible or contraindicated from a medical point of view. It is recognized that patients occasionally become so ill or emotionally distraught on disclosure as to foreclose a rational decision, or complicate or hinder the treatment, or perhaps even pose psychological damage to the patient. . . . Where that is so, the cases have generally held that the physician is armed with a privilege to keep the information from the patient, . . . and we think it clear that portents of that type may justify the physician in action he deems medically warranted. The critical inquiry is whether the physician responded to a sound medical judgment that communication of the risk information would present a threat to the patient's well-being.

. . . The physician's privilege to withhold information for therapeutic reasons must be carefully circumscribed, however, for otherwise it might devour the disclosure rule itself. The privilege does not accept the paternalistic notion that the physician may remain silent simply because divulgence might prompt the patient to forego therapy the physician feels the patient really needs. . . . That attitude presumes instability or perversity for even the normal patient, and runs counter to the foundation principle that the patient should and ordinarily can make the choice for himself. . . . Nor does the privilege contemplate operation save where the patient's reaction to risk information, as reasonable foreseen by the physician, is menacing. . . . And even in a situation of that kind, disclosure to a close relative with a view to securing consent to the proposed treatment may be the only alternative open to the physician. . . .

. . . No more than breach of any other legal duty does nonfulfillment of the physician's obligation to disclose alone establish liability to the patient. An unrevealed risk that should have been made known must materialize, for otherwise the omission, however unpardonable, is legally without consequence. Occurrence of the risk must be harmful to the patient, for negligence unrelated to injury is nonactionable. . . . And, as in malpractice actions generally, . . . there must be a causal relationship between the physician's failure to adequately divulge and damage to the patient. . . .

. . . A causal connection exists when, but only when, disclosure of significant risks incidental to treatment would have resulted in a decision against it. . . . The patient obviously has no complaint if he would have submitted to the therapy notwithstanding awareness that the risk was one of its perils. On the other hand, the very purpose of the disclosure rule is to protect the patient against consequences which, if known, he would have avoided by foregoing the treatment. . . . The more difficult question is whether the factual issue on causality calls for an objective or a subjective determination.

It has been assumed that the issue is to be resolved according to whether the factfinder believes the patient's testimony that he would not have agreed to the treatment if he had known of the danger which later ripened into injury. . . . We think a technique which ties the factual conclusion on causation simply to the assessment of the patient's credibility is unsatisfactory. To be sure, the objective of risk-disclosure is preservation of the patient's interest in intelligent self-choice on proposed treatment, a matter the patient is free to decide for any reason that appeals to him. . . . When, prior to commencement of therapy, the patient is sufficiently informed on risks and he exercises his choice, it may truly be said that he did exactly what he wanted to do. But when causality is explored at a post-injury trial with a professedly uninformed patient, the question whether he actually would have turned the treatment down if he had known the risks is purely hypothetical: "Viewed from the point at which he had to decide, would the patient have decided differently had he known something he did not know?" . . . And the answer which the patient supplies hardly represents more than a guess, perhaps tinged by the circumstance that the uncommunicated hazard has in fact materialized. . . .

In our view, this method of dealing with the issue on causation comes in second-best. It places the physician in jeopardy of the patient's hindsight and bitterness. It places the factfinder in the position of deciding whether a speculative answer to a hypothetical question is to be credited. It calls for a subjective determination solely on testimony of a patient-witness shadowed by the occurrence of the undisclosed risk. . . .

. . . Better it is, we believe, to resolve the causality issue on an objective basis: in terms of what a prudent person in the patient's position would have decided if suitably informed of all perils bearing significance. . . . If adequate disclosure could reasonably be expected to have caused that person to decline the treatment because of the revelation of the kind of risk or danger that resulted in harm, causation is shown, but otherwise not. . . . The patient's testimony is relevant on that score of course but it would not threaten to dominate the findings. . . .

. . . Appellant testified that Dr. Spence revealed to him nothing suggesting a hazard associated with the laminectomy. His mother testified that, in response to her specific inquiry, Dr. Spence informed her that the laminectomy was no more serious than any other operation. When, at trial, it developed from Dr. Spence's testimony that paralysis can be expected in one percent of laminectomies, it became the jury's responsibility to decide whether that peril was of sufficient magnitude to bring the disclosure duty into play. . . . There was no emergency to frustrate an opportunity to disclose, ... and Dr. Spence's expressed opinion that disclosure would have been unwise did not foreclose a contrary conclusion by the jury. There was no evidence that appellant's emotional makeup was such that concealment of the risk of paralysis was medically sound.[5] Even if disclosure to appellant himself might have bred ill consequences, no reason appears for the omission to communicate the information to his mother, particularly in view of his minority. . . .

In sum, judged by legal standards, the proof militated against a directed verdict in Dr. Spence's favor. . . .

Reversed and remanded for a new trial.

TRUMAN V. THOMAS*

Supreme Court of California (1980)

BIRD, Chief Justice. . . .

Respondent, Dr. Claude R. Thomas, is a family physician engaged in a general medical practice. He was first contacted in April 1963 by appellants' mother, Rena Truman, in connection with her second pregnancy. He continued

---

[5] . . . Dr. Spence's opinion—that disclosure is medically unwise—was expressed as to patients generally, and not with reference to traits possessed by appellant. His explanation was:

I think that I always explain to patients the operations are serious, and I feel that any operation is serious. I think that I would not tell patients that they might be paralyzed because of the small percentage, one per cent, that exists. There would be a tremendous percentage of people that would not have surgery and would not therefore be benefited by it, the tremendous percentage that get along very well, 99 per cent.

*611 P. 2d 902

to act as the primary physician for Mrs. Truman and her two children until March 1969. During this six-year period, Mrs. Truman not only sought his medical advice, but often discussed personal matters with him.

In April 1969, Mrs. Truman consulted Dr. Casey, a urologist, about a urinary tract infection which had been treated previously by Dr. Thomas. While examining Mrs. Truman, Dr. Casey discovered that she was experiencing heavy vaginal discharges and that her cervix was extremely rough. Mrs. Truman was given a prescription for the infection and advised to see a gynecologist as soon as possible. When Mrs. Truman did not make an appointment with a gynecologist, Dr. Casey made an appointment for her with a Dr. Ritter.

In October 1969, Dr. Ritter discovered that Mrs. Truman's cervix had been largely replaced by a cancerous tumor. Too far advanced to be removed by surgery, the tumor was unsuccessfully treated by other methods. Mrs. Truman died in July 1970 at the age of 30.

Appellants are Rena Truman's two children. They brought this wrongful death action against Dr. Thomas for his failure to perform a pap smear test on their mother. At the trial, expert testimony was presented which indicated that if Mrs. Truman had undergone a pap smear at any time between 1964 and 1969, the cervical tumor probably would have been discovered in time to save her life. . . .

Although Dr. Thomas saw Mrs. Truman frequently between 1964 and 1969, he never performed a pap smear test on her. Dr. Thomas testified that he did not "specifically" inform Mrs. Truman of the risk involved in any failure to undergo the pap smear test. Rather, "I said, 'You should have a pap smear.' We don't say by now it can be Stage Two [in the development of cervical cancer] or go through all of the different lectures about cancer. I think it is a widely known and generally accepted manner of treatment and I think the patient has a high degree of responsibility. We are not enforcers, we are advisors." However, Dr. Thomas' medical records contain no reference to any discussion or recommendation that Mrs. Truman undergo a pap smear test.

For the most part, Dr. Thomas was unable to describe specific conversations with Mrs. Truman. For example, he testified that during certain periods he "saw Rena very frequently, approximately once a week or so, and I am sure my opening remark was, 'Rena, you need a pap smear,' . . . I am sure we discussed it with her so often that she couldn't [have] fail[ed] to realize that we wanted her to have a complete examination, breast examination, ovaries and pap smear." Dr. Thomas also testified that on at least two occasions when he performed pelvic examinations of Mrs. Truman she refused him permission to perform the test, stating she could not afford the cost. Dr. Thomas offered to defer payment, but Mrs. Truman wanted to pay cash. . . .

The central issue for this court is whether Dr. Thomas breached his duty of care to Mrs. Truman when he failed to inform her of the potentially fatal consequences of allowing cervical cancer to develop undetected by a pap smear. . . .

... The scope of a physician's duty to disclose is measured by the amount of knowledge a patient needs in order to make an informed choice. All information material to the patient's decision should be given. . . .

... If a patient indicates that he or she is going to *decline* the risk-free test or treatment, then the doctor has the additional duty of advising of all material risks of which a reasonable person would want to be informed before deciding not to undergo the procedure. . . .

CLARK, Justice, dissenting.

I dissent.

The consent instruction demanded by plaintiffs will impose upon doctors the intolerable burden of having to explain diagnostic tests to healthy patients. To meet their new burden doctors will have to spend the greater part of their day not examining or treating patients, but explaining to them all information relevant to the purposes of diagnostic examinations and tests. Such burden is unreasonable, and the trial court properly refused the instruction. . . .

Carried to its logical end, the majority decision requires physicians to explain to patients who have not had a recent general examination the intricacies of chest examinations, blood analyses, X-ray examinations, electrocardiograms, urine analyses and innumerable other procedures. In short, today's ruling mandates doctors to provide each such patient with a summary course covering most of his or her medical education. Most medical tests—like pap smears—are designed to detect illness which might prove fatal absent timely treatment. Explaining the purposes of each procedure to each such patient will obviously take hours if not days.

Few, if any, people in our society are unaware that a general examination is designed to discover serious illness for timely treatment. While a lengthy explanation may result in general examinations for some patients who would otherwise decline or defer them, the onerous duty placed upon doctors by today's decision will result in reduced care for others. Requiring physicians to spend a large portion of their time teaching medical science before practicing it will greatly increase the cost of medical diagnosis—a cost ultimately paid by an unwanting public. Persons desiring treatment for specific complaints will be deterred from seeking medical advice once they realize they will be charged not only for treatment but also for lengthy lectures on the merits of their examination. . . .

When a patient chooses a physician, he or she obviously has confidence in the doctor and intends to accept proffered medical advice. When the doctor prescribes diagnostic tests, the patient is aware the tests are intended to discover illness. It is therefore reasonable to assume that a patient who refuses advice is aware of potential risk.

Moreover, the physician-patient relationship is based on trust, and forcing the doctor in a hard sell approach to his services can only jeopardize that relationship. . . .

STRUNK V. STRUNK*

Court of Appeals of Kentucky (1969)

OSBORNE, Judge.

The specific question involved upon this appeal is: Does a court of equity have the power to permit a kidney to be removed from an incompetent ward of the state upon petition of his committee, who is also his mother, for the purpose of being transplanted into the body of his brother, who is dying of a fatal kidney disease? We are of the opinion it does.

The facts of the case are as follows: Arthur L. Strunk, 54 years of age, and Ava Strunk, 52 years of age, of Williamstown, Kentucky, are the parents of two sons. Tommy Strunk is 28 years of age, married, an employee of the Penn State Railroad and a part-time student at the University of Cincinnati. Tommy is now suffering from chronic glomerulus nephritis, a fatal kidney disease. He is now being kept alive by frequent treatment on an artificial kidney, a procedure which cannot be continued much longer. . . .

Jerry Strunk is 27 years of age, incompetent, and through proper legal proceedings has been committed to the Frankfort State Hospital and School, which is a state institution maintained for the feeble-minded. He has an I.Q. of approximately 35, which corresponds with the mental age of approximately six years. He is further handicapped by a speech defect, which makes it difficult for him to communicate with persons who are not well acquainted with him. When it was determined that Tommy, in order to survive, would have to have a kidney the doctors considered the possibility of using a kidney from a cadaver if and when one became available or one from a live donor if this could be made available. The entire family, his mother, father and a number of collateral relatives were tested. Because of incompatibility of blood type or tissue none were medically acceptable as live donors. As a last resort, Jerry was tested and found to be highly acceptable. This immediately presented the legal problem as to what, if anything, could be done by the family, especially the mother and the father to procure a transplant from Jerry to Tommy. The mother as a committee petitioned the county court for authority to proceed with the operation. The court found that the operation was necessary, that under the peculiar circumstances of this case it would not only be beneficial to Tommy but also beneficial to Jerry because Jerry was greatly dependent upon Tommy, emotionally and psychologically, and that his well-being would be jeopardized more severely by the loss of his brother than by the removal of a kidney. . . .

A psychiatrist, in attendance to Jerry, who testified in the case, stated in his opinion the death of Tommy under these circumstances would have "an extremely traumatic effect upon him" (Jerry). . . .

*445 S.W. 2d 145

The Department of Mental Health of this Commonwealth has entered the case as amicus curiae and on the basis of its evaluation of the seriousness of the operation as opposed to the traumatic effect upon Jerry as a result of the loss of Tommy, recommended to the court that Jerry be permitted to undergo the surgery. Its recommendations are as follows:

> It is difficult for the mental defective to establish a firm sense of identity with another person and the acquisition of this necessary identity is dependent upon a person whom one can conveniently accept as a model and who at the same time is sufficiently flexible to allow the defective to detach himself with reasurances of continuity. His need to be social is not so much the necessity of a formal and mechanical contact with other human beings as it is the necessity of a close intimacy with other men, the desirability of a real community of feeling, an urgent need for a unity of understanding. Purely mechanical and formal contact with other men does not offer any treatment for the behavior of a mental defective; only those who are able to communicate intimately are of value to hospital treatment in these cases. And this generally is a member of the family.

> In view of this knowledge, we now have particular interest in this case. Jerry Strunk, a mental defective, has emotions and reactions on a scale comparable to that of [sic] normal person. He identifies with his brother Tom; Tom is his model, his tie with his family. Tom's life is vital to the continuity of Jerry's improvement at Frankfort State Hospital and School. The testimony of the hospital representative reflected the importance to Jerry of his visits with his family and the constant inquiries Jerry made about Tom's coming to see him. Jerry is aware he plays a role in the relief of this tension. We the Department of Mental Health must take all possible steps to prevent the occurrence of any guilt feelings Jerry would have if Tom were to die.

> The necessity of Tom's life to Jerry's treatment and eventual rehabilitation is clearer in view of the fact that Tom is his only living sibling and at the death of their parents, now in their fifties, Jerry will have no concerned, intimate communication so necessary to his stability and optimal functioning.

> The evidence shows that at the present level of medical knowledge, it is quite remote that Tom would be able to survive several cadaver transplants. Tom has a much better chance of survival if the kidney transplant from Jerry takes place.

Upon this appeal we are faced with the fact that all members of the immediate family have recommended the transplant. The Department of Mental Health has likewise made its recommendation. The county court has given its approval. The circuit court has found that it would be to the best interest of the ward of the state that the procedure be carried out. Throughout the legal proceedings, Jerry has been represented by a guardian ad litem, who has continually questioned the power of the state to authorize the removal of an organ from the body of an incompetent who is a ward of the state. . . .

The medical practice of transferring tissue from one part of the human body to another (autografting) and from one human being to another (homografting) is rapidly becoming a common clinical practice. In many cases the transplants take as well where the tissue is dead as when it is alive. This has made practicable the establishment of tissue banks where such material can be stored for future use.

Vascularized grafts of lungs, kidneys and hearts are becoming increasingly common. These grafts must be of functioning, living cells with blood vessels remaining anatomically intact. The chance of success in the transfer of these organs is greatly increased when the donor and the donee are genetically related. . . .

The renal transplant is becoming the most common of the organ transplants. This is because the normal body has two functioning kidneys, one of which it can reasonably do without, thereby making it possible for one person to donate a kidney to another. Testimony in this record shows that there have been over 2500 kidney transplants performed in the United States up to this date. The process can be effected under present techniques with minimal danger to both the donor and the donee. Doctors Hamburger and Crosneir describe the risk to the donor as follows:

> This discussion is limited to renal transplantation, since it is inconceivable that any vital organ other than the kidney might ever be removed from a healthy living donor for transplantation purposes. The immediate operative risk of unilateral nephrectomy in a healthy subject has been calculated as approximately 0.05 per cent. The long-term risk is more difficult to estimate, since the various types of renal disease do not appear to be more frequent or more severe in individuals with solitary kidneys than in normal subjects. On the other hand, the development of surgical problems, trauma, or neoplasms, with the possible necessity of nephrectomy, do increase the long-term risks in living donors; the long-term risk, on this basis, has been estimated at 0.07 per cent. . . . These data must, however, be considered in the light of statistical life expectancy which, in a healthy 35 year old adult, goes from 99.3 per cent to 99.1 per cent during the next five succeeding years; this is an increase in risk equal to that incurred by driving a car for 16 miles every working day.

> The risks incurred by the donor are therefore very limited, but they are a reality, even if, until now, there have been no reports of complications endangering the life of a donor anywhere in the world. Unfortunately, there is no doubt that, as the number of renal transplants increases, such an incident will inevitably be recorded. . . .

> . . . *The circuit court having found that the operative procedures in this instance are to the best interest of Jerry Strunk and this finding having been based upon substantial evidence, we are of the opinion the judgment should be affirmed.* . . .

STEINFELD, Judge (dissenting).

Apparently because of my indelible recollection of a government which, to the everlasting shame of its citizens, embarked on a program of genocide and experimentation with human bodies I have been more troubled in reaching a decision in this case than in any other. My sympathies and emotions are torn between a compassion to aid an ailing young man and a duty to fully protect unfortunate members of society. . . .

The majority opinion is predicated upon the finding of the circuit court that there will be psychological benefits to the ward but points out that the incompetent has the mentality of a six-year-old child. It is common knowledge beyond dispute that the loss of a close relative or a friend to a six-year-old child is not of major impact. Opinions concerning psychological trauma are at best most nebulous. Furthermore, there are no guarantees that the transplant will become a surgical success, it being well known that body rejection of transplanted organs is frequent. The life of the incompetent is not in danger, but the surgical procedure advocated creates some peril. . . .

Unquestionably the attitudes and attempts of the committee and members of the family of the two young men whose critical problems now confront us are commendable, natural and beyond reproach. However, they refer us to nothing indicating that they are privileged to authorize the removal of one of the kidneys of the incompetent for the purpose of donation, and they cite no statutory or other authority vesting such right in the courts. The proof shows that less compatible donors are available and that the kidney of a cadaver could be used, although the odds of operational success are not as great in such case as they would be with the fully compatible donor brother.

I am unwilling to hold that the gates should be open to permit the removal of an organ from an incompetent for transplant, at least until such time as it is conclusively demonstrated that it will be of significant benefit to the incompetent. The evidence here does not rise to that pinnacle. To hold that committees, guardians or courts have such awesome power even in the persuasive case before us, could establish legal precedent, the dire result of which we cannot fathom. Regretfully I must say no. . . .

SUPERINTENDENT OF BELCHERTOWN STATE SCHOOL V. SAIKEWICZ*

Supreme Judicial Court of Massachusetts (1977)

LIACOS, Justice. . . .

The judge below found that Joseph Saikewicz, at the time the matter arose, was sixty-seven years old, with an I.Q. of ten and a mental age of approximately two years and eight months. He was profoundly mentally retarded. The record discloses that, apart from his leukemic condition, Saikewicz enjoyed generally good health. He was physically strong and well built, nutritionally nourished, and ambulatory. He was not, however, able to communicate verbally—resorting to gestures and grunts to make his wishes known to others and responding only to gestures or physical contacts. In the course of treatment for various medical conditions arising during Saikewicz's residency at the school, he had been unable to respond intelligibly to inquiries

*370 N.E. 2d 417

such as whether he was experiencing pain. It was the opinion of a consulting psychologist, not contested by the other experts relied on by the judge below, that Saikewicz was not aware of dangers and was disoriented outside his immediate environment. As a result of his condition, Saikewicz had lived in State institutions since 1923 and had resided at the Belchertown State School since 1928. Two of his sisters, the only members of his family who could be located, were notified of his condition and of the hearing, but they preferred not to attend or otherwise become involved.

On April 19, 1976, Saikewicz was diagnosed as suffering from acute myeloblastic monocytic leukemia. Leukemia is a disease of the blood. It arises when organs of the body produce an excessive number of white blood cells as well as other abnormal cellular structures, in particular undeveloped and immature white cells. Along with these symptoms in the composition of the blood the disease is accompanied by enlargement of the organs which produce the cells, e.g., the spleen, lymph glands, and bone marrow. The disease tends to cause internal bleeding and weakness, and, in the acute form, severe anemia and high susceptibility to infection. Attorneys' Dictionary of Medicine. . . . The particular form of the disease present in this case, acute myeloblastic monocytic leukemia is so defined because the particular cells which increase are the myeloblasts, the youngest form of a cell which at maturity is known as the granulocytes. . . . The disease is invariably fatal.

Chemotherapy, as was testified to at the hearing in the Probate Court, involves the administration of drugs over several weeks, the purpose of which is to kill the leukemia cells. This treatment unfortunately affects normal cells as well. One expert testified that the end result, in effect, is to destroy the living vitality of the bone marrow. Because of this effect, the patient becomes very anemic and may bleed or suffer infections—a condition which requires a number of blood transfusions. In this sense, the patient immediately becomes much "sicker" with the commencement of chemotherapy, and there is a possibility that infections during the initial period of severe anemia will prove fatal. Moreover, while most patients survive chemotherapy, remission of the leukemia is achieved in only thirty to fifty per cent of the cases. Remission is meant here as a temporary return to normal as measured by clinical and laboratory means. If remission does occur, it typically lasts for between two and thirteen months although longer periods of remission are possible. Estimates of the effectiveness of chemotherapy are complicated in cases, such as the one presented here, in which the patient's age becomes a factor. According to the medical testimony before the court below, persons over age sixty have more difficulty tolerating chemotherapy and the treatment is likely to be less successful than in younger patients. . . . This prognosis may be compared with the doctors' estimates that, left untreated, a patient in Saikewicz's condition would live for a matter of weeks or, perhaps, several months. According to the testimony, a decision to allow the disease to run its natural course would not result in pain for the patient, and death would probably come without discomfort.

An important facet of the chemotherapy process, to which the judge below directed careful attention, is the problem of serious adverse side effects caused by the treating drugs. Among these side effects are severe nausea, bladder irritation, numbness and tingling of the extremities, and loss of hair. The bladder irritation can be avoided, however, if the patient drinks fluids, and the nausea can be treated by drugs. It was the opinion of the guardian ad litem, as well as the doctors who testified before the probate judge, that most people elect to suffer the side effects of chemotherapy rather than to allow their leukemia to run its natural course. . . .

Concluding that, in this case, the negative factors of treatment exceeded the benefits, the probate judge ordered on May 13, 1976, that no treatment be administered to Saikewicz for his condition of acute myeloblastic monocytic leukemia except by further order of the court. The judge further ordered that all reasonable and necessary supportive measures be taken, medical or otherwise, to safeguard the well-being of Saikewicz in all other respects and to reduce as far as possible any suffering or discomfort which he might experience. . . .

Saikewicz died on September 4, 1976, at the Belchertown State School hospital. Death was due to bronchial pneumonia, a complication of the leukemia. Saikewicz died without pain or discomfort. . . .

. . . To protect the incompetent person within its power, the State must recognize the dignity and worth of such a person and afford to that person the same panoply of rights and choices it recognizes in competent persons. If a competent person faced with death may choose to decline treatment which not only will not cure the person but which substantially may increase suffering in exchange for a possible yet brief prolongation of life, then it cannot be said that it is always in the "best interests" of the ward to require submission to such treatment. . . .

". . . Patients who request treatment know the risks involved and can appreciate the painful side effects when they arrive. They know the reason for the pain and their hope makes it tolerable." To make a worthwhile comparison, one would have to ask whether a majority of people would choose chemotherapy if they were told merely that something outside of their previous experience was going to be done to them, that this something would cause them pain and discomfort, that they would be removed to strange surroundings and possibly restrained for extended periods of time, and that the advantages of this course of action were measured by concepts of time and mortality beyond their ability to comprehend. . . .

We believe that both the guardian ad litem in his recommendation and the judge in his decision should have attempted (as they did) to ascertain the incompetent person's actual interests and preferences. In short, the decision in cases such as this should be that which would be made by the incompetent person, if that person were competent, but taking into account the present and future incompetency of the individual as one of the factors which would necessarily enter into the decision-making process of the competent person. Having recognized the right of a competent person to make for himself the same decision as the court made in this case, the question is, do the facts on the record support the proposition that Saikewicz himself would have made the decision under the standard set forth. We believe they do. . . .

. . . The probate judge identified six factors weighing against administration of chemotherapy. Four of these—Saikewicz's age . . . the probable side effects of treatment, the low chance of producing remission, and the certainty that treatment will cause immediate suffering—were clearly established by the medical testimony to be considerations that any individual would weigh carefully. A fifth factor—Saikewicz's inability to cooperate with the treatment—introduces those considerations that are unique to this individual and which therefore are essential to the proper exercise of substituted judgment. The judge heard testimony that Saikewicz would have no comprehension of the reasons for the severe disruption of his formerly secure and stable environment occasioned by the chemotherapy. He therefore would experience fear without the understanding from which other patients draw strength. The inability to anticipate and prepare for the severe side effects of the drugs leaves room only for confusion and disorientation. The possibility that such a naturally uncooperative patient would have to be physically restrained to allow the slow intravenous administration of drugs could only compound his pain and fear, as well as possibly jeopardize the ability of his body to withstand the toxic effects of the drugs. . . .

. . . The sixth factor identified by the judge as weighing against chemotherapy was "the quality of life possible for him even if the treatment does bring about remission." To the extent that this formulation equates the value of life with any measure of the quality of life, we firmly reject it. A reading of the entire record clearly reveals, however, the judge's concern that special care be taken to respect the dignity and worth of Saikewicz's life precisely because of his vulnerable position. The judge, as well as all the parties, were keenly aware that the supposed ability of Saikewicz, by virtue of his mental retardation, to appreciate or experience life had no place in the decision before them. Rather than reading the judge's formulation in a manner that demeans the value of the life of one who is mentally retarded, the vague, and perhaps ill-chosen, term "quality of life" should be understood as a reference to the continuing state of pain and disorientation precipitated by the chemotherapy treatment. Viewing the term in this manner, together with the other factors properly considered by the judge, we are satisfied that the decision to withhold treatment from Saikewicz was based on a regard for his actual interests and preferences and that the facts supported this decision. . . .

IN THE MATTER OF KAREN QUINLAN*

Supreme Court of New Jersey (1976)

HUGHES, C. J. . . .

The central figure in this tragic case is Karen Ann Quinlan, a New Jersey resident. At the age of 22, she lies in a debilitated and allegedly moribund state at Saint Clare's Hospital in Denville, New Jersey. The litigation has to do, in final analysis, with her life,—its continuance or cessation,—and the responsibilities, rights and duties, with regard to any fateful decision concerning it, of her family, her guardian, her doctors, the hospital, the State through its law enforcement authorities, and finally the courts of justice. . . .

The matter is of transcendent importance, involving questions related to the definition and existence of death, the prolongation of life through artificial means developed by medical technology undreamed of in past generations of the practice of the healing arts;[1] the impact of such durationally indeterminate and artificial life prolongation on the rights of the incompetent, her family and society in general; the bearing of constitutional right and the scope of judicial responsibility, as to the appropriate response of an equity court of justice to the extraordinary prayer for relief of the plaintiff. Involved as well is the right of the plaintiff, Joseph Quinlan, to guardianship of the person of his daughter. . . .

On the night of April 15, 1975, for reasons still unclear, Karen Quinlan ceased breathing for at least two 15 minute periods. She received some ineffectual mouth-to-mouth resuscitation from friends. She was taken by ambulance to Newton Memorial Hospital. There she had a temperature of 100 degrees, her pupils were unreactive and she was unresponsive even to deep pain. The history at the time of her admission to that hospital was essentially incomplete and uninformative.

*355 A. 2d 647
[1]Dr. Julius Korein, a neurologist, testified:

A. . . . [Y]ou've got a set of possible lesions that prior to the era of advanced technology and advances in medicine were no problem inasmuch as the patient would expire. They could do nothing for themselves and even external care was limited. It was—I don't know how many years ago they couldn't keep a person alive with intravenous feedings because they couldn't give enough calories. Now they have these high caloric tube feedings that can keep people in excellent nutrition for years so what's happened is these things have occurred all along but the technology has now reached a point where you can in fact start to replace anything outside of the brain to maintain something that is irreversibly damaged.

Q. Doctor, can the art of medicine repair the cerebral damage that was sustained by Karen?

A. In my opinion, no. . . .

Q. Doctor, in your opinion is there any course of treatment that will lead to the improvement of Karen's condition?

A. No.

Three days later, Dr. Morse examined Karen at the request of the Newton admitting physician, Dr. McGee. He found her comatose with evidence of decortication, a condition relating to derangement of the cortex of the brain causing a physical posture in which the upper extremities are flexed and the lower extremities are extended. She required a respirator to assist her breathing. Dr. Morse was unable to obtain an adequate account of the circumstances and events leading up to Karen's admission to the Newton Hospital. Such initial history or etiology is crucial in neurological diagnosis. Relying as he did upon the Newton Memorial records and his own examination, he concluded that prolonged lack of oxygen in the bloodstream, anoxia, was identified with her condition as he saw it upon first observation. When she was later transferred to Saint Clare's Hospital she was still unconscious, still on a respirator and a tracheotomy had been performed. On her arrival Dr. Morse conducted extensive and detailed examinations. An electroencephalogram (EEG) measuring electrical rhythm of the brain was performed and Dr. Morse characterized the result as "abnormal but it showed some activity and was consistent with her clinical state." Other significant neurological tests, including a brain scan, an angiogram, and a lumbar puncture were normal in result. Dr. Morse testified that Karen has been in a state of coma, lack of consciousness, since he began treating her. He explained that there are basically two types of coma, sleep-like unresponsiveness and awake unresponsiveness. Karen was originally in a sleep-like unresponsive condition but soon developed "sleep-wake" cycles, apparently a normal improvement for comatose patients occurring within three to four weeks. In the awake cycle she blinks, cries out and does things of that sort but is still totally unaware of anyone or anything around her.

Dr. Morse and other expert physicians who examined her characterized Karen as being in a "chronic persistent vegetative state." Dr. Fred Plum, one of such expert witnesses, defined this as a "subject who remains with the capacity to maintain the vegetative parts of neurological function but who . . . no longer has any cognitive function."

Dr. Morse, as well as the several other medical and neurological experts who testified in this case, believed with certainty that Karen Quinlan is not "brain dead." They identified the Ad Hoc Committee of Harvard Medical School report . . . as the ordinary medical standard for determining brain death, and all of them were satisfied that Karen met none of the criteria specified in that report and was therefore not "brain dead" within its contemplation.

In this respect it was indicated by Dr. Plum that the brain works in essentially two ways, the vegetative and the sapient. He testified:

We have an internal vegetative regulation which controls body temperature which controls breathing, which controls to a considerable degree blood pressure, which controls to some degree heart rate, which controls chewing, swallowing and which controls sleeping and waking. We have a more highly developed brain which is uniquely human which controls our relation to the outside world, our capacity to talk, to see, to feel, to sing, to think. Brain death necessarily must mean the death of both of these functions of the brain, vegetative and the sapient. Therefore, the presence of any function which is regulated or governed or controlled by the deeper parts of the brain which in laymen's terms might be considered purely vegetative would mean that the brain is not biologically dead.

Because Karen's neurological condition affects her respiratory ability (the respiratory system being a brain stem function) she requires a respirator to assist her breathing. From the time of her admission to Saint Clare's Hospital Karen has been assisted by an MA-1 respirator, a sophisticated machine which delivers a given volume of air at a certain rate and periodically provides a "sigh" volume, a relatively large measured volume of air designed to purge the lungs of excretions. Attempts to "wean" her from the respirator were unsuccessful and have been abandoned.

The experts believe that Karen cannot now survive without the assistance of the respirator; that exactly how long she would live without it is unknown; that the strong likelihood is that death would follow soon after its removal, and that removal would also risk further brain damage and would curtail the assistance the respirator presently provides in warding off infection.

It seemed to be the consensus not only of the treating physicians but also of the several qualified experts who testified in the case, that removal from the respirator would not conform to medical practices, standards and traditions.

The further medical consensus was that Karen in addition to being comatose is in a chronic and persistent "vegetative" state, having no awareness of anything or anyone around her and existing at a primitive reflex level. Although she does have some brain stem function (ineffective for respiration) and has other reactions one normally associates with being alive, such as moving, reacting to light, sound and noxious stimuli, blinking her eyes, and the like, the quality of her feeling impulses is unknown. She grimaces, makes stereotyped cries and sounds and has chewing motions. Her blood pressure is normal.

Karen remains in the intensive care unit at Saint Clare's Hospital, receiving 24-hour care by a team of four nurses characterized, as was the medical attention, as "excellent." She is nourished by feeding by way of a nasal-gastro tube and is routinely examined for infection, which under these circumstances is a serious life threat. The result is that her condition is considered remarkable under the unhappy circumstances involved.

Karen is described as emaciated, having suffered a weight loss of at least 40 pounds, and undergoing a continuing deteriorative process. Her posture is described as fetal-like and grotesque; there is extreme flexion-rigidity of the arms, legs and related muscles and her joints are severely rigid and deformed.

From all of this evidence, and including the whole testimonial record, several basic findings in the physical area are mandated. Severe brain and associated damage, albeit of uncertain etiology, has left Karen in a chronic and persistent vegetative state. No form of treatment which can cure or improve that condition is known or available. As nearly as may be determined, considering the guarded area of remote uncertainties characteristic of most medical science predictions, she can *never* be restored to cognitive or sapient life. Even with regard to the vegetative level and improvement therein (if such it may be called) the prognosis is extremely poor and the extent unknown if it should in fact occur.

She is debilitated and moribund and although fairly stable at the time of argument before us (no new information having been filed in the meanwhile in expansion of the record), no physician risked the opinion that she could live more than a year and indeed she may die much earlier. Excellent medical and nursing care so far has been able to ward off the constant threat of infection, to which she is peculiarly susceptible because of the respirator, the tracheal tube and other incidents of care in her vulnerable condition. Her life accordingly is sustained by the respirator and tubal feeding, and removal from the respirator would cause her death soon, although the time cannot be stated with more precision.

The determination of the fact and time of death in past years of medical science was keyed to the action of the heart and blood circulation, in turn dependent upon pulmonary activity, and hence cessation of these functions spelled out the reality of death.[2]

Developments in medical technology have obfuscated the use of the traditional definition of death. Efforts have been made to define irreversible coma as a new criterion for death, such as by the 1968 report of the Ad Hoc Committee of the Harvard Medical School (the Committee comprising ten physicians, an historian, a lawyer and a theologian), which asserted that:

> From ancient times down to the recent past it was clear that, when the respiration and heart stopped, the brain would die in a few minutes; so the obvious criterion of no heart beat as synonymous with death was sufficiently accurate. In those times the heart was considered to be the central organ of the body; it is not surprising that its failure marked the onset of death. This is no longer valid when modern resuscitative and supportive measures are used. These improved activities can now restore "life" as judged by the ancient standards of persistent respiration and continuing heart beat. This can be the case even when there is not the remotest possibility of an individual recovering consciousness following massive brain damage. . . .

The Ad Hoc standards, carefully delineated, included absence of response to pain or other stimuli, pupilary reflexes, corneal, pharyngeal and other reflexes, blood pressure, spontaneous respiration, as well as "flat" or isoelectric electroencephalograms and the like, with all tests repeated "at least 24 hours later with no change." In such circumstances, where all of such criteria have been met as showing "brain death," the Committee recommends with regard to the respirator:

[2]Death. The cessation of life; the ceasing to exist; defined by physicians as a total stoppage of the circulation of the blood, and a cessation of the animal and vital functions consequent thereon, such as respiration, pulsation, etc. *Black's Law Dictionary.* . . .

The patient's condition can be determined only by a physician. When the patient is hopelessly damaged as defined above, the family and all colleagues who have participated in major decisions concerning the patient, and all nurses involved, should be so informed. Death is to be declared and *then* the respirator turned off. The decision to do this and the responsibility for it are to be taken by the physician-in-charge, in consultation with one or more physicians who have been directly involved in the case. It is unsound and undesirable to force the family to make the decision. . . .

But, as indicated, it was the consensus of medical testimony in the instant case that Karen, for all her disability, met none of these criteria, nor indeed any comparable criteria extant in the medical world and representing, as does the Ad Hoc Committee report, according to the testimony in this case, prevailing and accepted medical standards.

We have adverted to the "brain death" concept and Karen's disassociation with any of its criteria, to emphasize the basis of the medical decision made by Dr. Morse. When plaintiff and his family, finally reconciled to the certainty of Karen's impending death, requested the withdrawal of life support mechanisms, he demurred. His refusal was based upon his conception of medical standards, practice and ethics described in the medical testimony, such as in the evidence given by another neurologist, Dr. Sidney Diamond, a witness for the State. Dr. Diamond asserted that no physician would have failed to provide respirator support at the outset, and none would interrupt its life-saving course thereafter, except in the case of cerebral death. In the latter case, he thought the respirator would in effect be disconnected from one already dead, entitling the physician under medical standards and, he thought, legal concepts, to terminate the supportive measures. We note Dr. Diamond's distinction of major surgical or transfusion procedures in a terminal case not involving cerebral death, such as here:

> The subject has lost human qualities. It would be incredible, and I think unlikely, that any physician would respond to a sudden hemorrhage, massive hemorrhage or a loss of all her defensive blood cells, by giving her large quantities of blood. I think that . . . major surgical procedures would be out of the question even if they were known to be essential for continued physical existence.

This distinction is adverted to also in the testimony of Dr. Julius Korein, a neurologist called by plaintiff. Dr. Korein described a medical practice concept of "judicious neglect" under which the physician will say:

> Don't treat this patient anymore, . . . it does not serve either the patient, the family, or society in any meaningful way to continue treatment with this patient.

Dr. Korein also told of the unwritten and unspoken standard of medical practice implied in the foreboding initials DNR (do not resuscitate), as applied to the extraordinary terminal case:

Cancer, metastatic cancer, involving the lungs, the liver, the brain, multiple involvements, the physician may or may not write: Do not resuscitate. . . . [I]t could be said to the nurse: if this man stops breathing don't resuscitate him. . . . No physician that I know personally is going to try and resuscitate a man riddled with cancer and in agony and he stops breathing. They are not going to put him on a respirator. . . . I think that would be the height of misuse of technology.

While the thread of logic in such distinctions may be elusive to the non-medical lay mind, in relation to the supposed imperative to sustain life at all costs, they nevertheless relate to medical decisions, such as the decision of Dr. Morse in the present case. We agree with the trial court that the decision was in accord with Dr. Morse's conception of medical standards and practice.

We turn to that branch of the factual case pertaining to the application for guardianship, as distinguished from the nature of the authorization sought by the applicant. The character and general suitability of Joseph Quinlan as guardian for his daughter, in ordinary circumstances, could not be doubted. The record bespeaks the high degree of familial love which pervaded the home of Joseph Quinlan and reached out fully to embrace Karen, although she was living elsewhere at the time of her collapse. The proofs showed him to be deeply religious, imbued with a morality so sensitive that months of tortured indecision preceded his belated conclusion (despite earlier moral judgments reached by the other family members, but unexpressed to him in order not to influence him) to seek the termination of life-supportive measures sustaining Karen. A communicant of the Roman Catholic Church, as were other family members, he first sought solace in private prayer looking with confidence, as he says, to the Creator, first for the recovery of Karen and then, if that were not possible, for guidance with respect to the awesome decision confronting him. . . .

. . . To confirm the moral rightness of the decision he was about to make he consulted with his parish priest and later with the Catholic chaplain of Saint Clare's Hospital. He would not, he testified, have sought termination if that act were to be morally wrong or in conflict with the tenets of the religion he so profoundly respects. He was disabused of doubt, however, when the position of the Roman Catholic Church was made known to him. . . .

. . . The judge was bound to measure the character and motivations in all respects of Joseph Quinlan as prospective guardian; and insofar as these religious matters bore upon them, they were properly scrutinized and considered by the court.

Thus germane, we note the position of that Church as illuminated by the record before us. We have no reason to believe that it would be at all discordant with the whole of Judeo-Christian tradition, considering its central respect and reverence for the sanctity of human life. It was in this sense of relevance that we admitted as *amicus curiae* the New Jersey Catholic Conference, essentially the spokesman for the various Catholic bishops of New Jersey, organized to give witness to spiritual values in public affairs in the statewide community. The position statement of Bishop Lawrence B. Casey, reproduced in the *amicus* brief, projects these views:

(a) The verification of the fact of death in a particular case cannot be deduced from any religious or moral principle and, under this aspect, does not fall within the competence of the church;—that dependence must be had upon traditional and medical standards, and by these standards Karen Ann Quinlan is assumed to be alive.

(b) The request of plaintiff for authority to terminate a medical procedure characterized as "an extraordinary means of treatment" would not involve euthanasia. This upon the reasoning expressed by Pope Pius XII in his "allocutio" (address) to anesthesiologists on November 24, 1957, when he dealt with the question:

Does the anesthesiologist have the right, or is he bound, in all cases of deep unconsciousness, even in those that are completely hopeless in the opinion of the competent doctor, to use modern artificial respiration apparatus, even against the will of the family?

His answer made the following points:

1. In ordinary cases the doctor has the right to act in this manner, but is not bound to do so unless this is the only way of fulfilling another certain moral duty.

2. The doctor, however, has no right independent of the patient. He can act only if the patient explicitly or implicitly, directly or indirectly gives him the permission.

3. The treatment as described in the question constitutes extraordinary means of preserving life and so there is no obligation to use them nor to give the doctor permission to use them.

4. The rights and the duties of the family depend on the presumed will of the unconscious patient if he or she is of legal age, and the family, too, is bound to use only ordinary means.

5. This case is not to be considered euthanasia in any way; that would never be licit. The interruption of attempts at resuscitation, even when it causes the arrest of circulation, is not more than an indirect cause of the cessation of life, and we must apply in this case the principle of double effect.

So it was that the Bishop Casey statement validated the decision of Joseph Quinlan:

Competent medical testimony has established that Karen Ann Quinlan has no reasonable hope of recovery from her comatose state by the use of any available medical procedures. The continuance of mechanical (cardiorespiratory) supportive measures to sustain continuation of her body functions and her life constitute extraordinary means of treatment. *Therefore, the decision of Joseph . . . Quinlan to request the discontinuance of this treatment is, according to the teachings of the Catholic Church, a morally correct decision.* (emphasis in original)

And the mind and purpose of the intending guardian were undoubtedly influenced by factors included in the following reference to the interrelationship of the three disciplines of theology, law and medicine as exposed in the Casey statement:

> The right to a natural death is one outstanding area in which the disciplines of theology, medicine and law overlap; or, to put it another way, it is an area in which these three disciplines convene.
>
> Medicine with its combination of advanced technology and professional ethics is both able and inclined to prolong biological life. Law with its felt obligation to protect the life and freedom of the individual seeks to assure each person's right to live out his human life until its natural and inevitable conclusion. Theology with its acknowledgment of man's dissatisfaction with biological life as the ultimate source of joy . . . defends the sacredness of human life and defends it from all direct attacks.
>
> These disciplines do not conflict with one another, but are necessarily conjoined in the application of their principles in a particular instance such as that of Karen Ann Quinlan. Each must in some way acknowledge the other without denying its own competence. The civil law is not expected to assert a belief in eternal life; nor, on the other hand, is it expected to ignore the right of the individual to profess it, and to form and pursue his conscience in accord with that belief. Medical science is not authorized to directly cause natural death; nor, however, is it expected to prevent it when it is inevitable and all hope of a return to an even partial exercise of human life is irreparably lost. Religion is not expected to define biological death; nor, on its part, is it expected to relinquish its responsibility to assist man in the formation and pursuit of a correct conscience as to the acceptance of natural death when science has confirmed its inevitability beyond any hope other than that of preserving biological life in a merely vegetative state.

And the gap in the law is aptly described in the Bishop Casey statement:

> In the present public discussion of the case of Karen Ann Quinlan it has been brought out that responsible people involved in medical care, patients and families have exercised the freedom to terminate or withhold certain treatments as extraordinary means in cases judged to be terminal, i. e., cases which hold no realistic hope for some recovery, in accord with the expressed or implied intentions of the patients themselves. To whatever extent this has been happening it has been without sanction in civil law. Those involved in such actions, however, have ethical and theological literature to guide them in their judgments and actions. Furthermore, such actions have not in themselves undermined society's reverence for the lives of sick and dying people. . . .

We have no doubt, in these unhappy circumstances, that if Karen were herself miraculously lucid for an interval (not altering the existing prognosis of the condition to which she would soon return) and perceptive of her irreversible condition, she could effectively decide upon discontinuance of the life-support apparatus, even if it meant the prospect of natural death. To this extent we may distinguish *Heston* . . . which concerned a severely injured young woman (Delores Heston), whose life depended on surgery and blood transfusion; and who was in such extreme shock that she was unable to express an informed choice (although the Court apparently considered the case as if the patient's own religious decision to resist transfusion were at stake), but most importantly a patient apparently salvable to long life and vibrant health;—a situation not at all like the present case.

We have no hesitancy in deciding, in the instant diametrically opposite case, that no external compelling interest of the State could compel Karen to endure the unendurable, only to vegetate a few measurable months with no realistic possibility of returning to any semblance of cognitive or sapient life. We perceive no thread of logic distinguishing between such a choice on Karen's part and a similar choice which, under the evidence in this case, could be made by a competent patient terminally ill, riddled by cancer and suffering great pain; such a patient would not be resuscitated or put on a respirator in the example described by Dr. Korein, and *a fortiori* would not be kept *against his will* on a respirator. . . .

The agitation of the medical community in the face of modern life prolongation technology and its search for definitive policy are demonstrated in the large volume of relevant professional commentary. . . .

The wide debate thus reflected contrasts with the relative paucity of legislative and judicial guides and standards in the same field. The medical profession has sought to devise guidelines such as the "brain death" concept of the Harvard Ad Hoc Committee mentioned above. But it is perfectly apparent from the testimony we have quoted of Dr. Korein, and indeed so clear as almost to be judicially noticeable, that humane decisions against resuscitative or maintenance therapy are frequently a recognized *de facto* response in the medical world to the irreversible, terminal, pain-ridden patient, especially with familial consent. And these cases, of course, are far short of "brain death."

We glean from the record here that physicians distinguish between curing the ill and comforting and easing the dying; that they refuse to treat the curable as if they were dying or ought to die, and that they have sometimes refused to treat the hopeless and dying as if they were curable. In this sense, as we were reminded by the testimony of Drs. Korein and Diamond, many of them have refused to inflict an undesired prolongation of the process of dying on a patient in irreversible condition when it is clear that such "therapy" offers neither human or humane benefit. We think these attitudes represent a balanced implementation of a profoundly realistic perspective on the meaning of life and death and that they respect the whole Judeo-Christian tradition of regard for human life. No less would they seem consistent with the moral matrix of medicine, "to heal," very much in the sense of the endless mission of the law, "to do justice."

Yet this balance, we feel, is particularly difficult to perceive and apply in the context of the development by advanced technology of sophisticated and artificial life-sustaining devices. For those possibly curable, such devices are of great value, and, as ordinary medical procedures, are essential. Consequently, as pointed out by Dr. Diamond, they are necessary because of the ethic of medical practice. But in light of the situation in the present case (while the record here is somewhat hazy in distinguishing between "ordinary" and "extraordinary" measures), one would have to think that the use of the same respirator or life support could be considered "ordinary" in the context of the possibly curable patient but "extraordinary" in the context of the forced sustaining by cardio-respiratory processes of an irreversibly doomed patient. . . .

. . . there must be a way to free physicians, in the pursuit of their healing vocation, from possible contamination by self-interest or self-protection concerns which would inhibit their independent medical judgments for the well-being of their dying patients. We would hope that this opinion might be serviceable to some degree in ameliorating the professional problems under discussion.

A technique aimed at the underlying difficulty (though in a somewhat broader context) is described by Dr. Karen Teel, a pediatrician and a director of Pediatric Education, who writes in the *Baylor Law Review* under the title "The Physician's Dilemma: A Doctor's View: What The Law Should Be." Dr. Teel recalls:

> Physicians, by virtue of their responsibility for medical judgments are, partly by choice and partly by default, charged with the responsibility of making ethical judgments which we are sometimes ill-equipped to make. We are not always morally and legally authorized to make them. The physician is thereby assuming a civil and criminal liability that, as often as not, he does not even realize as a factor in his decision. There is little or no dialogue in this whole process. The physician assumes that his judgment is called for and, in good faith, he acts. Someone must and it has been the physician who has assumed the responsibility and the risk.

> I suggest that it would be more appropriate to provide a regular forum for more input and dialogue in individual situations and to allow the responsibility of these judgments to be shared. Many hospitals have established an Ethics Committee composed of physicians, social workers, attorneys, and theologians, . . . which serves to review the individual circumstances of ethical dilemma and which has provided much in the way of assistance and safeguards for patients and their medical caretakers. Generally, the authority of these committees is primarily restricted to the hospital setting and their official status is more that of an advisory body than of an enforcing body.

> The concept of an Ethics Committee which has this kind of organization and is readily accessible to those persons rendering medical care to patients, would be, I think, the most promising direction for further study at this point. . . . [This would allow] some much needed dialogue regarding these issues and [force] the point of exploring all of the options for a particular patient. It diffuses the responsibility for making these judgments. Many physicians, in many circumstances, would welcome this sharing of responsibility. I believe that such an entity could lend itself well to an assumption of a legal status which would allow courses of action not now undertaken because of the concern for liability. . . .

The most appealing factor in the technique suggested by Dr. Teel seems to us to be the diffusion of professional responsibility for decision, comparable in a way to the value of multi-judge courts in finally resolving on appeal difficult questions of law. Moreover, such a system would be protective to the hospital as well as to the doctor in screening out, so to speak, a case which might be contaminated by less than worthy motivations of family or physician. In the real world and in relationship to the momentous decision contemplated, the value of additional views and diverse knowledge is apparent. . . .

... The trial court was apparently convinced of the high character of Joseph Quinlan and his general suitability as guardian under other circumstances, describing him as "very sincere, moral, ethical and religious." The court felt, however, that the obligation to concur in the medical care and treatment of his daughter would be a source of anguish to him and would distort his "decision-making processes." We disagree, for we sense from the whole record before us that while Mr. Quinlan feels a natural grief, and understandably sorrows because of the tragedy which has befallen his daughter, his strength of purpose and character far outweighs these sentiments and qualifies him eminently for guardianship of the person as well as the property of his daughter. Hence we discern no valid reason to overrule the statutory intendment of preference to the next of kin. . . .

We ... remand this record to the trial court to implement (without further testimonial hearing) the following decisions:

1. To discharge, with the thanks of the Court for his service, the present guardian of the person of Karen Quinlan, Thomas R. Curtin, Esquire, a member of the Bar and an officer of the court.
2. To appoint Joseph Quinlan as guardian of the person of Karen Quinlan with full power to make decisions with regard to the identity of her treating physicians.

We repeat for the sake of emphasis and clarity that upon the concurrence of the guardian and family of Karen, should the responsible attending physicians conclude that there is no reasonable possibility of Karen's ever emerging from her present comatose condition to a cognitive, sapient state and that the life-support apparatus now being administered to Karen should be discontinued, they shall consult with the hospital "Ethics Committee" or like body of the institution in which Karen is then hospitalized. If that consultative body agrees that there is no reasonable possibility of Karen's ever emerging from her present comatose condition to a cognitive, sapient state, the present life-support system may be withdrawn and said action shall be without any civil or criminal liability therefor on the part of any participant, whether guardian, physician, hospital or others. . . .

PEOPLE V. PRIVITERA*

California Court of Appeal, Fourth District (1977)

STANIFORTH, Associate Justice.
Under California Health and Safety Code section 1707.1 ... it is a misdemeanor to sell, deliver, prescribe or administer any drug or device to be used in the diagnosis, treatment, alleviation or cure of cancer which has not been approved by the designated federal agency ... or by a state board. . . .

*App., 141 Cal. Rptr. 764

. . . Defendants, James Robert Privitera, Jr., a medical doctor, William David Turner, Phyllis Blanche Disney, Winifred Agnes Davis, and Carroll Ruth Leslie, were convicted by jury of a felony, conspiracy to sell, to prescribe, an unapproved drug, laetrile, intended for the alleviation or cure of cancer. . . . Davis and Turner were convicted of selling laetrile to be used for the alleviation or cure of cancer. . . .

. . . The defendants were involved in a common plan to import distribute and prescribe laetrile (also referred to as amygdalin or vitamin B–17) to cancer patients. Defendants Turner and Davis were the importers and chief suppliers of the drug. Defendants Leslie and Disney worked as the distribution network in various residential areas. Dr. Privitera prescribed amygdalin for cancer victims (or to undercover state agents represented to be cancer victims). Dr. Privitera referred patients to Turner and Davis to buy the amygdalin; Disney referred patients to Dr. Privitera for treatment. . . .

The defendants told the prospective users of the drug that amygdalin was an effective treatment or cure for cancer. Substantial evidence supports the jury finding of a common plan or agreement to supply and prescribe amygdalin as a cancer cure. Laetrile has not been "approved" by a designated governmental agency. . . .

. . . Amygdalin is a by-product of apricot pits. The substance has been the subject of widespread public dispute as to its efficacy for the treatment of cancer. Orthodox medicine, as represented by the American Cancer Society, places it in the area of nostrums. Its proponents vary in their claims from that as a cure for cancer or as simply a nutritional aid causing the patient to gain weight, have a better appetite, and a better emotional outlook. It is generally conceded that amygdalin is non-toxic; it does not fall within the general ban of drugs which are toxic, habit forming, addictive, or otherwise distort reality. Conventional medicine regards the "evidence," "proof," of the curative effect of amygdalin as anecdotal in nature and contends the drug has never been established by scientific methodology to have any effect whatsoever upon either the cure or retardation of cancer growth. Despite the pros and cons of the experts in the field of medicine, and others from non-medical fields taking side on this issue, cancer victims in large numbers have sought the relief, whatever its nature, which is available from the use of this drug. Where, as in Mexico and in West Germany, the drug is available through doctors and clinics, cancer victims, able to travel, seek out and obtain the treatment.

Dr. Privitera points out that many cancer victims have investigated and evaluated the merits of surgery, radiation therapy or chemotherapy with the aid of competent medical advice and have made the highly personal decision; the benefits from such therapy is not sufficient to justify the risks which include disfigurement, debilitation, and accelerated death and for this reason have chosen to seek amygdalin as a treatment, other cancer victims have been advised that their condition is hopeless, their case is terminal and as a last resort before certain death, seek amygdalin.

Dr. Privitera contends many conceded cancer victims, competent and responsible adults, seek and use amygdalin as a food substance to ameliorate the horrifying physical wasting away of the body (cachexia) which accompanies cancer. Thus they seek amygdalin not only for its possible cancer curative benefits, but also for its known nutritional benefits. Cancer victims cannot be certain amygdalin will either cure or control cancer but they believe, based upon the anecdotal, personal experience approach, the drug provides relief from the terrible pain, mental malaise, the emotional depression and weight loss which mark the progression of their disease.

The People assert, contrary to Dr. Privitera's contentions, not a single accredited medical school in the State of California teaches amygdalin might be effective in the controlling or curing of cancer. Further the use of amygdalin as a form of nutritional therapy is officially regarded by the State Department of Health, the California Medical Association, the National Cancer Institute and a great block of practicing physicians, to be of no value whatsoever in the controlling or curing of cancer.

Dr. Privitera specifically contends section 1707.1 of the Health and Safety Code is unconstitutional. It is a denial of one aspect of individual "liberty" protected by the due process clause of the Fourteenth Amendment.

The patient, he asserts, has a right of "privacy" or "a guarantee of certain areas or zones of privacy." This is the individual right of independence in making certain kinds of important decisions. The very nature of the relationship, the act to be performed, the decision to be made, precludes unjustified state presence. It is "the right of the individual to be free in action, thought, experience and belief from governmental compulsion." (Kurland, "The Private I," University of Chicago Magazine . . .) . . . It is that right voiced by Justice Brandeis in his dissent in *Olmstead v. United States* . . . "the right to be let alone," "the right most valued by civilized men." . . .

Historically this right of privacy was first articulated as a constitutional right in *Griswold* v. *Connecticut* . . . a decision holding unconstitutional a statute prohibiting the use of contraceptives. However, the recognition of the existence, innate in every human being, of a zone of privacy is older than the Bill of Rights, older than our political parties, older than the state's concern with the nature of treatment to be received by cancer-ridden patients. It is in the nature of man that such right exists. . . .

At the heart of the People's defense of Health and Safety Code section 1707.1 is the premise, Legislature declared . . . that early and accurate diagnosis of cancer materially reduces the likelihood of death, prolongs useful life; where false or misleading representations are made to the public, large numbers rely upon such falsities, and needlessly die of cancer.

The People contend the California Legislature in enacting the statutory scheme made this implicit finding: Ineffective cancer remedies are more hazardous to the patient than the state-sanctioned alternatives. . . .

To require the doctor to use only orthodox "state sanctioned" methods of treatment under threat of criminal penalty for variance is to invite a repetition in California of the Soviet experience with "Lysenkoism."[1] The mention of a requirement that licensed doctors must prescribe, treat, within "state sanctioned alternatives" raises the spector of medical stagnation at best, statism, paternalistic Big Brother at worst. It is by the alternatives to orthodoxy that medical progress has been made. A free, progressive society has an enormous stake in recognizing and protecting this right of the physician. . . .

The nineteen witnesses testifying for Dr. Privitera conveyed a felt imminency of death. One senses a mortal fear of both the disease and the orthodox alternatives. This is a desperate utterly human seeking to avoid the pain and to prolong life. . . .

To these nineteen cancer victims the enforcement of Health and Safety Code section 1707.1, the denial to them of medical treatment albeit unorthodox, albeit unapproved by a state agency, must surely take on a Kafkaesque, a nightmare, quality. No demonstrated public danger, no compelling interest of the state, warrants an Orwellian intrusion into the most private of zones of privacy. . . .

The state has in the name of protecting the cancer victim criminalized the doctor who is willing to innovate, willing to try an unapproved drug with the consent of his patient. From the terminal patient's viewpoint a new depth of inhumanity is reached by a broad sweep of this law so interpreted. No compelling interest of the state requires Dr. Privitera's nineteen cancer patients to endure the unendurable, to die, even forbidden hope. . . .

Judgments reversed.

COLOGNE, Associate Justice, dissenting. . . .

Why is it a fundamental right to have unproven treatment when effective treatment may be available?

My concern with the majority view is not with the proposition we must place great importance upon the right of choice of medical treatment. My concern is that we give it so much importance we deny reason and the best medical judgment as the standard for health care. . . .

Preventing the administration of ineffective treatment methods to sick persons, particularly those with a fear-inducing and desperation-producing illness such as cancer, is a reasonable legislative purpose. Taking legislative action to accomplish this purpose promotes the use of effective treatment methods to the end of the physical and economic well-being of all the people. . . .

---

[1]Soviet geneticist T. D. Lysenko, controversial dictator of "communistic" biology during the Stalin period, stultified the science of genetics in the U.S.S.R. for at least a generation. He imposed the "state-sanctioned alternative," the curious idea that environmentally acquired characteristics of an organism could be transmitted to the offspring through inheritance. Thus, the Stalinist concept of ideological conformity politically implanted in genetics paralyzed this important branch of Soviet science.

This preventative legislative action naturally tends to enable many persons suffering from the ailment to get well by having effective treatment methods applied at an early stage. There are proven effective treatment methods for many forms of cancer particularly in cases of early detection. The Legislature has been made mindful of the human and economic waste attending a cancer patient's receipt of ineffective treatment and attending the offering of false hope to the frightened or desperate patient. I cannot charge wrongdoing by the manufacturers, distributors and physicians who may profit from the dispensing of laetrile if they merely provide hope to the terminally ill who have no recognized cure available . . . but there is a grievous wrong committed when they consciously or unconsciously deny proper treatment to those who could benefit by early effective treatment. Diverting the patient's attention and resources from use of an effective remedy at a time when the cancer might be cured under approved treatment programs is cruel and inhuman. Such a diversion is surely dangerous to the patient, at best giving him a gamble an unproven treatment *might* be effective and at worst resulting in wasted resources and death. There is also a wrong in taking money from patients for possibly worthless drugs, thereby unduly taxing cancer victims and also depriving them or their families of funds necessary for support. . . .

The majority tells us the effect of the prohibition of Health and Safety Code section 1707.1 is to chill innovative treatment by a licensed doctor. I cannot ignore the conclusion reached by Congress after its hearings that the clinical impressions and beliefs of practicing physicians are "treacherous," are poorly controlled experiments and do not constitute an adequate basis for establishing efficacy. . . . If we use the method of developing medical knowledge suggested by the majority opinion we discard the scientific approach thus opening the door to experimentation using a variety of disjointed cancer "treatments" of unproven or unprovable value, undocumented for general use and without control mechanisms. Better reasoning calls for an orderly collection of cancer treatment methods of scientifically proven worth before the public is used as the guinea pig. Certainly it is the research scientist, knowledgeable in the field and aware of related studies, who is the one to be given this freedom, not the manufacturer, distributor and general practitioner as the majority would advocate. Unrestricted sale and experimentation is one thing, scientific determination is quite another. . . . The law provides a method of developing such research. The innovative physician is free to take advantage of Health and Safety Code section 1708 which establishes a means of conducting investigations into the safety and therapeutic value of a cancer drug, medicine, compound or device without fear of penalty. . . .

. . . There is ample evidence available to show a well-meaning licensed medical practitioner can innocently become an instrument of a drug promotion program without intent to jeopardize the public health and safety. In fact, a licensed medical doctor administering unproven cancer cures which do not work may likely have a more deadly impact on the public health than the nonlicensed promoter. . . .

... A patient in these circumstances of trust is likely to stay with the physician to the end. When the end is a needless death, an unnecessarily shortened life or a prolonged illness, the remedies of malpractice or license revocation take on a hollow ring to the patient or his heirs. . . .

IN THE MATTER OF ROBERT QUACKENBUSH, AN ALLEGED INCOMPETENT*

Morris County (N.J.) Courts, Probate Division (1978)

MUIR, A. J. S. C.

Morristown Memorial Hospital petitions for the appointment of a guardian for Robert Quackenbush, an alleged mental incompetent and patient at the hospital, to authorize the guardian to consent to an operation to amputate the legs of Quackenbush and to consent to other medical treatment necessary due to gangrenous conditions in both his legs. . . .

The facts elicited at the hearing indicate that Robert Quackenbush is 72 years old and has lived as a semi-recluse for the last ten years in a trailer in Chester, New Jersey. He is divorced, has no children, his parents and siblings are deceased and he is unable to provide any significant information concerning relatives except for a Mrs. Kagan, an 83-year-old cousin with whom he lived in the trailer. The cousin is presently in a nursing care facility.

A local rescue squad brought Quackenbush to the hospital emergency room at the request of his neighbors. He refused treatment and was rambunctious and belligerent. Because of the refusal to accept treatment, hospital officials attempted to send him home, but all available agencies for transportation refused to transport him. Finally, he was admitted at the direction of Dr. Ames Filippone, who became his treating physician.

Dr. Filippone, mainly through other sources, but with some information from the patient, learned that Quackenbush was hospitalized about two months prior to his admission. At that time he was diagnosed as suffering from arteriosclerosis in the legs and advised to have an operation, but he refused and left the hospital. Aside from that hospitalization and medical attention, he shunned medical treatment for the prior 40 years. Dr. Filippone described him as a conscientious objector to medical therapy.

A medical examination by Dr. Filippone indicates that Quackenbush has gangrene in both legs. On his left leg the skin is black from the knee down, is partially mummified and the foot is dangling, about to fall off. On the left leg, there is an open sore, which is draining fluid and in which the tibia (shinbone) and

*383 A. 2d 785

tendons are exposed. His right leg is in a similar condition except that the black skin and mummified condition extend from midcalf down.

Neither leg has a normal pulse behind the knee or ankle, indicating total absence of blood flow. The blood is being seeded with bacteria from inflammed areas adjoining the gangrene. Cultures of the blood indicate the presence of gas-forming bacteria. Such bacteria can lead to gas gangrene, a more fulminating type infection than gangrene. The existence of bacteria multiplying in the blood is described as septicemia.

The diagnosis is that the gangrene is caused by arteriosclerosis (a thickening and hardening of arteries and other vessels leading to acute diminishment of blood flow) inducing high fever, dehydration and profound anemia (number of red blood cells being less than normal). At the time of admission to the hospital Quackenbush had a 102° fever and an abnormally high pulse rate.

After commencement of treatment, which consisted of bandaging and heavy doses of two antibiotics, penicillin and gentamicin, the patient's temperature and pulse rate gradually became normal. Dr. Filippone described the doses of antibiotics as heroic measures, meaning quantities in highly unusual amounts. He indicated concentrated use of gentamicin could cause kidney failure.

Realizing his patient's aversion to an operation, Dr. Filippone discussed with Quackenbush carefully over a period of days the nature and extent of the illness, the nature and extent of the surgery, the risk involved in the operation and the risks involved if there is no operation. On January 5 Quackenbush signed a form consenting to the operation but later that day withdrew the consent.

Dr. Filippone's prognosis is that Mr. Quackenbush must have the operation or he will die within about three weeks. The antibiotics can control the infection only if the source of the infection is removed through amputation. If the source of the infection is not removed, the formation of bacteria in the blood will build to the point where abscesses will occur on the legs, lungs, brain and other places. Fever will develop, become uncontrollable and ultimately lead to a comatose condition. The abscesses and fever will eventually result in death.

Death may be averted if the operation is performed. The operation will consist of removal of both legs just above the knee at the very least, and possibly removal of both legs entirely. Whether both legs must be removed entirely cannot be decided until the operation is underway. The probability of recovery from the amputation is good and the risks involved are limited.

The extent of the amputation will dictate whether Quackenbush will be confined to a wheelchair for the rest of his life or be a candidate for rehabilitation. If the amputations are of the entire legs, wheelchair confinement is the only alternative. If the amputations are restricted, leaving portions of the legs, he may be fitted with artificial legs for use in moving about. In either event, he will need nursing care which the hospital cannot provide.

A social worker from the hospital indicates it could take up to six months to place Mr. Quackenbush in a nursing home after the operation. She was unable to state with any certainty that the nursing home of placement would have rehabilitation facilities. She did say it was unlikely that Quackenbush could get into a complete rehabilitation facility due to his age and the fact that such a facility is normally for temporary treatment, not permanent, care.

The testimony concerning Quackenbush's mental condition was elicited from two psychiatrists. The first, appearing for the hospital, was Dr. Michael Giuliano. Dr. Giuliano, licensed to practice in 1971, saw Quackenbush once on January 6. The doctor's conclusions are that Quackenbush is suffering from an organic brain syndrome with psychotic elements. He asserts that the organic brain syndrome is acute—i. e., subject to change—and could be induced by the septicemia. He bases his opinion on the patient's disorientation as to place—not aware of being in a hospital; his disorientation as to the people around him—not aware of talking to a nurse and doctor during the interview; his visual hallucinations—seeing but not hearing people in the room who are not there, and the inappropriateness of his responses to the discussions on the gravity of his condition and what might result. Dr. Giuliano did acknowledge that the hallucinations could be induced by conditions related to the septicemia but concluded that Quackenbush's mental condition was not sufficient to make an informed decision concerning the operation.

Dr. Abraham S. Lenzner, a Board-certified psychiatrist for 25 years and specialist in geriatric psychiatry, testified as an independent witness at the request of the court. Dr. Lenzner is Chief of Psychiatry at the Memorial Hospital and a professor at the New Jersey College of Medicine and Dentistry.

Dr. Lenzner is of the opinion, based upon reasonable medical certainty, that Quackenbush has the mental capacity to make decisions, to understand the nature and extent of his physical condition, to understand the nature and extent of the operations, to understand the risks involved if he consents to the operation, and to understand the risks involved if he refuses the operation. He bases that opinion on an interview with Quackenbush held on January 11. At the interview the doctor and Quackenbush thoroughly discussed the patient's condition, illness and ramifications involved in the options of having the operation. The doctor indicates that Quackenbush knows he has gangrene and fully appreciates the magnitude of the illness. Quackenbush told him he hoped for a miracle and that he is a coward about making decisions. The doctor found no hallucinations. He did find some fluctuations in mental lucidity. Quackenbush would lose his train of thought, and his discussion would wander off, but the doctor says this is to be expected under the circumstances and is not a sign of mental incompetency.

I visited with Quackenbush for about ten minutes on January 12. During that period he did not hallucinate, his answers to my questions were responsive and he seemed reasonably alert. His conversation did wander occasionally but to no greater extent than would be expected of a 72-year-old man in his circumstances. He spoke somewhat philosophically about his circumstances and desires. He hopes for a miracle but realizes there is no great likelihood of its occurrence. He indicates a desire—plebeian, as he described it—to return to his trailer and live out his life. He is not experiencing any pain and indicates that if he does, he could change his mind about having the operation. . . .

. . . The matter may be tried before a judge without a jury. My findings pursuant to this authority are that Robert Quackenbush is competent and capable of exercising informed consent on whether or not to have the operation. I do not question the events and conditions described by Dr. Giuliano but find they were of a temporary, curative, fluctuating nature, and whatever their cause the patient's lucidity is sufficient for him to make an informed   choice.

The hospital argues, however, that the court must make the decision in favor of compelling the operation. It describes the decision of Quackenbush in refusing the operation as an aberration from normal behavior. It equates the refusal to suicide and asserts a compelling state interest in preventing Quackenbush from refusing vital medical care and treatment. The hospital relies on *John F. Kennedy Memorial Hosp.* v. *Heston*. . . .

Quackenbush asserts a constitutional right of privacy and right of self-determination, relying on *In re Quinlan*. . . .

The *Heston* case involved a 22-year-old unmarried woman who, as the result of an automobile accident, required surgery. A blood transfusion was essential to the success of the operation. The blood transfusion was refused on religious grounds. The refusal was made through the woman's parents since she was in shock at the time. (She later affirmed her parents' decision after successful surgery.)

The Supreme Court, in affirming the trial Court's decision to permit the transfusion, found that a compelling State interest in the preservation of life and the right of a physician to administer medical treatment according to his best judgment prevailed over the patient's religious claim justifying the Court's refusal to permit the patient (through her parents) to reject life-saving medical assistance. . . .

In *Quinlan* a 22-year-old girl was in a comatose condition on a respirator. The respirator, at the time, was essential to keep her alive. She was described by the testimony of doctors to be in a chronic persistent vegetative state which meant she had no cognitive functioning and no reasonable prospect of returning to a cognitive or sapient life. There was no medical procedure available to improve her condition.

Chief Justice Hughes, after recognizing the unwritten constitutional right of privacy, stated in *Quinlan*:

> Presumably this right is broad enough to encompass a patient's decision to decline medical treatment under certain circumstances, in much the same way as it is broad enough to encompass a woman's decision to terminate pregnancy under certain conditions. . . .

He then pointed out the State's interest weakens and the individual's right of privacy grows as the degree of bodily invasion increases and the prognosis dims, until the ultimate point when the individual's rights overcome the State's interest in preserving life. . . . The *Quinlan* decision distinguished *Heston*, noting that a blood transfusion is a minimal bodily invasion and that the woman had a potential for vibrant health and long life. That distinction is viable in this case. Quackenbush is confronted with a significant bodily invasion and does not have the long life and vibrant health potential.

. . . The extent of the bodily invasion required to overcome the State's interest is not defined in *Quinlan*. Further, there is a suggestion of a need for a combination of significant bodily invasion *and* a dim prognosis before the individual's right of privacy overcomes the State's interest in preservation of life. Under the circumstances of this case, I hold that the extensive bodily invasion involved here—the amputation of both legs above the knee and possibly the amputation of both legs entirely—is sufficient to make the State's interest in the preservation of life give way to Robert Quackenbush's right of privacy to decide his own future regardless of the absence of a dim prognosis.[1]

No decision of this nature is easily made. Always present is the predominant interest in the preservation of life. But constitutional and decisional law invest Quackenbush with rights that overcome that interest.

Quackenbush, therefore, as a mentally competent individual, has the right to make his informed choice concerning the operation and I will not interfere with that choice.

PEEK V. CICCONE*

U.S. District Court for the Western District of Missouri (1968)

BECKER, Chief judge.

Petitioner, a federal convict confined in the United States Medical Center for Federal Prisoners, Springfield, Missouri, filed in this Court a petition for a writ of mandamus "for production of witnesses and documents to substantuate (sic) denial of due process of law and cruel and inhumane treatment. . . .

In the petition the petitioner states that he is a convict serving a "long sentence"; that his transfer to the federal prison at Leavenworth, Kansas, from McNeil Island and then to the Medical Center was "cruel and [in] humane

---

[1]Dim prognosis is interpreted to mean no successful operation can take place that will return the patient to a cognitive sapient life. The operation in this case is projected to be successful. Dim prognosis is not interpreted to mean a successful operation with possible lifetime confinement to a wheelchair or, alternatively, dependence upon artificial legs and prosthetic devices in remaining years that will be spent at a nursing home. If the latter interpretation was considered, then certainly, in Quackenbush's eyes, there is a dim prognosis.

*288 F. Supp. 329

treatment because it resulted in brutality and mental and physical suffering"; that he has been forced to take drugs which "muddle a man's mind preventing him from writing clearly to courts, politicians or relatives"; that various reports of his "stability" or "instability" which allegedly have been forwarded to the late Senator Robert F. Kennedy are prejudicial reports made by "prison officials"; that he is not allowed to see these reports and this is a denial of "legal representation"; that his work assignment at the Medical Center is " 'forced slave labor' under the guise of 'rehabilitation' "; and that he has been brutally treated, confined in the "hole," a building where no "heat or too much heat is applied, small rations of water and a starvation diet, plus deprivation of hygiene facilities."

After considering petitioner's complaints, this Court determined that the nature of the petition was habeas corpus. The respondent was ordered to show cause why a writ of habeas corpus awarding injunctive relief should not be granted.

Respondent's response to the order to show cause states that on January 31, 1962, petitioner received a total sentence of twenty-five years. . . . that his initial commitment was in the United States Penitentiary, McNeil Island, Washington, on February 2, 1962; that he was transferred to the United States Penitentiary, Leavenworth, Kansas, on December 5, 1965; that on March 24, 1966, petitioner was transferred to the Medical Center; that upon entering the Medical Center, "petitioner was housed in Ward 10A 2, which provides close individual custody for psychiatric patients"; that upon his entry to the Medical Center, he refused to accept a work assignment and on April 1, 1966, he "was placed in Ward 21E in a strip cell for discipline and maximum security"; that on April 2, 1966, he "refused to accept food and water and demanded that he be personally waited upon by custodial personnel"; that on April 9, 1966, because of petitioner's changed attitude, he was scheduled to be moved to Ward 10B where he would be allowed more freedom and comfort but that he refused oral medication which had been ordered for him and the custodial personnel were required to administer the medication intramuscularly and with force; and that petitioner was not injured, but one custodial officer was injured and, therefore, petitioner's scheduled transfer to Ward 10B was cancelled.

Respondent's response further stated the following:

"On April 12, 1966, petitioner was transferred to Ward 10B which is maximum control for acutely ill and chronic psychotics. Residents of this ward are kept in their rooms at all times except that exercise in the yard is provided on a regular basis with

---

[1]The official files and records in this case show that after a jury trial, petitioner was sentenced by the United States District Court for the Western District of Washington, Southern Division; that he was charged with "robbery of federal funds" . . . in Count I and with "assault with a dangerous weapon and wounding in the commission of a robbery of money of the United States" . . . in Counts II and III; that he was found guilty on all three Counts of the indictment; that the sentence on Count I was 15 years; that the sentences on Counts II and III were each 25 years; and that all three sentences were to run concurrently and not consecutively.

personal escort. On April 13, 1966, petitioner reported that he had passed out, fallen to the floor and cut his eye. This injury required one stitch to close. The injury to petitioner's eye which he complains of occurred in this manner, not at the time when medication was administered forcibly. On April 20, 1966, petitioner was moved to Ward 10D which again is a maximum control ward where the residents are housed in individual rooms. During the day the doors to these rooms are left open and the residents are allowed to go and come in the ward with some degree of freedom. Television is available. On May 11, 1966, petitioner was transferred to Ward 10F which is a ward for younger aggressive prisoners. This ward again provides individual rooms which are locked only at night and the residents are permitted to exercise in the yard, watch television, attend movies and have gymnasium privileges. At this time prisoner was assigned to work in the food service at the main kitchen. On May 19, 1966, petitioner refused to continue to work in food service and was reprimanded and warned but reassigned as an orderly in the craft shop, where he is currently assigned. On July 22, 1966, petitioner was removed from 10F and transferred to the regular prison population.

"The medication received by petitioner is as follows: April 6, 1966, 5 mg. Permitil, twice daily. This is a tranquilizing drug. As petitioner had refused this medication, Thorazine was administered in its place intramuscularly. April 23, 1966, the dosage was reduced to 4 mg.; April 29, 1966, reduced to 3 mg. and May 5, 1966, reduced to 2 mg. This medication was of a tranquilizing nature and was ordered by the medical staff of the institution for petitioner's benefit. It was reduced in strength in a continuing pattern and has been of substantial benefit to petitioner in that his psychiatric condition has improved to the degree where he has been recommended for transfer to a regular prison institution. . . .

"Petitioner's complaint regarding brute force apparently refers to forcible administration of medication on April 9, 1966. The drugs involved were ordered by his assigned doctor and determined necessary for treatment of his condition. Petitioner was not injured and undue force was not used. One of the medical center personnel was, however, injured in this incident. Petitioner's eye injury apparently resulted from a fall and was not occasioned by acts of medical center personnel. Force is sometimes required to obtain compliance with Medical Center rules and regulations and to assure as much as possible the safety of other inmates, personnel and the public at large. All of the acts of the personnel at the United States Medical Center has [sic] been done in petitioner's best interests which is evidenced by his improved condition. The care provided is in line with the present day medical knowledge and penal administration. Undue force has not been used nor has the petitioner been mistreated in any way. It is respectfully submitted that all of the matters referred to by petitioner are within the sound administrative discretion of the Bureau of Prisons."

Petitioner's traverse of the response to the order to show cause entitled "Rebuttal Brief to the Opposition" stated that the administration of drugs by members of the Medical Center staff who were not "certified doctors" or "registered medical assistants" was unlawful and improper; that petitioner had not received a psychiatric hearing as provided by Section 4241, Title 18, U.S.C.; that his transfer to the Medical Center was unlawful because "prison officials" had misrepresented his "psychiatric record of illness"; that his confinement at the Medical Center prevented him from obtaining legal relief from custody. . . .

. . . During the course of the hearing, petitioner informed this Court that he had had a religious experience in which it was revealed to him that he was the reincarnation of Jesus Christ. Petitioner claims to have had this experience on February 5, 1962, while he was in prison at McNeil Island; that he underwent a "mind regeneration" from February 5, 1962, until November 27, 1965, when his own soul and the soul of the "Christos" (sic) began to operate through the same mind; and that this event was predicted or prophesied in 1917 by the revelations of the Virgin Mary to a group of children in Fatima, Portugal. The incident is reported in The Columbia Encyclopedia as follows:

"*Fatima*, hamlet, W. Portugal, near Leiria. At the nearby Cova da Iria is the national shrine of Our Lady of the Rosary of Fatima. This became a great Roman Catholic center of pilgrimage after the six reported apparitions of the Virgin Mary to three shepherd children, May 13–Oct. 13, 1917. The oldest of these children was named Lucia de Jesus Santos. An impressive basilica was built in 1944."

Petitioner claims that one or more of the Fatima revelations were never publicly disclosed but were kept secret and transferred in writing to the Pope through the Bishop of Leiria. Petitioner testified that the secret of Fatima was revealed to him and, in substance, is as follows: that after two world wars and the rise of Russian communism, Christ or his "messenger of love" would appear on earth in the body of a thief and would bring world-wide peace. Petitioner further testified that he is a thief and the "Christos" (sic) referred to by the Virgin Mary in the secret prophecy of Fatima. . . .

. . . During the course of the hearing at which testimony was received on the issues of whether or not petitioner had been subjected to cruel and unusual punishment by prison officials and to the administration of drugs by unlicensed personnel while confined in the Medical Center, it became clear that petitioner was not being subjected to invidiously discriminatory or cruel and unusual punishment at the time of the filing of the petition herein or thereafter, nor was there a probability that petitioner would be subjected to such punishment.

Officer Brinkley testified that he had been employed by the Bureau of Prisons for 19 years; that he recalled one occasion when petitioner refused a request to take oral medication prescribed and ordered by a doctor; that he may have told the petitioner that the medication would be administered by force if necessary; that force was used to administer the medication, but that he did not give the petitioner the injection; that he and three other officers helped to hold the petitioner while officer Robert Randolph administered the injection; and that he suffered injuries to his nose while struggling to hold petitioner so that the injection could be given.

Officer Randolph testified that on April 9, 1966, after petitioner refused to take the oral medication, he administered 50 milligrams of Thorazine (a tranquilizer) to the petitioner intramuscularly; that he was not a doctor or a registered nurse; that he is not a registered pharmacist but although not an expert, he has had medical training and experience in administering intramuscular injections while employed at the Medical Center; that Dr. Walinsky of the Medical Center had ordered the injection of 50 milligrams of Thorazine if petitioner refused the oral medication; that the oral medication (Permitil) is received from the ward supervisor in small cups showing the person's name and number who is to receive it; that the drug Thorazine might cause one not accustomed to it to become dizzy; that force was used to give the petitioner the injection of Thorazine; that he did not know of any unnecessary force used to administer the injection to the petitioner and that there was no indication that petitioner was injured; and that the day after force was used to administer the Thorazine to petitioner, petitioner apologized and thereafter accepted the oral medication without incident.

Dr. Louis Moreau, M.D., Deputy Chief of Psychiatry at the Medical Center, testified that the medical history of petitioner received at the Medical Center from Leavenworth Penitentiary indicated that petitioner suffered from chronic schizophrenia; that he interviewed and examined petitioner when admitted to the Medical Center to determine his ward and job assignment; that petitioner had not been certified as psychotic at the time of entering the Medical Center and had not been certified psychotic since his arrival at the Medical Center; that petitioner was assigned to ward 21E for refusing to accept his work assignment; that both the oral and injected types of medication prescribed for the petitioner were tranquilizers administered to reduce the petitioner's anxiety and hostility; that they are non-narcotic and not habit forming; that the medication prescribed for petitioner was ordered by Doctor Walinsky; that the dosage prescribed for the petitioner was a reasonable dosage; that the treatment of petitioner was reasonable and ordinary; that petitioner improved after receiving the treatment; that force may be used to administer medication only as a last resort; and that he was not aware of the use of force to administer Thorazine to the petitioner on April 9, 1966.

Petitioner testified that when he was admitted to the Medical Center he was assigned to work in the kitchen; that he refused to accept this assignment because he had a weight problem; that Dr. Moreau examined him and talked to him about this problem; that because of refusing to accept this work assignment, he was isolated from the Medical Center population and given drugs; that he requested an assignment to the craft shop so that he could rehabilitate himself; that he later was assigned to the craft shop and is presently working there; that the drugs he received at the Medical Center made him dizzy and on occasion have caused him to faint; and that once he fainted and injured himself. . . .

After hearing the testimony on the issue of whether petitioner had been treated cruelly, unusually, or otherwise unlawfully by the officials of the Medical Center, it is found that he has not been so treated. The officers of the Medical Center (subordinates of the Attorney General) were not attempting to punish or harm the petitioner by forcibly administering under medical direction the intramuscular injection of Thorazine to petitioner on April 9, 1966. Petitioner was physically restrained by the prison officials only after he refused the oral medication and had been advised that he would be given the medication by injection if he did not consent to taking it orally. Under these circumstances, it cannot be said that petitioner was subjected to cruel or unusual treatment within the prohibition of the Eighth Amendment, nor was he treated in an invidiously discriminatory manner by such administration of medication.

Petitioner's contention that he was illegally required to submit to the administration of drugs and medicine by unlicensed personnel of the Medical Center is also without merit. Officer Randolph and Dr. Moreau both testified that Dr. Walinsky, a competent medical practitioner, had prescribed the medication and the dosage to be given. The medication was properly prepared by a competent person other than the one administering the medicine or drug. Further, officer Randolph as a result of his training is shown by the evidence to be competent to give intramuscular injections.

> *Therefore, these acts, based on Dr. Walinksy's orders, are not within the prohibitions of the Eighth Amendment or otherwise unlawful. . . .*

ROCKFORD CLUTCH DIVISION, BORG-WARNER CORPORATION V. INDUSTRIAL COMMISSION*

Supreme Court of Illinois (1966)

SCHAEFER, Justice. . . .
On February 14, 1961 the claimant suffered an injury when a stack of round iron plates on which he was working fell over on him. His back was injured as he attempted to hold them up. The record shows that for some time prior to his injury the claimant suffered from what is described in the record as "a cardiac condition," and because of that condition had been assigned to light work. The company doctor took X rays of Zabawa, prescribed a corset for his back, and told him to go to bed. After several weeks of examination and treatment, the doctor recommended that Zabawa undergo a laminectomy and possibly a spinal fusion to correct his disability. The employer offered to pay all medical and surgical costs of the operation, but Zabawa refused.

In the fall of 1961, the doctor advised both the employer and Zabawa that he could go back to work if he was assigned light duties. On January 8, 1962, Zabawa appeared for work, but shortly after arriving he announced that he was not going to work and he left. He has never returned to work since the day he sustained his injuries.

*215 N.E. 2d 209

On January 9, 1962, Zabawa filed an application for adjustment of claim with the Industrial Commission. The arbitrator made an award based on total permanent disability in November 1962, and the commission confirmed the award on June 5, 1963. . . .

It is undisputed that the doctor to whom the employer referred the claimant found that an operation on his back was necessary. The claimant's witness, Dr. Parker C. Hardin, testified that claimant suffers from a ruptured lumbar and lumbosacro spine intervertebral disc and that he has small bilateral, indirect inguinal herniae which also resulted from the injury. Dr. Hardin testified that the standard treatment for the claimant's back condition is a laminectomy and, if necessary, a spinal fusion. He also testified that there was no guaranty that surgery would improve the condition but that in his experience 80 to 95 per cent of those who undergo disc surgery are sufficiently improved that they are very pleased they had the operation. Three to five per cent are not improved or are made worse by the operation. He testified that a laminectomy is a serious major operation, that he had never heard of anyone dying from the operation, but that this man had a heart condition which would increase the risk. He did not examine the claimant's heart because he did not consider himself a cardiologist or a person qualified to express an opinion about the heart.

On review before the commission, the employer offered in evidence two letters signed by Dr. R. Gregory Green, which stated that he had examined the claimant in March, April, and May of 1961. The first letter stated that when the patient was re-examined on April 17, 1961, his left achilles tendon reflex was still absent. "It was felt that the patient's condition was becoming worse and it was decided to refer the patient to Dr. Courtney Hamlin, specialist in internal medicine, for a complete cardiac evaluation to see if the patient would be able to tolerate surgery. For that reason I authorized Dr. Hamlin to carry out this examination at company expense. I am sure you are aware that this patient was treated for several months by Dr. Hamlin for a cardiac condition." The second letter stated that shortly after May 2, "we received a letter dated April 25, 1961, from Dr. Hamlin in which he stated that he thought that the patient could tolerate surgery if necessary." . . .

. . . Dr. Hardin, claimant's witness, testified that a laminectomy is a "serious, large, important major operation" which may involve quite a prolonged procedure. There is danger of injury to the aorta. He testified that in his experience 85 per cent of the people who undergo an operation for the condition from which the claimant suffered are improved. The employer offered a letter from Dr. Eugene E. Herzberger. This letter stated that the patient had been referred to Dr. George Barry who "did not find any evidence of organic heart disease." The letter continued: "In view of the obvious disability of the patient and the persistence of symptoms and signs, it is felt that the patient should be operated upon and the herniated intervertebral disc removed. However, prior to the operation a myelographic study should be carried out, for precise visualization of the level of the herniation of the nucleus pulposus. As the patient's heart condition does not appear to represent any contrary indication, it is felt that it would be advisable to subject the patient to surgery as soon as possible. As most of our operations of this kind are carried out under local anesthesia and as the patients invariably walk on the day of the operation following such a procedure, there is no reason to consider the surgical procedure in any way particularly worrisome in the light of the patient's general condition. The patient has been advised as to these facts and will have to make his own decision on the matter. If this patient is not treated surgically, it is very likely that he is going to remain with considerable permanent disability, which of course could be avoided with proper surgery." . . .

The employer urges the applicability of section 19(d) of the Worker's Compensation Act . . . which provides that if an injured employee refuses "to submit to such medical, surgical, or hospital treatment as is reasonably essential to promote his recovery, the Commission may, in its discretion, reduce or suspend the compensation of any such injured employee." . . .

. . . Under our decisions, however, in the absence of bad faith, it is for the claimant to choose whether to continue to suffer from a disability or to submit to a major operation designed to cure it. . . .

The employer's attorney conceded in oral argument that he knew of no case in any jurisdiction in which compensation had been reduced or denied for failure to submit to a laminectomy. His difficulty may be explained by the fact that when an intervertebral disc operation is at issue, "most courts will not at present disturb a finding that refusal to submit to the operation is reasonable." (. . . Larson, Law of Workmen's Compensation . . .) This treatise cites a number of cases in which, despite testimony that an operation on an injured disc would be beneficial, the operation was not required as a condition of compensation. . . .

. . . The Workmen's Compensation Act is not designed simply to protect employees who follow the best medical opinion of the day. It is designed for employees with divergent personalities, beliefs, and fears. If a claimant's response to an offer of treatment is within the bounds of reason, his freedom of choice should be preserved even when an operation might mitigate the employer's damages.

> . . . Further testimony from independent medical exerts would not, in our opinion, add anything significant to the record in this case. The claimant should be entitled to decide on the basis of whatever competent medical advice he chooses to follow whether he should submit to major surgery. The record contains ample evidence of the serious character of the proposed operation, and under the circumstances, no futher evidence could render his refusal unreasonable. . . .

4

EXPERIMENTATION

Both this and the preceding chapter concern informed consent. But here, the focus is upon the experimental rather than the clinical. These cases depict research as well as, or instead of, care.

The first case, *United States* v. *Karl Brandt*—a war crimes case prosecuted at the end of World War II—does not so much provide us material for debate as a warning that even finely educated men are capable of extraordinary treachery and self-excuse. For the doctors whose crimes were joined with Brandt's in this case were "outstanding men of science . . . trained in the highest traditions of German medicine," to use the words of the judge.

These medical experiments were clearly inexcusable. But does this mean that the findings should never be released? If there is something of scientific value in the studies, should we ignore it out of respect for the victims and disgust for the doctors? (This was in fact a point of controversy after the trial.)

Although the case presents an historical horror rather than a current crisis, it does contain an item of lasting interest, the Nuremberg Code. Is it well framed? Were they too hasty in suggesting controls? Or is it morally slack in places?

In *Kaimowitz* v. *Department of Mental Health*, Louis Smith's statement of informed consent to experimental psychosurgery seems to be acceptable. But the judge is not satisfied. First he objects to psychosurgery in general. He reasons that the state cannot allow people to so clearly imperil their ability to think and speak.

Second, he says that Smith's prison setting invalidates his consent. Tantalized by prospects of release and stripped of dignity, he might well find the doctors' offer irresistible. The situation is, in a word, coercive. The pressures are such that he would choose things he would not consider on the outside.

Is the judge overstating the problem? Or is this an enlightened ruling? Should the threat of death or serious impairment from disease also invalidate an informed consent statement? For one could argue that the situation is coercive. For example, a desperate cancer patient could agree to an experiment with a new anticancer drug. Should his agreement count? At what level is the pressure so great as to rule out informed consent?

As scientists and doctors become increasingly familiar with the workings of the brain, surgical and chemical adjustments become more attractive. While the topic here is informed consent, this case may also serve as the occasion to consider the practice of psychosurgery. Is there any warrant for the sort of work these Michigan doctors chose? Are they on the right track, or is there something treacherous in their program, apart from the question of coercion?

Hyman v. *Jewish Chronic Disease Hospital* takes us back to the matter of informing, the other aspect of informed consent. With all the proper backing and clearance, Drs. Southern and Levin injected patients with cancer cells. They wanted to study the rejection rate from bodies already suffering from cancer. So as not to alarm the subjects, they did not tell them the precise nature of the injections. Besides, they were confident that there was nothing to fear. Should they have let the subjects decide what was or was not worth fearing? Or would that have pointlessly destroyed a valuable experiment? In many experiments, particularly the psychological ones, the subject must not fully understand the nature of the test. Otherwise, the results will be skewed. How much secrecy, if any, is permissible? Do the guidelines in *Canterbury* v. *Spence* apply as well to experimental situations?

New Jersey Society for the Prevention of Cruelty to Animals v. *Board of Education of the City of East Orange* gives us another situation in which informed consent is impossible: animals are unable to decline or agree to experimental treatment.

How shall we assess their suffering? Surely they lack the imagination, knowledge, and self-consciousness which is so much a part of human suffering. We enhance our pain by horror and reflection. They do not. But few would say that they are simply unfeeling mechanisms on the order of soft drink machines. So how shall we proceed?

We speak of human rights. Are we prepared to speak of animal rights?

Can we afford to suspend the enormous use of lab animals in medical research? If we believe that animals may be so used, does it follow that anything goes? Or are there moral distinctions to be drawn in the choice of techniques?

This consideration of the rights and suffering of animals could easily lead to a discussion of bull fights, fox hunts, steel traps, livestock shipping conditions, and the many other situations in which animals may be abused. Where must we draw the line in the defense of animals?

UNITED STATES V. KARL BRANDT*

Nuremberg Military Tribunal (1947)

Between September 1939 and April 1945 all of the defendants herein unlawfully, willfully, and knowingly committed war crimes [and crimes against humanity] . . . in that they were principals in, accessories to, ordered, abetted, took a consenting part in, and were connected with plans and enterprises involving medical experiments without the subjects' consent, upon [German civilians and] civilians and members of the armed forces of nations then at war with the German Reich . . . in the course of which experiments the defendants committed murders, brutalities, cruelties, tortures, atrocities, and other inhuman acts. Such experiments included, but were not limited to the following:

High-altitude experiments.   From about March 1942 to about August 1942 experiments were conducted at the Dachau concentration camp, for the benefit of the German Air Force, to investigate the limits of human endurance and existence at extremely high altitudes. The experiments were carried out in a low-pressure chamber in which the atmospheric conditions and pressures prevailing at high altitude (up to 68,000 feet) could be duplicated. The experimental subjects were placed in the low-pressure chamber and thereafter the simulated altitude therein was raised. Many victims died as a result of these experiments and others suffered grave injury, torture, and ill-treatment. . . .

Freezing experiments.   From about August 1942 to about May 1943 experiments were conducted at the Dachau concentration camp, primarily for the benefit of the German Air Force, to investigate the most effective means of treating persons who had been severely chilled or frozen. In one series of experiments the subjects were forced to remain in a tank of ice water for periods up to 3 hours. Extreme rigor developed in a short time. Numerous victims died in the course of these experiments. After the survivors were severely chilled, rewarming was attempted by various means. In another series of experiments, the subjects were kept naked outdoors for many hours at temperatures below freezing. The victims screamed with pain as parts of their bodies froze. . . .

Malaria experiments.   From about February 1942 to about April 1945 experiments were conducted at the Dachau concentration camp in order to investigate immunization for and treatment of malaria. Healthy concentration-camp inmates were infected by mosquitoes or by injections of extracts of the

Trials of War Criminals Before the Nuremberg Military Tribunals, The Medical Case (Washington, D.C.: U.S. Government Printing Office, 1948).

mucous glands of mosquitoes. After having contracted malaria the subjects were treated with various drugs to test their relative efficacy. Over 1,000 involuntary subjects were used in these experiments. Many of the victims died and others suffered severe pain and permanent disability. . . .

Sulfanilamide experiments. From about July 1942 to about September 1943 experiments to investigate the effectiveness of sulfanilamide were conducted at the Ravensbrueck concentration camp for the benefit of the German Armed Forces. Wounds deliberately inflicted on the experimental subjects were infected with bacteria such as streptococcus, gas gangrene, and tetanus. Circulation of blood was interrupted by tying off blood vessels at both ends of the wound to create a condition similar to that of a battlefield wound. Infection was aggravated by forcing wood shavings and ground glass into the wounds. The infection was treated with sulfanilamide and other drugs to determine their effectiveness. Some subjects died as a result of these experiments and others suffered serious injury and intense agony. . . .

Epidemic jaundice experiments. From about June 1943 to about January 1945 experiments were conducted at the Sachsenhausen and Natzweiler concentration camps, for the benefit of the German Armed Forces, to investigate the causes of, and inoculations against, epidemic jaundice. Experimental subjects were deliberately infected with epidemic jaundice, some of whom died as a result, and others were caused great pain and suffering. . . .

Spotted fever [typhus] experiments. From about December 1941 to about February 1945 experiments were conducted at the Buchenwald and Natzweiler concentration camps, for the benefit of the German Armed Forces, to investigate the effectiveness of spotted fever and other vaccines. At Buchenwald numerous healthy inmates were deliberately infected with spotted fever virus in order to keep the virus alive; over 90 percent of the victims died as a result. Other healthy inmates were used to determine the effectiveness of different spotted fever vaccines and of various chemical substances. In the course of these experiments 75 percent of the selected number of inmates were vaccinated with one of the vaccines or nourished with one of the chemical substances and, after a period of 3 to 4 weeks, were infected with spotted fever germs. The remaining 25 percent were infected without any previous protection in order to compare the effectiveness of the vaccines and the chemical substances. As a result, hundreds of persons experimented upon died. . . .

Experiments with poison. In or about December 1943, and in or about October 1944, experiments were conducted at the Buchenwald concentration camp to investigate the effect of various poisons upon human beings. The poisons were secretly administered to experimental subjects in their food. The victims died as a result of the poison or were killed immediately in order to permit autopsies. In or about September 1944 experimental subjects were shot with poison bullets and suffered torture and death. . . .

Between June 1943 and September 1944 the defendants Rudolf Brandt and Sievers . . . were principals in, accessories to, ordered, abetted, took a consenting part in, and were connected with plans and enterprises involving the murder of civilians and members of the armed forces of nations then at war with the German Reich and who were in the custody of the German Reich in exercise of belligerent control. One hundred twelve Jews were selected for the purpose of completing a skeleton collection for the Reich University of Strasbourg. Their photographs and anthropological measurements were taken. Then they were killed. Thereafter, comparison tests, anatomical research, studies regarding race, pathological features of the body, form and size of the brain, and other tests, were made. The bodies were sent to Strasbourg and defleshed. . . .

A sort of rough pattern is apparent on the face of the indictment. Experiments concerning high altitude, the effect of cold, and the potability of processed sea water have an obvious relation to aeronautical and naval combat and rescue problems. The mustard gas and phosphorous burn experiments, as well as those relating to the healing value of sulfanilamide for wounds, can be related to air-raid and battlefield medical problems. It is well known that malaria, epidemic jaundice, and typhus were among the principal diseases which had to be combated by the German Armed Froces and by German authorities in occupied territories.

To some degree, the therapeutic pattern outlined above is undoubtedly a valid one, and explains why the Wehrmacht, and especially the German Air Force, participated in these experiments. Fanatically bent upon conquest, utterly ruthless as to the means or instruments to be used in achieving victory, and callous to the sufferings of people whom they regarded as inferior, the German militarists were willing to gather whatever scientific fruit these experiments might yield.

But our proof will show that a quite different and even more sinister objective runs like a red thread through these hideous researches. We will show that in some instances the true object of these experiments was not how to rescue or to cure, but how to destroy and kill. The sterilization experiments were, it is clear, purely destructive in purpose. The prisoners at Buchenwald who were shot with poisoned bullets were not guinea pigs to test an antidote for the poison; their murderers really wanted to know how quickly the poison would kill. This destructive objective is not superficially as apparent in the other experiments, but we will show that it was often there.

Mankind has not heretofore felt the need of a word to denominate the science of how to kill prisoners most rapidly and subjugated people in large numbers. This case and these defendants have created this gruesome question for the lexicographer. For the moment we will christen this macabre science "thanatology," the science of producing death. The thanatological knowledge, derived in part from these experiments, supplied the techniques for genocide, a policy of the Third Reich, exemplified in the "euthanasia" program and in the widespread slaughter of Jews, gypsies, Poles, and Russians. This policy of mass extermination could not have been so effectively carried out without the active participation of German medical scientists. . . .

The 20 physicians in the dock range from leaders of German scientific medicine, with excellent international reputations, down to the dregs of the German medical profession. All of them have in common a callous lack of consideration and human regard for, and an unprincipled willingness to abuse their power over the poor, unfortunate, defenseless creatures who had been deprived of their rights by a ruthless and criminal government. All of them violated the Hippocratic commandments which they had solemnly sworn to uphold and abide by, including the fundamental principles never to do harm— "*primum non nocere.*"

Outstanding men of science, distinguished for their scientific ability in Germany and abroad, are the defendants Rostock and Rose. Both exemplify, in their training and practice alike, the highest traditions of German medicine. Rostock headed the Department of Surgery at the University of Berlin and served as dean of its medical school. Rose studied under the famous surgeon, Enderlen, at Heidelberg and then became a distinguished specialist in the fields of public health and tropical diseases. Handloser and Schroeder are outstanding medical administrators. Both of them made their careers in military medicine and reached the peak of their profession. Five more defendants are much younger men who are nevertheless already known as the possessors of considerable scientific ability, or capacity in medical administration. These include the defendants Karl Brandt, Ruff, Beiglboeck, Schaefer, and Becker-Freyseng.

A number of the others such as Romberg and Fischer are well trained, and several of them attained high professional position. But among the remainder few were known as outstanding scientific men. Among them at the foot of the list is Blome who has published his autobiography entitled "Embattled Doctor" in which he sets forth that he eventually decided to become a doctor because a medical career would enable him to become "master over life and death." . . .

These experiments revealed nothing which civilized medicine can use. It was, indeed, ascertained that phenol or gasoline injected intravenously will kill a man inexpensively and within 60 seconds. This and a few other "advances" are all in the field of thanatology. . . .

Apart from these deadly fruits, the experiments were not only criminal but a scientific failure. It is indeed as if a just deity had shrouded the solutions which they attempted to reach with murderous means. The moral shortcomings of the defendants and the precipitous ease with which they decided to commit murder in quest of "scientific results," dulled also that scientific hesitancy, that thorough thinking-through, that responsible weighing of every single step which alone can insure scientifically valid results. Even if they had merely been forced to pay as little as two dollars for human experimental subjects, such as American investigators may have to pay for a cat, they might have thought twice before wasting unnecessary numbers, and thought of simpler and better ways to solve their problems. The fact that these investigators had free and unrestricted access to human beings to be experimented upon misled them to the dangerous and fallacious conclusion that the results would thus be better and more quickly obtainable than if they had gone through the labor of preparation, thinking, and meticulous preinvestigation.

A particularly striking example is the sea-water experiment. I believe that three of the accused . . . will today admit that this problem could have been solved simply and definitively within the space of one afternoon. On 20 May 1944 when these accused convened to discuss the problem, a thinking chemist could have solved it right in the presence of the assembly within the space of a few hours by the use of nothing more gruesome than a piece of jelly, a semipermeable membrane and a salt solution, and the German Armed Forces would have had the answer on 21 May 1944. But what happened instead? The vast armies of the disenfranchised slaves were at the beck and call of this sinister assembly; and instead of thinking, they simply relied on their power over human beings rendered rightless by a criminal state and government. . . .

. . . Who could German medicine look to to keep the profession true to its traditions and protect it from the ravaging inroads of Nazi pseudo-science? This was the supreme responsibility of the leaders of German medicine—men like Rostock and Rose and Schroeder and Handloser. That is why their guilt is greater than that of any of the other defendants in the dock. They are the men who utterly failed their country and their profession, who showed neither courage nor wisdom nor the vestiges of moral character. . . .

TESTIMONY OF DEFENSE EXPERT WITNESS DR. FRANZ VOLLHARDT

Direct Examination

DR. MARX: Please, would you briefly tell the Tribunal what your scientific activities have been and in what special field you have taken a particularly great interest, and since when?

WITNESS VOLLHARDT: I am Professor of Internal Medicine at Frankfurt and predominantly I have dealt with the questions of circulation, metabolism, blood pressure, and kidney diseases.

Q: Which foreign academies and foreign societies have you been a member of? . . .

A: I am Honorary Doctor of the Sorbonne, Paris, of Goettingen and Freiburg; and, as far as societies are concerned, there are a lot of them, Medical Society at Edinburgh, at Geneva, at Luxembourg. I am an Honorary Member of the University at Santiago, and so on and so forth.

Q: Now, Professor, have you sufficient insight into the planning and carrying out of the so-called sea-water experiments to give an expert opinion on that subject?

A: I think that scientifically speaking the planning was excellent and I have no objection to the entire plan. It was good
to add a hunger-and-thirst group because we know by
experience that thirst can be borne less well than hunger,
and if people are suffering from hunger and thirst too, they
do not suffer from hunger, but do suffer from thirst; and
that resembles what shipwrecked persons would be subjected to because they only suffer from thirst. It was excellent
that Wofatit was to be introduced into the experiments too,
although it was expected from the beginning that this wonderful discovery would show its value. . . .

Q: Could the aim of these experiments have been achieved
with a semipermeable membrane?

A: I don't understand how one can imagine this. What we
are concerned with is the question of how long the
human body can survive without water and under the
excess quantity of salt. Now, that is subject to the water
content of the body and it depends first of all, upon
whether water is only used by the intermediary tissues or
whether the cell liquid too is being used up. In the latter
case, there is a danger which becomes apparent through
excess potassium quantities, and this was also continu-
ously observed and checked during such experiments,
and there were no excess potassium quantities such as
can be expected after 6 days.

Q: Nor would it be right to say that these experiments were
not planned scientifically and medically, is that correct?

A: Absolutely not.

Q: Could they have been planned differently?

A: I couldn't imagine how.

Q: Were these experiments in the interests of active warfare,
or in the interests of the care of shipwrecked sailors or
soldiers?

A: The latter.

Q: In other words, for aviators and sailors who were shipwrecked or might be shipwrecked?

A: Towards the end of the war there was an increase in the
number of pilots shot down as well as of shipwrecked
personnel, and it was, therefore, the duty of the hygiene
department concerned to consider the question of how
one could best deal with such cases of shipwrecked personnel. . . .

Q: Now, Professor, the experiments we were talking about;
did they have a practical valuable aim and did they
show a corresponding result?

A: Yes, that is correct. For instance an important observation was made which Eppinger had expected; he wanted to see if the kidneys did concentrate salt under such extreme conditions to an even higher extent than one expected previously. One thought that it would be something like 2.0 percent but 2.6 or 2.7 percent and record figures of 3.0, 3.5, 3.6, and 4 percent are shown, so that the fortunate man who is in a position to concentrate 3.6 percent or 4 percent of salt would be able to live on sea water for quite a long period.

Finally, one unsuspected fact was shown which may be connected with this, and that is that the drinking of small quantities of sea water up to 500 cc. given over a lengthy period turned out to be better than unalleviated thirst.

Q: So, you think that the result of these experiments is not only of importance in wartime, but is also of importance for the problems of seafaring nations?

A: Quite right, it is a wonderful thing for all seafaring nations.

JUDGMENT

BEALS, SEBRING, CRAWFORD, J.J.: . . . Judged by any standard of proof the record clearly shows the commission of war crimes and crimes against humanity. . . . Beginning with the outbreak of World War II criminal medical experiments on non-German nationals, both prisoners of war and civilians, including Jews and "asocial" persons, were carried out on a large scale in Germany and the occupied countries. These experiments were not the isolated and casual acts of individual doctors and scientists working solely on their own responsibility, but were the product of coordinated policy-making and planning at high governmental, military, and Nazi Party levels, conducted as an integral part of the total war effort. They were ordered, sanctioned, permitted, or approved by persons in positions of authority who under all principles of law were under the duty to know about these things and to take steps to terminate or prevent them.

The great weight of the evidence before us is to the effect that certain types of medical experiments on human beings, when kept within reasonably well-defined bounds, conform to the ethics of the medical profession generally. The protagonists of the practice of human experimentation justify their views on the basis that such experiments yield results for the good of society that are unprocurable by other methods or means of study. All agree, however, that certain basic principles[1] must be observed in order to satisfy moral, ethical, and legal concepts:

1. The voluntary consent of the human subject is absolutely essential.

[1]These ten principles are now known as the Nuremberg Code.

This means that the person should have legal capacity to give consent; should be so situated as to be able to exercise free power of choice, without the intervention of any element of force, fraud, deceit, duress, over-reaching, or other ulterior form of constraint or coercion; and should have sufficient knowledge and comprehension of the elements of the subject matter involved as to enable him to make an understanding and enlightened decision. This latter element requires that before the acceptance of an affirmative decision by the experimental subject there should be made known to him the nature, duration, and purpose of the experiment; the method and means by which it is to be conducted; all inconveniences and hazards reasonably to be expected; and the effects upon his health or person which may possibly come from his participation in the experiment.

The duty and responsibility for ascertaining the quality of the consent rests upon each individual who initiates, directs, or engages in the experiment. It is a personal duty and responsibility which may not be delegated to another with impunity.

2. The experiment should be such as to yield fruitful results for the good of society, unprocurable by other methods or means of study, and not random and unnecessary in nature.

3. The experiment should be so designed and based on the results of animal experimentation and a knowledge of the natural history of the disease or other problem under study that the anticipated results will justify the performance of the experiment.

4. The experiment should be so conducted as to avoid all unnecessary physical and mental suffering and injury.

5. No experiment should be conducted where there is an a priori reason to believe that death or disabling injury will occur; except, perhaps, in those experiments where the experimental physicians also serve as subjects.

6. The degree of risk to be taken should never exceed that determined by the humanitarian importance of the problem to be solved by the experiment.

7. Proper preparations should be made and adequate facilities provided to protect the experimental subject against even remote possibilities of injury, disability, or death.

8. The experiment should be conducted only by scientifically qualified persons. The highest degree of skill and care should be required through all stages of the experiment of those who conduct or engage in the experiment.

9. During the course of the experiment the human subject should be at liberty to bring the experiment to an end if he has reached the physical or mental state where continuation of the experiment seems to him to be impossible.

10. During the course of the experiment the scientist in charge must be prepared to terminate the experiment at any stage, if he has probable cause to believe, in the exercise of the good faith, superior skill, and careful judgment required of him that a continuation of the experiment is likely to result in injury, disability, or death to the experimental subject. . . .

KAIMOWITZ V. DEPARTMENT OF MENTAL HEALTH FOR THE STATE OF MICHIGAN*

State of Michigan in the Circuit Court for the County of Wayne (1973)

This case came to this Court originally on a complaint for a writ of Habeas Corpus brought by Plaintiff Kaimowitz on behalf of John Doe and the Medical Committee for Human Rights, alleging that John Doe was being illegally detained in the Lafayette Clinic for the purpose of experimental psychosurgery.[1]

John Doe had been committed by the Kalamazoo County Circuit Court on January 11, 1955, to the Ionia State Hospital as a Criminal Sexual Psychopath, without a trial of criminal charges, under the terms of the then existing Criminal Sexual Psychopathic law. . . . He had been charged with the murder and subsequent rape of a student nurse at the Kalamazoo State Hospital while he was confined there as a mental patient.

In 1972, Drs. Ernst Rodin and Jacques Gottlieb of the Lafayette Clinic, a facility of the Michigan Department of Mental Health, had filed a proposal "For the Study of Treatment of Uncontrollable Aggression." . . .

This was funded by the Legislature of the State of Michigan for the fiscal year 1972. After more than 17 years at the Ionia State Hospital, John Doe was transferred to the Lafayette Clinic in November of 1972 as a suitable research subject for the Clinic's study of uncontrollable aggression.

Under the terms of the study, 24 criminal sexual psychopaths in the State's mental health system were to be subjects of the experiment. The experiment was to compare the effects of surgery on the amygdaloid portion of the limbic system of the brain with the effect of the drug cyproterone acetate on the male hormone flow. The comparison was intended to show which, if either, could be used in controlling aggression of males in an institutional setting, and to afford lasting permanent relief from such aggression to the patient. . . .

Substantial difficulties were encountered in locating a suitable patient population for the surgical procedures and a matched controlled group for the treatment by the anti-androgen drug. . . . As a matter of fact, it was concluded that John Doe was the only known appropriate candidate available within the state mental health system for the surgical experiment.

John Doe signed an "informed consent" form to become an experimental subject prior to his transfer from the Ionia State State Hospital.[2] . . . He had

---

*Civil Action, No. 73-19434-AW

[1]The name John Doe has been used through the proceedings to protect the true identity of the subject involved. After the institution of this action and during proceedings his true identity was revealed. His true name is Louis Smith. For the purpose of the Opinion, however, he will be referred to throughout as John Doe.

[2]"Since conventional treatment efforts over a period of several years have not enabled me to control my outbursts of rage and anti-social behavior, I submit an application to be a subject in a

obtained signatures from his parents giving consent for the experimental and innovative surgical procedures to be performed on his brain, . . . and two separate three-man review committees were established by Dr. Rodin to review the scientific worthiness of the study and the validity of the consent obtained from Doe.

The Scientific Review Committee, headed by Dr. Elliot Luby, approved of the procedure, and the Human Rights Review Committee, consisting of Ralph Slovenko, a Professor of Law and Psychiatry at Wayne State University, Monsignor Clifford Sawher, and Frank Moran, a Certified Public Accountant, gave their approval to the procedure.

Even though no experimental subjects were found to be available in the state mental health system other than John Doe, Dr. Rodin prepared to proceed with the experiment on Doe, and depth electrodes were to be inserted into his brain on or about January 15, 1973. . . .

Violent behavior not associated with brain disease should not be dealt with surgically. At best, neurosurgery rightfully should concern itself with medical problems and not the behavior problems of a social etiology. . . .

Psychosurgery flattens emotional responses, leads to lack of abstract reasoning ability, leads to a loss of capacity for new learning and causes general sedation and apathy. It can lead to impairment of memory, and in some instances unexpected responses to psychosurgery are observed. It has been found, for example, that heightened rage reaction can follow surgical intervention on the amygdala, just as placidity can. . . .

research project which may offer me a form of effective therapy. This therapy is based upon the idea that episodes of anti-social rage and sexuality might be triggered by a disturbance in certain portions of my brain. I understand that in order to be certain that a significant brain disturbance exists, which might relate to my anti-social behavior, an initial operation will have to be performed. This procedure consists of placing fine wires into my brain, which will record the electrical activity from those structures which play a part in anger and sexuality. These electrical waves can then be studied to determine the presence of an abnormality.

"In addition electrical stimulation with weak currents passed through these wires will be done in order to find out if one or several points in the brain can trigger my episodes of violence or unlawful sexuality. In other words this stimulation may cause me to want to commit an aggressive or sexual act, but every effort will be made to have a sufficient number of people present to control me. If the brain disturbance is limited to a small area, I understand that the investigators will destroy this part of my brain with an electrical current. If the abnormality comes from a larger part of my brain, I agree that it should be surgically removed, if the doctors determine that it can be done so, without risk of side effects. Should the electrical activity from the parts of my brain into which the wires have been placed reveal that there is no significant abnormality, the wires will simply be withdrawn.

"I realize that any operation on the brain carries a number of risks which may be slight, but could be potentially serious. These risks include infection, bleeding, temporary or permanent weakness or paralysis of one or more of my legs or arms, difficulties with speech and thinking, as well as the ability to feel, touch, pain and temperature. Under extraordinary circumstances, it is also possible that I might not survive the operation.

"Fully aware of the risks detailed in the paragraphs above, I authorize the physicians of Lafayette Clinic and Providence Hospital to perform the procedures as outlined above.

Simply stated, on this record there is no scientific basis for establishing that the removal or destruction of an area of the limbic brain would have any direct therapeutic effect in controlling aggressivity or improving tormenting personal behavior, absent the showing of a well-defined clinical syndrome such as epilepsy.

To advance scientific knowledge, it is true that doctors may desire to experiment on human beings, but the need for scientific inquiry must be reconciled with the inviolability which our society provides for a person's mind and body. Under a free government, one of a person's greatest rights is the right to inviolability of his person, and it is axiomatic that this right necessarily forbids the physician or surgeon from violating, without permission, the bodily integrity of his patient. . . .

Generally, individuals are allowed free choice about whether to undergo experimental medical procedures. But the State has the power to modify this free choice concerning experimental medical procedures when it cannot be freely given, or when the result would be contrary to public policy. For example, it is obvious that a person may not consent to acts that will constitute murder, manslaughter, or mayhem upon himself. . . . In short, there are times when the State for good reason should withhold a person's ability to consent to certain medical procedures. . . .

Institutionalization tends to strip the individual of the support which permit him to maintain his sense of self-worth and the value of his own physical and mental integrity. . . . He finds himself stripped of customary amenities and defenses. Free movement is restricted. He becomes a part of communal living subject to the control of the institutional authorities. . . .

Involuntarily confined mental patients live in an inherently coercive institutional environment. Indirect and subtle psychological coercion has profound effect upon the patient population. Involuntarily confined patients cannot reason as equals with the doctors and administrators over whether they should undergo psychosurgery. They are not able to voluntarily give informed consent because of the inherent inequality in their position. . . .

Freedom of speech and expression, and the right of all men to disseminate ideas, popular or unpopular, are fundamental to ordered liberty. Government has no power or right to control men's minds, thoughts, and expressions. This is the command of the First Amendment. And we adhere to it in holding an involuntarily detained mental patient may not consent to experimental psychosurgery.

For, if the First Amendment protects the freedom to express ideas, it necessarily follows that it must protect the freedom to generate ideas. Without the latter protection, the former is meaningless.

Experimental psychosurgery, which is irreversible and intrusive, often leads to the blunting of emotions, the deadening of memory, the reduction of affect, and limits the ability to generate new ideas. Its potential for injury to the creativity of the individual is great, and can impinge upon the right of the individual to be free from interference with his mental processes.

The State's interest in performing psychosurgery and the legal ability of the involuntarily detained mental patient to give consent must bow to the First

Amendment, which protects the generation and free flow of ideas from unwarranted interference with one's mental processes. . . .

HYMAN V. JEWISH CHRONIC DISEASE HOSPITAL*

New York Supreme Court, Appellate Division (1964)

Before BELDOCK, P. J., and CHRIST, BRENNAN, HILL and HOPKINS, JJ.

PER CURIAM. . . .

As the result of approximately ten years of reseach, Dr. Chester M. Southam of the Sloan-Kettering Institute for Cancer Research found that cancer patients did not have as marked a defense against cancer as did non-cancer patients. It is a biological law that human beings will reject cells which are transplanted from another human being unless both persons are of precisely the same genetic constitution (e. g., identical twins). It was found that, when a healthy individual was injected with the cancer cells of another individual, the healthy person promptly rejected the transplant, whereas when a cancer patient was injected with such foreign cancer cells, rejection of the transplant was delayed. What was not known was whether the foreign cancer cells lived longer in cancer patients (as contrasted with non-cancer patients) as the result of the pre-existing cancer or as the result of the patient's general weakness and debilitation. It was this question which Dr. Southam attempted to answer by the experiments conducted at the Jewish Chronic Disease Hospital; and it is these experiments which are involved in the present appeal.

The experiments showed that the sick and debilitated non-cancer patients had the same response to foreign cancer cells as healthy volunteers, that is, there was a prompt rejection of the transplant. This in turn opened a wide possibility that, if there be such a biological mechanism as a defense against cancer, it may be possible to stimulate it either before cancer strikes or perhaps even later when the cancer has taken hold.

The project was financed by the United States Public Health Service and by the American Cancer Society. It was undertaken by Drs. Southam and Levin of the Sloan-Kettering Institute at the Jewish Chronic Disease Hospital, with the permission of Dr. Mandel, Director of the Department of Medicine and Director of Medical Education of the Hospital. . . .

On July 16, 1963, under the supervision of Drs. Southam and Levin, 22 patients at the hospital were injected with foreign cancer cells on the anterior surface of one thigh at two sites just beneath the skin. The patients were not told

*251 N.Y.S. 2d 818

that the injection was of cancer cells because the doctors did not wish to stir up any unnecessary anxieties in the patients. The doctors felt there was no need to tell the patients that the injected material contained cancer cells because: (a) it was of no consequence to the patients; (b) the precise nature of the foreign cells was irrelevant to the bodily reactions which could be expected to occur; (c) it was not germane to the reaction being studied; and (d) it was not a cause of increased risk to the patient.

However, the patients were told that an injection of a cell suspension was planned as a skin test for immunity or response. The patients were also told that within a few days a lump would form and would last for several weeks and gradually disappear. The patients were observed for several weeks after the injection of July 16, 1963. As expected, the lump developed and disappeared within an average period of from six to eight weeks.

The Hospital and the doctors in charge of the experiment claim that each patient gave his oral consent. Petitioner, however, claims that the patients were either incompetent to give their consents or that they did not understand to what it was they were being asked to consent. . . .

. . . The Hospital's future policy will be in accordance with petitioner's contention that experiments such as the one here involved should be done only with the patient's written consent after the patient has been properly informed. . . .

NEW JERSEY SOCIETY FOR THE PREVENTION OF CRUELTY TO ANIMALS V. BOARD OF EDUCATION OF THE CITY OF EAST ORANGE*

Essex County (N.J.) Court, Law Division (1966)

BARRETT, J. C. C.

In this action The New Jersey Society for the Prevention of Cruelty to Animals (S.P.C.A.) . . . seeks recovery against the Board of Education of the City of East Orange (board) of penalties at the rate of $100 per alleged violation arising primarily out of cancer-inducing experiments conducted by a student in its high school on live chickens. . . .

. . . I conclude that if there is a truly useful motive, a real and valid purpose, there can . . . be acts done to animals which are ostensibly cruel or which ostensibly cause pain.[1] . . .

---

*219 A. 2d 200

[1]Most of the witnesses in the case professed themselves as unable to say the two chickens which developed cancer were in pain as a result of their tumor. Evidently no one has yet been able either to determine scientifically the existence of or the measurement of pain in chickens or animals of this type.

The experiment here involved was in biology which, of course, is the study of life, and the purposes of the defendants in this and other experiments are as follows:

"1. To offer the student an opportunity to observe life processes which lead to a sympathetic respect for life.

2. To provide future citizens with some knowledge of the nature of science and of the techniques and principles of scientific inquiry.

3. To provide future citizens with some knowledge of the principles of health, disease, and medicine and of some aspects of agriculture.

4. To identify the talented student in this field.

5. To motivate selected students to become the medical and biological scientists of the future."

The experiment itself was conducted by Barry Fugere, at that time a 17-year-old sophomore in the East Orange High School. He was an outstanding student, very superior, as the high school principal testified. He was in the top seven of all East Orange students and two or three years above his age in ability. He ultimately graduated eighth out of 404. Before his request to conduct the experiment was granted, his first-year biology teacher, Donald Robertshaw, gave Fugere extensive reading assignments which were followed by Fugere, and Robertshaw examined him carefully as to what he had read, checked carefully into his motives, and satisfied himself that Fugere was fully capable of conducting the experiment in all phases. Fugere was strongly motivated toward a career in medical research as a doctor and virologist, and at present is a pre-medical student at Drew University. Robertshaw, I conclude, is a fully qualified science teacher, well able to permit and supervise an experiment of this type. In addition to his work at East Orange High School, Robertshaw teaches science at Upsala College.

The experiment Fugere desired to conduct and did conduct involved the Rous sarcoma virus. Discovered many years ago, this preparation is known to produce cancerous tumors in chickens, particularly young chickens, and has been the subject of many experiments over the years. From a well respected nonprofit culture collection in Washington, Fugere asked for and obtained the virus and information on it, being sent a letter outlining the procedures in connection with the virus, and he generally followed this letter in the conduct of his experiment.

He bought four 6–8-week-old chickens, constructed two cages therefor and, because he was ill, did not inject them at 2–8 weeks, the suggested procedure, but waited until they were several weeks older. Fugere had had prior experience in injecting with a needle and therefore knew the technique. The chickens were

---

Yet, for the purpose of this case, I am satisfied the chickens certainly suffered some discomfort and probably some pain. At any rate, our Legislature, by the very enactment of this statute, would have seemed to have considered the subject and placed prohibitions on needless or unnecessary discomfort or pain, or whatever the feeling of the chickens may be termed. In any event, there was in this case some mutilation and killing.

injected with the virus on January 28, 1964. On February 10, 1964 two chickens first showed signs of developing a tumor, and on March 7, 1964, one chicken was bleeding from the tumor, which had enlarged considerably. On the advice of Robertshaw, Fugere put the chicken to death by ether. The second chicken developed a tumor which grew and spread, and this chicken died from the tumor on March 17, 1964. The other two chickens have never developed any signs of cancer.

Fugere prepared slides of the matter from the tumors of the two dead chickens and studied their chest cavities and other parts of their remains. On all steps of the procedure, briefly outlined above, Robertshaw kept a close check. He had obtained permission for the whole experiment, not only from the head of his science department, but from the principal of the school, both of whom were generally aware of the progress of the experiment.

Fugere outlined in detail in his testimony the purposes that moved him to conduct the experiment and his motives in continuing it and in preparing his slides and examining them. He was particularly interested in the fact that two chickens resisted the virus and in the cause of such resistance. I am completely satisfied that his motives and those of his superiors in connection with the experiment were of the highest calibre and were purely scientific and educational in nature.

The two surviving chickens, together with details of the experiment, were, at the suggestion of another science teacher of East Orange High School, entered in the Newark Science Fair held April 6 and 7, 1964. There the matter came to the attention of Mr. Don R. Maxfield, New Jersey Executive Director of The American Humane Society, and ultimately these proceedings were instituted.

Much point was made by plaintiff of the fact that the experiment on the chickens was delayed until they were several weeks older than the suggested time of injection. The testimony satisfied me that this delay was valuable to the experiment rather than harmful.

The experiment obtained honorable mention in the Newark Science Fair and first place in a later Science Fair in East Orange. The articles Fugere read and the advance studies he made and all the steps of the experiment are fully detailed in the evidence.

It is not in dispute in the case, and indeed from the evidence could not be disputed, that apart from the nature of the experiment itself, with which plaintiff quarrels, the chickens were given proper care and feeding during the course of the experiment in the high school animal room, an area specially constructed for such purpose.

. . . The issue remains as to whether the high purposes of the experiment took it out of the statutory prohibition against needless mutilation or killing or unnecessary cruelty. To this issue the greater part of the testimony in the case was directed.

On this vital point defendants produced many distinguished witnesses, including scientists, educators, writers or collaborators or directors of a new series, "Biological Sciences Curriculum Studies." This project, as developed in the testimony of its director, Dr. Arnold B. Grobman, was a result of Federal Government grants of some eight million dollars and involved long effort on the part of leaders in the field. In the books and pamphlets of this project for science teaching in the high schools of this country there are featured the advantages of living animal experiments to be conducted by students under appropriate supervision. Suffice it to say that this project has resulted in the production of books and pamphlets which are probably among the most widely used in the country in the teaching of high school science. The blue book in the series was copyrighted in 1963, and I gather the other books and pamphlets appeared around that time.

The testimony of Dr. Grobman, presently Dean of the College of Arts and Sciences at Rutgers, is illustrative of the views of virtually all of the other expert witnesses produced on the subject by defendants. He said that the use of living animals is essential at the high school level for biological studies in that it (1) helps students have sympathy for living things; (2) helps make them literate in the scientific field; (3) motivates other students to scientific careers; and (4) eliminates study by rote. Other witnesses detailed other good purposes.

According to Dr. Grobman and the other expert defense witnesses, the goal of present high school science teachers should be to encourage laboratory work with plants and with animals, both dead and alive. Many of the experiments, according to these witnesses, use live chickens and other live animals. They agree that what Barry Fugere did was necessary for his educational development.

As against this array of testimony, plaintiff produced an educator in the field, Robert M. Frey, Professor of Biology at Plymouth State College, University of New Hampshire, a doctor of education. Dr. Frey viewed Fugere's experiment as unnecessary and he emphatically stated he does not recommend animal experimentation at the high school level. He felt some students would be scared away from science by this type of work, and believed it should be postponed until the students are more mature. He felt such experiments have no educational value. He believed lecture demonstrations with models, films and slides would be the best possible method for high school students. He said that animal experimentation at his college is commenced in the junior year.

As to the use of models, films and slides, defendants' experts concede they have a place, but were of the opinion that these were far inferior to living animal experimentation under proper circumstances and under suitable supervision by qualified high school science teachers.

Testifying for plaintiff, James T. Mehorter, Professor of Psychology at Montclair State College, asserted that an experiment such as was here conducted, or any experiment upon living animals at the high school level, would have an adverse effect on the mental health of adolescents. He presented an impressive argument for this point of view. Nonetheless, he did not discuss any specific example of such an adverse result having occurred.

In opposition to Professor Mehorter's views, defendants presented Bertram D. Cohen, Professor of Psychology at the College, Graduate School and Medical School of Rutgers University. Dr. Cohen has a distinguished background, with many publications and much work in the field to his credit. In his view, no harm would come to a student who engages in such experimentation; on the contrary, he felt that the student would be benefited. From his extensive work in clinics dealing with juveniles, Dr. Cohen said that a science experiment would not cause mental disturbances of the type envisioned by Professor Mehorter. I accept whole-heartedly Dr. Cohen's views.

S.P.C.A. contends that even if a properly conducted scientific experiment performed on live animals would not *per se* constitute a violation of the statute, the particular experiment involved here was improperly conducted. I am satisfied from the evidence that this experiment was in fact properly conducted, but even if there were mistakes, I am convinced by the evidence that they did not diminish the educational value of the experiment and may have actually added to the learning process.

I am further convinced from all the testimony that the type of experiment in this case, conducted as it was under the careful supervision of qualified people, did not constitute either an abuse or a needless mutilation or killing or unnecessary cruelty upon and of living animals or creatures. . . .

. . . In the person of its first two witnesses, S.P.C.A. produced testimony indicating that the two well chickens exhibited at the Newark Science Fair were to some degree inadequately caged and were without water and food for $3\frac{1}{2}$ hours. Maybe the cage used at the Newark Science Fair, which was smaller than the one used during the experiment, could have been a little larger, because in it the chickens had to stoop a bit. Yet, for the short period of their confinement I find the cage to have been entirely satisfactory. As to the lack of food and water for $3\frac{1}{2}$ hours, Barry Fugere outlined in detail what he himself had done and what prepa-ration he had made. He fed and watered the chickens on two occasions on their first day there, and again at 6 P.M. on the second and last day. He had antici-pated being at the Fair at 4 or 4:30 P.M. on the second day, but was delayed in transit by an automobile accident. Moreover, he had made arrangements with an attendant there to supply them with food and water if he should be absent, but the attendant apparently failed to act for a short period.

Under these circumstances I hold that the board of education did not violate N.J. S.A. 4:22–26 in connection with the exhibit at the Newark Science Fair, even if the chickens suffered unduly. However, I find they did not suffer unduly and that whatever discomfort they had was of a transitory, temporary nature and was not cruelty or anything else prohibited by the statute.

S.P.C.A. further argues that the particular virus could be of some danger to human beings. From the evidence on this score, I find this particular strain of Rous sarcoma virus apparently presented no danger to humans, although certain present strains of the virus might, according to the "Potential Biohazards in Can-cer Research," conceivably present such danger. Future experiments with cancer virus might well be conducted with this thought in mind, so that adequate precau-tions can, if deemed necessary, be taken for the human beings involved.

In the course of the trial I stated that the injection of the chickens did not, in my opinion, cause pain of any significance in so far as the statute is concerned. If any pain there was at the time of the injections, it was *de minimis*. I adhere to such ruling. . . .

S.P.C.A. . . . argues that the result, if defendant board is successful, would be that the science teacher would determine when the experiment was justified, balancing his evaluation of the pain and cruelty against the educational value to be derived. This, indeed, would place a heavy responsibility in the hands of the teacher, but then again, the minds of our children are also placed in his hands. . . .

5

PRIVACY

Some feel that people concerned about privacy must be wrongdoers. For if a person has done nothing wrong, he has nothing to fear from disclosure.

But is this naive? Information can be misunderstood, twisted, and regimented in countless unfortunate ways. So should we not seek control over access to our personal lives?

Even when the information is not misused and we have nothing to hide, exposure can unsettle us. It can strip us of the dignity we need to live effectively and confidently in the world.

As we pursue and guard ourselves against dangerous persons, what zones of personal control and privilege must we respect? And under what circumstances, if any, are these boundaries properly ignored?

In *People* v. *One 1941 Mercury Sedan* we find that personally damaging evidence was forced from the mouth of Frank Williams, but Judge Peters does not think that this violated Williams' constitutional right against self-incrimination. For in this case, it was marijuana rather than oral testimony which was drawn from the suspect. Is there a morally relevant difference between the two sorts of "interrogation"?

The judge's opinion takes note of a variety of means for checking the body for evidence—fingerprinting, fingernail scraping, urinalysis, blood test, enema, and, in the present case, stomach pumping. We can add to these the surgical search for an incriminating bullet and the roadside breathalyzer test.

Is there something barbaric about any of these techniques? Do they ignore the sanctity of one's body? Or are they perfectly reasonable exercises of police power, not unlike searching a coat lining, as Judge Peters suggests?

The alleged invasion in *Whalen* v. *Roe* does not make us as queasy as its predecessor, but Roe (a fictitious name, for the sake of his privacy) is still incensed. For the court upholds the constitutionality of a computer drug-use file which, in Roe's judgment, invades the privacy of New York's citizens. Justice Stevens is convinced that the proper safeguards are in place and that the file serves an important purpose. Do you share his confidence? If this file is not a problem, what sort of file would be?

Simonsen v. *Swenson* leads us to consider the proper limits to doctor-patient confidentiality. Dr. Swenson's understanding of the transmission of syphilis is dated, but may we say the same for his sense of duty? Did he violate a trust in reporting Simonsen's condition to Mrs. Bristol? Or did Simonsen have no right to expect absolute secrecy from the doctor?

How great must the danger be before the doctor may speak? Or we could ask how great it must be before he *must* speak. For those who are infected because they are not warned may well sue him on account of his silence.

*PEOPLE V. ONE 1941 MERCURY SEDAN**

California District Court of Appeal, First District (1946)

PETERS, Presiding Justice.

This proceeding was instituted by the state . . . to declare a forfeiture of the interests of one Frank Williams, the registered owner, . . . in a designated automobile, on the ground that such automobile was on April 18, 1944, used unlawfully to conceal, convey, carry or transport marihuana in violation of law. . . .

The record discloses that on April 18, 1944, an inspector of the State Division of Narcotic Enforcement followed the Williams car for some distance. He testified that he then knew the car was being used to transport marihuana. The inspector picked up two police officers and then stopped the Williams car then being driven by Williams. Williams got out of the car. The inspector handcuffed one of the passengers and then came over to where the police officers were attempting to search Williams. As he approached, Williams, who had some brown paper in his hands, put the paper in his mouth and tried to pull away from the officers. The inspector asked Williams what he had put in his mouth and was told

*168 P. 2d 443

it was gum. The inspector tried to force Williams' mouth open, and in doing so got his finger between Williams' teeth. Williams bit down on the inspector's finger, and, in the ensuing struggle, Williams succeeded in swallowing what he had in his mouth. One of the officers during the struggle succeeded in handcuffing Williams' hands behind his back.

Williams, still handcuffed, was then put in the inspector's car and taken by the officers to the emergency hospital. He was there placed on an operating table with his hands cuffed in front of him. He was told that the doctor there present was going to pump out his stomach, and, if necessary, they would strap him to the table and use force. Williams stated that would not be necessary. A doctor thereupon forced a tube through Williams' mouth and down his throat and proceeded to pump out the contents of his stomach. Towards the end of this operation Williams began to kick his legs about and the officers then held his legs down on the table.

The substances pumped out of Williams' stomach were placed in jars by the inspector and later delivered by him to another inspector of the State Division of Narcotic Enforcement whose duty it was to make analyses of narcotic drugs. This chemist made an analysis of the contents of the jars and found that they contained marihuana.

The state was permitted to make this preliminary proof, but when the jars were offered in evidence the trial court sustained an objection on the grounds that the evidence had been unlawfully secured, and on the further ground that to permit such evidence would be to compel Williams to be a witness against himself in violation of . . . the California Constitution.

The inspector also testified that after Williams had had his stomach pumped out and his handcuffs removed he had a conversation with Williams in the lobby of the hospital; that in response to questions Williams admitted that on the day in question he had purchased five marihuana cigarettes for an unidentified friend; that he had these cigarettes in his possession when he was stopped by the police; that it was these cigarettes that he had swallowed when the police started to search him.

On this evidence the trial court based its findings and judgment that the state had failed to prove a violation of law sufficient to warrant the forfeiture. The correctness of this judgment admittedly turns upon the correctness of the trial court's ruling excluding the proffered evidence.

The overwhelming number of cases hold that the mere fact that the evidence, other than testimonial evidence, had its origin with defendant, even where taken against his will, is no ground for its exclusion. . . .

In *People* v. *Sallow* . . . the defendent contended that by requiring her to have her fingerprints taken, and the receipt in evidence of such fingerprints, she was required, in violation of her constitutional rights to be a witness against herself in a criminal case. The court said . . . :

> The taking of finger prints is not a violation of the spirit or purpose of the constitutional inhibition. "The scope of the privilege, in history and in principle," says

Greenleaf, "includes only the process of testifying, by word of mouth or in writing; i.e., the process of disclosure by utterance. It has no application to such physical, evidential circumstances as may exist on the witness' body or about his person." . . . It would be a forced construction to hold that by finger printing the defendant was required to furnish evidence against herself. . . .

. . . In *State* v. *McLaughlin* . . . a detective was allowed to testify that on the day of defendant's arrest, which was the date of the homicide, he, with another detective, visited defendant and took certain scrapings from his fingernails; that he placed the scrapings together and turned them over to the assistant chief of detectives. The scrapings were taken in order to ascertain whether they contained human blood. It was shown on the trial that they did. The court on appeal held that the testimony was properly admitted and violated no constitutional right of the defendant. . . .

. . . the majority of courts have held that the privilege against self-incrimination is not violated by producing in court through witnesses other than the accused the results of medical examinations, even where done forcefully. A few typical cases will suffice to illustrate the point. In *State* v. *Gatton* . . . the question arose over the admissibility of evidence as to the refusal of the defendant to submit to a blood test or urinalysis where he had been charged with operating a motor vehicle while intoxicated. The evidence was admitted and he was convicted. On appeal he contended that the admission of such testimony violated the privilege against self-incrimination. In holding that the privilege was limited to disclosure by utterance the court stated . . . :

> It will be observed in the instant case that the evidence offered was not required to be given by the defendant himself, but was given by the deputy sheriff and the doctor called by the deputy to make the examination of defendant. We are unable to observe any merit in the defendant's claim that the introduction of such evidence violated his constitutional rights, and we believe, and hold, that the constitutional inhibition against self-incrimination relates only, as stated by Greenleaf, to disclosure by utterance. No such disclosure was required of defendant in this case. . . .

The case of *State* v. *Cram* . . . is one where the defendant was charged with manslaughter committed while under the influence of intoxicating liquor. The accused was rendered unconscious by the accident, and while still unconscious he was arrested and a sample of blood was taken from him for the purpose of having it analyzed to determine its alcoholic content, if any. At his trial the doctor testified as to such content. The court on appeal held the evidence was admissible and stated . . .

> We need not consider how far a court would go in requiring a man to submit to a blood test. . . .

> Here the blood has already been extracted; defendant is not being called upon to submit to an examination.

The defendant was not deprived of any of his constitutional rights by the admission of the testimony here in question. He was not compelled to testify against himself. Evidence of the results of the analysis of the blood sample was not his testimony but that of Dr. Beeman, distinct from anything the defendant may have said or done. The blood sample was obtained without the use of any process against him as a witness. He was not required to establish the authenticity, identity or origin of the blood; those facts were proved by other witnesses. . . .

A case quite similar, factually, to the instant case is *Ash* v. *State*. . . . There the accused, who had been charged with receiving stolen property, swallowed several of the stolen rings. He was taken to the hospital and the rings located by fluoroscopic examination. Against his will and over his vigorous objections he was compelled to submit to an enema, and the stolen property thus recovered. This property was identified and produced in evidence at his trial over his objections. He was convicted and appealed, contending the privilege had been violated. The court stated . . . :

It will be noted from the facts of this case that the officers had information pointing to the appellant's guilt; that after he came under their observation they saw him place a metallic object in his mouth which they took to be the rings in question, or one of them. This proved to be correct. His possession of the rings and secreting them in the presence of the officers is the gist of the offense. He was, therefore, committing a felony in their presence. This gave them a legal right to arrest him and search his person. . . .

. . . Where then should they end this search? If the rings remained in the appellant's mouth, they would have had as much right to search his mouth and secure the rings as if they were in his pocket. He swallowed them. They determined this by seeing him make three or four efforts to swallow something, which took place in their presence and which warranted them in continuing their search. There is no contention that the officers resorted to any cruel or inhuman method of determining the presence of the rings, nor in extracting them. They applied the most approved method of doing so. Under the directions of a skilled operator they located the rings in the appellant's bowels. Could it be said that if a thief has stolen property, sewed it up in his pocket, or in the lining of his coat, that the officers would have no right to cut the stitches or even to injure his clothing for the purpose of securing the valuables belonging to another and that when they did so there would be a question about the admissibility of the evidence thus obtained? The evidence is replete with the conduct of the appellant in fighting the officers physically resisting every effort made by them to procure the rings, but there is no evidence to indicate any cruelty or unusual treatment on their part in doing so. They gave him an enema, a very normal and natural thing to do, thereby extracting the rings which the appellant had chosen to secrete in this most unusual manner. If the act of the officers should be considered unusual, it was brought about by reason of the act of the accused party. We think that the officers had a legal right to arrest appellant and to search him and to continue that search to such a reasonable degree as to permit them to ascertain whether or not the appellant possessed the stolen property, which they had a right to believe he had.

The modern and majority rule has been approved by the Model Code of Evidence drafted by the American Law Institute. Rule 205 . . . reads as follows:

No person has a privilege under Rule 203 to refuse

(a) to submit his body to examination for the purpose of discovering or recording his corporal features and other identifying characteristics, or his physical or mental condition, or (b) to furnish or to permit the taking of samples of body fluids or substances for analysis.

. . . In line with the weight of authority it is our opinion that the privilege against self-incrimination does not preclude the introduction of physical disclosures the defendant is forced to make, or the results of tests to which he has involuntarily submitted. It is our view that the privilege only protects the individual from any forced disclosures made by him, whether oral or written. It is limited to the protection against testimonal compulsion. The privilege protects the accused from the process of extracting from his own lips against his will an admission of guilt, but it does not extend to the exclusion of his body as evidence when such evidence may be relevant and material. The privilege is aimed at preventing the compulsory oral examination of the accused before or during trial. Experience of many years has demonstrated that when statements are extorted from an accused there is a strong likelihood that the extorted evidence would be unreliable. But the reason for the rule no longer exists when physical evidence is considered. In the present case the evidence as to the narcotic content of Williams' stomach in no way depended upon the testimonial utterances of Williams for its probative force. Williams was not required to establish the identity, origin, or authenticity of the evidence, nor was he required in any way to testify concerning its analysis. This was done by other witnesses. Under the circumstances, for reasons already stated, the evidence was not privileged and should have been admitted. . . .

WHALEN, COMMISSIONER OF HEALTH OF NEW YORK V. ROE*

U.S. Supreme Court (1977)

MR. JUSTICE STEVENS delivered the opinion of the Court.

The constitutional question presented is whether the State of New York may record, in a centralized computer file, the names and addresses of all persons who have obtained, pursuant to a doctor's prescription, certain drugs for which there is both a lawful and an unlawful market.

The District Court enjoined enforcement of the portions of the New York State Controlled Substances Act of 1972 which require such recording on the ground that they violate appellees' constitutionally protected rights of privacy. . . .

*429 U.S. 589

Many drugs have both legitimate and illegitimate uses. In response to a concern that such drugs were being diverted into unlawful channels, in 1970 the New York Legislature created a special commission to evaluate the State's drug-control laws. . . . The commission found the existing laws deficient in several respects. There was no effective way to prevent the use of stolen or revised prescriptions, to prevent unscrupulous pharmacists from repeatedly refilling prescriptions, to prevent users from obtaining prescriptions from more than one doctor, or to prevent doctors from over-prescribing, either by authorizing an excessive amount in one prescription or by giving one patient multiple prescriptions. . . . In drafting new legislation to correct such defects, the commission consulted with enforcement officials in California and Illinois where central reporting systems were being used effectively. . . .

The new New York statute classified potentially harmful drugs in five schedules. . . . Drugs, such as heroin, which are highly abused and have no recognized medical use, are in Schedule I; they cannot be prescribed. Schedules II through V include drugs which have a progressively lower potential for abuse but also have a recognized medical use. Our concern is limited to Schedule II, which includes the most dangerous of the legitimate drugs.[1]

With an exception for emergencies, the Act requires that all prescriptions for Schedule II drugs be prepared by the physician in triplicate on an official form. . . . The completed form identifies the prescribing physician; the dispensing pharmacy; the drug and dosage; and the name, address, and age of the patient. One copy of the form is retained by the physician, the second by the pharmacist, and the third is forwarded to the New York State Department of Health in Albany. A prescription made on an official form may not exceed a 30-day supply, and may not be refilled. . . .

The District Court found that about 100,000 Schedule II prescription forms are delivered to a receiving room at the Department of Health in Albany each month. They are sorted, coded, and logged and then taken to another room where the data on the forms is recorded on magnetic tapes for processing by a computer. Thereafter, the forms are returned to the receiving room to be retained in a vault for a five-year period and then destroyed as required by the statute. . . . The receiving room is surrounded by a locked wire fence and protected by an alarm system. The computer tapes containing the prescription data are kept in a locked cabinet. When the tapes are used, the computer is run "off-line," which means that no terminal outside of the computer room can read or record any information. Public disclosure of the identity of patients is expressly prohibited by the statute and by a Department of Health regulation. . . . Willful violation of these prohibitions is a crime punishable by up to one year in prison and a $2,000 fine. . . . At the time of trial there were 17 Department of Health employees with

---

[1]These include opium and opium derivatives, cocaine, methadone, amphetamines, and methaqualone. . . . These drugs have accepted uses in the amelioration of pain and in the treatment of epilepsy, narcolepsy, hyperkinesia, schizo-affective disorders, and migraine headaches.

access to the files; in addition, there were 24 investigators with authority to investigate cases of overdispensing which might be identified by the computer. Twenty months after the effective date of the Act, the computerized data had only been used in two investigations involving alleged overuse by specific patients. . . .

Appellees contend that the statute invades a constitutionally protected "zone of privacy." . . . The cases sometimes characterized as protecting "privacy" have in fact involved at least two different kinds of interests. . . . One is the individual interest in avoiding disclosure of personal matters, . . . and another is the interest in independence in making certain kinds of important decisions. . . . Appellees argue that both of these interests are impaired by this statute. The mere existence in readily available form of the information about patients' use of Schedule II drugs creates a genuine concern that the information will become publicly known and that it will adversely affect their reputations. This concern makes some patients reluctant to use, and some doctors reluctant to prescribe, such drugs even when their use is medically indicated. It follows, they argue, that the making of decisions about matters vital to the care of their health is inevitably affected by the statute. Thus, the statute threatens to impair both their interest in the nondisclosure of private information and also their interest in making important decisions independently.

We are persuaded, however, that the New York program does not, on its face, pose a sufficiently grievous threat to either interest to establish a constitutional violation.

Public disclosure of patient information can come about in three ways. Health Department employees may violate the statute by failing, either deliberately or negligently, to maintain proper security. A patient or a doctor may be accused of a violation and the stored data may be offered in evidence in a judicial proceeding. Or, thirdly, a doctor, a pharmacist, or the patient may voluntarily reveal information on a prescription form.

The third possibility existed under the prior law and is entirely unrelated to the existence of the computerized data bank. Neither of the other two possibilities provides a proper ground for attacking the statute as invalid on its face. There is no support in the record, or in the experience of the two States that New York has emulated, for an assumption that the security provisions of the statute will be administered improperly. . . . And the remote possibility that judicial supervision of the evidentiary use of particular items of stored information will provide inadequate protection against unwarranted disclosures is surely not a sufficient reason for invalidating the entire patient-identification program. . . .

Even without public disclosure, it is, of course, true that private information must be disclosed to the authorized employees of the New York Department of Health. Such disclosures, however, are not significantly different from those that were required under the prior law. Nor are they meaningfully distinguishable from a host of other unpleasant invasions of privacy that are associated with many facets of health care. Unquestionably, some individuals' concern for their own privacy may lead them to avoid or to postpone needed mdical attention. Nevertheless, disclosures of private medical information to doctors, to hospital personnel, to insurance companies, and to public health agencies are often an essential part of modern medical practice even when the disclosure may reflect unfavorably on the character of the patient. . . . Requiring such disclosures to representatives of the State having responsibility for the health of the community, does not automatically amount to an impermissible invasion of privacy.

Appellees also argue, however, that even if unwarranted disclosures do not actually occur, the knowledge that the information is readily available in a computerized file creates a genuine concern that causes some persons to decline needed medication. The record supports the conclusion that some use of Schedule II drugs has been discouraged by that concern; it also is clear, however, that about 100,000 prescriptions for such drugs were being filled each month prior to the entry of the District Court's injunction. Clearly, therefore, the statute did not deprive the public of access to the drugs.

Nor can it be said that any individual has been deprived of the right to decide independently, with the advice of his physician, to acquire and to use needed medication. Although the State no doubt could prohibit entirely the use of particular Schedule II drugs, . . . it has not done so. This case is therefore unlike those in which the Court held that a total prohibition of certain conduct was an impermissible deprivation of liberty. Nor does the State require access to these drugs to be conditioned on the consent of any state official or other third party. . . . Within dosage limits which appellees do not challenge, the decision to prescribe, or to use, is left entirely to the physician and the patient.

We hold that neither the immediate nor the threatened impact of the patient-identification requirements in the New York State Controlled Substances Act of 1972 on either the reputation or the independence of patients for whom Schedule II drugs are medically indicated is sufficient to constitute an invasion of any right or liberty protected by the Fourteenth Amendment. . . .

A final word about issues we have not decided. We are not unaware of the threat to privacy implicit in the accumulation of vast amounts of personal information in computerized data banks or other massive governmental files. . . . The collection of taxes, the distribution of welfare and social security benefits, the supervision of public health, the direction of our Armed Forces, and the enforcement of the criminal laws all require the orderly preservation of great quantities of information, much of which is personal in character and potentially embarrassing or harmful if disclosed. The right to collect and use such data for public purposes is typically accompanied by a concomitant statutory or regulatory duty to avoid unwarranted disclosures. Recognizing that in some circumstances that duty arguably has its roots in the Constitution, nevertheless New York's statutory scheme, and its implementing administrative procedures, evidence a proper concern with, and protection of, the individual's interest in privacy. We therefore need not, and do not, decide any question which might be presented by the unwarranted disclosure of accumulated private data—whether intentional or unintentional—or by a system that did not contain comparable security provisions. We simply hold that this record does not establish an invasion of any right or liberty protected by the Fourteenth Amendment.

Reversed.

SIMONSEN V. SWENSON*

Supreme Court of Nebraska (1920)

FLANSBURG, C. . . .

Plaintiff, with other employes of a telephone company, was working at Oakland, Neb. He was a stranger at the place, and was stopping with these men at a small hotel operated by a Mrs. Bristol. He became afflicted with sores on his body, and went to the defendant, a practicing physician at that place, who took the history of plaintiff's trouble, gave him a physical examination, and informed him that he believed his disease to be syphilis. He further stated, however, that it was impossible to be positive without making certain Wasserman tests, for which he had no equipment.

Defendant was the physician of the Bristol family, and acted as their hotel doctor when one was needed. He told plaintiff that there would be much danger of his communicating the disease to others in the hotel if he remained there, and requested that he leave the next day, which plaintiff promised to do.

On the following day the defendant, while making a professional call upon Mr. Bristol, who was ill, learned that plaintiff had not moved from the hotel. He therefore warned Mrs. Bristol that he thought plaintiff was afflicted with a "contagious disease," and for her to be careful, to disinfect his bedclothing, and to wash her hands in alcohol afterwards. Mrs. Bristol, acting upon this warning, placed all of plaintiff's belongings in the hallway, and fumigated his room. Plaintiff was forced to leave.

The testimony of the physicians disclosed that this particular disease is very readily transmitted in its early stages, and could be carried through drinking cups, eating utensils, and other articles handled or used by the diseased person.

After leaving Oakland, plaintiff consulted another physician. He gave to this physician a history, showing that he might have been exposed a few weeks before to such a disease, and was given a physical examination by this doctor. One Wasserman test was made, which proved negative. That test alone, however, this physician testified, proved nothing, since the presence or absence of such disease could not be positively known without extended tests. These had not been made,

*177 N.W. 831

and this doctor said that it was impossible for him to say whether the plaintiff had or had not the disease when he examined him. He went on further to say that the symptoms and information upon which the defendant acted were, however, reasonably sufficient to cause the defendant to believe as he did.

The testimony is practically without conflict; plaintiff having called the defendant to testify as his own witness.

The plaintiff contends that, having shown the relationship of physician and patient, the law prohibits absolutely a disclosure of any confidential communication, at any time or under any circumstances, and that a breach of this duty of secrecy, on the part of the physician, gives rise to a cause of action in damages in favor of the patient.

At common law there was no privilege as to communications between physician and patient, and this rule still prevails when not changed by statute. *Thrasher v. State.* . . .

There is a . . . provision of our statute, . . . providing that no physician shall practice medicine without a license from the board of health, and that such a license may be revoked when a physician is found guilty of "unprofessional or dishonorable conduct." Among the acts of such misconduct, defined by the statute, is the "betrayal of a professional secret to the detriment of a patient."

By this statute, it appears to us, a positive duty is imposed upon the physician, both for the benefit and advantage of the patient as well as in the interest of general public policy. The relation of physician and patient is necessarily a highly confidential one. It is often necessary for the patient to give information about himself which would be most embarrassing or harmful to him if given general circulation. This information the physician is bound, not only upon his own professional honor and the ethics of his high profession, to keep secret, but by reason of the affirmative mandate of the statute itself. A wrongful breach of such confidence, and a betrayal of such trust, would give rise to a civil action for the damages naturally flowing from such wrong. Is such a rule of secrecy then, subject to any qualifications or exceptions? The doctor's duty does not necessarily end with the patient, for on the other hand, the malady of his patient may be such that a duty may be owing to the public and, in some cases, to other particular individuals. . . .

No patient can expect that if his malady is found to be of a dangerously contagious nature he can still require it to be kept secret from those to whom, if there was no disclosure, such disease would be transmitted. The information given to a physician by his patient, though confidential, must, it seems to us, be given and received subject to the qualification that if the patient's disease is found to be of a dangerous and so highly contagious or infectious a nature that it will necessarily be transmitted to others unless the danger of contagion is disclosed to them, then the physician should, in that event, if no other means of protection is possible, be privileged to make so much of a disclosure to such persons as is necessary to prevent the spread of the disease. A disclosure in such case would, it follows, not be a betrayal of the confidence of the patient, since the patient must know, when he imparts the information or subjects himself to the examination, that, in the exception stated, his disease may be disclosed.

In order that such a privilege of making a disclosure be available to a physician, however, he must have had ordinary skill and learning of a physician, and must have exercised ordinary diligence and care in making his diagnosis; otherwise he could be subjected to an action for negligence in making a wrongful report. *Harriott* v. *Plimpton*. . . .

In making such disclosure a physician must also be governed by the rules as to qualifiedly privileged communications in slander and libel cases. He must prove that a disclosure was necessary to prevent spread of disease, that the communication was to one who, it was reasonable to suppose, might otherwise be exposed, and that he himself acted in entire good faith, with reasonable grounds for his diagnosis and without malice. . . .

It appears to us that the facts disclosed by the record in this case show that the occasion was privileged; that the defendant had reasonable grounds for his belief; that he made no further disclosure than was reasonably necessary under the circumstances; and that he acted in good faith and without malice. . . .

6

PROFESSIONAL STANDARDS

If it were not for the watchcare of the medical boards and the government, the public would be easy prey for medical charlatans and hucksters. The complexity of medical science and the terror of disease make the average citizen vulnerable to medical fraud and abuse. And, of course, well-meaning amateurs can do their share of damage.

While the threats are significant, libertarians urge that we must deregulate medicine and embrace the risk of harm in the interest of personal freedom. Others oppose state control because they believe that the regulatory decisions of medical boards are self-serving.

Medical practitioners must respect not only the judgment of medical boards, but also the threat of malpractice suits. Doctors may keep their licenses while suffering financially ruinous episodes in the courts. And so they must keep up with the litigation if they want to maintain rewarding and undistracted practices. Here, too, standards are set.

People v. *Amber* is a conflict over licensing. The question—"Who should be licensed to practice medicine?"—may be interpreted in two ways, First, "Who should be required to seek a license?" For example, does the lady piercing ears at the local beauty parlor or department store need to be licensed as a surgeon?

The second is, "Among those who seek a license to practice medicine, who should get one?" Here the question could pertain to the status of chiropractors.

The first interpretation more nearly fits this case, but this court opinion serves nicely to introduce both issues. On the one hand, is the theoretical base for acupuncture so utterly different from that of Western medical science that acupuncture fails to count as regulable medical practice? On the other, are acupuncturists quacks? What, indeed, counts as quackery?

Lying behind this dispute is the more general question raised in *People* v. *Privitera*, "What right does the government have to interfere with our choice of treatment?"

Health Systems Agency of Northern Virginia v. *Virginia State Board of Medicine* again shows a medical board at work in its role as a policeman. This state board considers the publication of doctors' fees a form of advertizing, which is forbidden in the profession. Is this really advertising? If so, so what? Is the appended statement of the American Medical Association's Judicial Council compelling? Has Judge Butzner blundered in granting permission for the directory?

Virginia State Board of Pharmacy v. *Virginia Citizens Consumer Council, Inc.* extends the controversy to pharmacy. Since prescription medicine is so expensive, the burden of justification falls upon those who would undermine competition among those who sell it. The Virginia State Board of Pharmacy takes up the challenge and defends its ban on advertizing in the name of professional standards and the public good. The court must decide whether such advertizing is the sort of speech whose freedom is protected by the Constitution. Justices Blackmun and Rehnquist square off on the issue.

Leaving behind the work of regulatory boards, we see patient in direct conflict with doctor in *Helling* v. *Carey*. In many such malpractice cases, the court tries to determine whether the doctor failed to meet professional standards. And so other doctors are called to testify for and against him. But here, Judge Hunter calls those professional standards into question. It is not good enough that Dr. Carey acted as an ophthalmologist typically would. He should, so the court reasons, have gone beyond the accepted standard.

Should doctors be required to shoulder this much responsibility? And what right does a judge who is not a physician have to tell a physician, indeed a whole medical specialty, what counts as good medicine?

PEOPLE V. *AMBER**

New York Supreme Court (1973)

WILLIAM C. BRENNAN, Justice.

In a fifteen-count indictment defendant is charged with the illegal practice of medicine; unlawfully holding himself out as being able to practice medicine, and illegally using the title "physician." The charges stem from the fact that defendant, who is not a licensed physician, allegedly engaged in the practice of acupuncture. . . .

The constitutional attack is two-pronged: first, that the statute is overbroad, and, second, that it is vague. The general power of the state under its police powers to regulate the right to practice medical arts in New York has been upheld against prior constitutional challenge. In *People* v. *Mulford* . . . the court held that when the defendant engaged in the practice of what he advertised as "suggestive therapeutics," his treatment consisting of laying on of hands and manipulation, breathing and rubbing his hands together in the treatment of physical ailments without giving or prescribing medicine, he was practicing medicine within the definition of the statute; and that the Legislature had the right to enact such provisions of law and that same do not violate the provisions of the Constitution. . . .

. . . many of the hypothetical instances raised by the defendant wherein he asserts that the actions taken would subject the actor to criminal sanction (e. g., athletic trainer during a football game treats an injured player; a cab driver who delivers a child in his taxi, etc.) would appear to be resolved by the application of . . . exceptions. . . .

. . . The counts remaining in this indictment are those accusing defendant of the illegal practice of medicine. Squarely presented . . . is a question of novel impression—whether or not acupuncture is the practice of medicine. It is necessary for the proper determination of this issue to inquire into the nature of acupuncture. Counsel for the defendant has provided this court with a memorandum of law which in considerable detail traces the history, philosophy and techniques of acupuncture. In this treatise the court is informed substantially as follows:

> The earliest accounts of Chinese acupuncture date back to the third or fourth century B.C. The word "acupuncture" is derived from the Latin words "acus," the needle, and "puncture," a pricking, and means "a puncturing of bodily tissue." Acupuncture is based on an energy concept. Traditionally, Chinese medicine is based on the concept that man is a microcosmic image of the universe and subject to identical laws. The immutable course of nature is thought to be guided by Tao, the Way. The two forces through which Tao acts were named Yin and Yang. Yin, also called the female element, possesses all the "negative" energy qualities, and Yang, the male element, possesses the "positive" energy qualities.

*349 N.Y.S. 2d 604

In the human body the vital essence termed "ch'i," consisting of a harmonious mixture of Yin and Yang is believed to be conveyed through twelve pairs of main ducts, plus two trunk ducts which run in the front and back midline of the body. These ducts, known as organ or median vessel meridians, are associated with a special inner organ function, process or system. The meridians emerge at the surface of the body at a certain number of designated points where vital energy can be predictably influenced by manipulation. These are known as acupuncture points. By palpating six pulses on each wrist, the acupuncturist is able to read the condition of the twelve organs and to determine the existence of energy imbalances, deficiencies, excesses, blockages and escapes. In response to individual symptoms, specific acupuncture points are then chosen for piqure. Out of the 670 points of the meridians, 31 are forbidden to piqures, and there are other points where a piqure is dangerous and may only be made after special precautions have been taken.

The piqure is made by the use of acupuncture needles. Those currently in general use are required to be very fine, hairlike, flexible, unbreakable and stainless. The lengths vary according to the usage; the long needle (three inches or more) is used for deep piqure in the region of the buttocks; the medium needle (two to three inches) is used for the deep points of the limbs and trunk; and the short needle (one to two inches) or the very short needle (less than one inch) is used on superficial points. The piqure, once placed, must remain there for a determined time at a determined depth.

The piqures are inserted and manipulated in accordance with the "great law of Pu-Hsieh and the rule of Shou Fa," which constitute the keystone of acupuncture, its procedure being to supply energy where it is lacking or to calm or retire an excess of energy where such excess is present. Ideally, it restores the equilibrium of the Yin and Yang and as a consequence the person's state of health is restored.

Acupuncture includes cauterizations, referred to as "a burning therapy" for which laws were established about a thousand years ago under the Northern Sung Dynasty. Sixty-six points are forbidden to cauterization, but are permitted to piqures. Six points are forbidden to both.

The application of cauterizations and piqures or insertions of needles into the human body is performed in the practice of acupuncture and is necessarily a form of treatment intended to relieve the patient of pain or other physical trouble by a method and theory quite different from the treatment provided by the members of the medical profession with which we are familiar. Because it is so different the argument is made that control of the practice of acupuncture was not contemplated in the laws, the violation of which is charged to this defendant, while at the same time defendant argues that the very same laws are so broad and embrace so many activities that they are unconstitutional.

As can be seen from the nature of the treatment in the instances briefly described in cases above cited, a statute intended to regulate, limit or control the diagnosis and treatment of ailments must necessarily be broad enough to include the gamut of those known, whether or not recognized and even those not yet conjured.

Defendant contends that only practices which constitute Western allopathic medicine come within the purview of the statute. Allopathy is defined as the treatment of disease by remedies that produce effects different from or opposite to those produced by the disease. Defendant argues that Chinese acupuncture is not Western allopathic medicine and therefore does not come within the contemplation of the practice of medicine as proscribed in the Education Law. The court does not read the statutes that way. There appears little doubt that acupuncture differs from allopathic medicine in its philosophy, practice and technique. Assuming the accuracy of the premise, the court cannot agree with the conclusion. To say that the statute is so limited by the failure of the legislature to envision the practice of acupuncture in this state is an implausible interpretation. The court finds nothing in the pertinent provisions of the Education Law which exclude, directly or by implication, any manner of diagnosis or treatment which is not embraced within the definition of "Western allopathic medicine." On the contrary, and to put it more positively, the definition of medicine as set forth in . . . the Education Law specifically includes the "diagnosing, treating, operating or prescribing for any human disease, pain, injury, deformity or physical condition." Whether actions constitute the practice of medicine is dependent upon the facts and not upon the name of the procedure, its origins or legislative lack of clairvoyance.

The term "diagnosis" is derived from the Greek prefix "dia" meaning between, and "gignoskein" meaning to discern. It is, in modern terminology a "sizing up" or a comprehending of the physical or mental status of a patient. It is the conclusion itself rather than the procedures upon which the conclusion is based which constitutes a diagnosis per se. No particular language need be used and no disease need be mentioned, for the diagnostician may make or draw his conclusion in his own way. (People v. Zinke. . . .)

In defendant's lengthy and informative memorandum of law, from which the court has gleaned its familiarity with the subject of acupuncture and the respects in which it differs from the Western allopathic medicine, scrupulously avoided is the fact that a patient is necessarily involved and that such patient seeks treatment, not out of curiosity but only because he is suffering pain or other physical ailment; that before he, the patient, can expect the anticipated relief from the harmonious workings of the dual forces of Yin and Yang, a diagnosis must be made, if not to recognize a "Western" disease, then at least to determine the existence of a disharmony brought about by the disequilibrium of Yin and Yang; that a proper diagnosis or determination necessarily involves an expert ability to palpate the twelve pulses in order to read the condition of the twelve organs and thus determine which of the twelve meridians must be used to convey the Yin and Yang to the seat of disharmony with the object of restoring the vital essence of "ch'i," which is described as an harmonious mixture of Yin and Yang. Following such diagnosis or determination, requiring skill and practice, and in response to "individual symptoms," specific points must be chosen for needling, that is, the insertion and manipulation of needles, the insertion referred to as a "piqure." Further judgment must be used to determine the need and the locale for cauterization. Such decisions, whether or not defendant would agree that they be called "diagnosis" or the result of diagnosis, and the application of cauterization and insertion of needles, in this court's opinion, constitute the practice of medicine as defined in the statutes. The performance of one or more of such functions comes within the statutes.

In the view of this court the statutes under consideration were designed to prevent such conduct as the indiscriminate application of cauterization and the sticking of needles into human beings by unskilled and unlicensed practitioners. The defendant's argument that the application of such treatment by knowledgeable practitioners actually effects cure and that the charges against him are therefore ill-founded is entirely untenable. No matter how skilled, even a thoroughly qualified physician may not practice without being licensed to do so. . . .

HEALTH SYSTEMS AGENCY OF NORTHERN VIRGINIA V. VIRGINIA STATE BOARD OF MEDICINE*

U.S. District Court for the Eastern District of Virginia (1976)

BUTZNER, Circuit Judge:
The principal issue in this case is whether the plaintiffs have a constitutional right to gather, publish, and receive information about the services and fees of physicians practicing in their community. The defendants assert that physicians who furnish information to be published in a medical directory, as proposed by the plaintiffs, would violate . . . the Virginia Code. This statute provides in part:

Any practitioner of medicine . . . shall be considered guilty of unprofessional conduct if he:

. . . Advertises to the public directly or indirectly in any manner his professional services, their costs, prices, fees, credit terms or quality."

. . . The plaintiff, Health Systems Agency of Northern Virginia, a nonprofit Virginia corporation, has been designated by the United States Department of Health, Education, and Welfare as the health planning agency for northern Virginia. . . . The Agency plans to publish a directory of factual information to help persons select physicians. . . .

*424 F. Supp. 267

The defendants are the Virginia State Board of Medicine and its members. The Board is empowered, by . . . the Virginia Code, to discipline any physician "guilty of immoral conduct, or of unprofessional conduct." . . . Consequently, it can enforce the statute's prohibition against advertising by physicians. . . .

The Agency investigated the information about physicians available from the telephone directory, the local medical societies, the *American Medical Directory*, the *Directory of Medical Specialists*, and the *Washington Physicians Directory*. . . . It found that a resident of northern Virginia cannot readily obtain any information other than the name, address, telephone number, and speciality of a physician. Professional directories, which include educational credentials, are generally unavailable to the public. . . .

In this case, the Agency does not seek special access to information unavailable to the general public. It asks, instead, to gather and publish information which the defendants concede is available from physicians, albeit in bits and pieces, upon the request of prospective patients. There is no suggestion that physicians give this information in confidence. The recipient can freely disclose it whether or not he or she becomes an actual patient. . . .

. . . The defendants' opposition to the directory also rests on the premise that even truthful advertising by physicians could be confusing. They contend that information about costs is inherently misleading because of the variety of professional services performed by physicians. They also argue that people will select physicians purely on the basis of cost without considering the quality of professional care. . . .

. . . The Agency, we believe, has taken adequate precautions to allay the concern that the Board expresses. The directory would contain factual information furnished by physicians. The Agency would neither recommend any physician nor include any promotional statements. All physicians practicing in the area would have the opportunity to be listed under the same format without charge. Included in the information about each physician would be his or her fees for house calls and for routine office and hospital visits. In addition, the introduction to the directory would explain that, although each physician has an established fee schedule for different kinds of visits, fees vary depending on such things as the time that the physician spends with the patient and the number of laboratory tests needed. . . .

APPENDIX . . .

Statement of the Judicial Council [of the American Medical Association], Re: Advertising and Solicitation

This statement reaffirms the long-standing policy of the Judicial Council on advertising and solicitation by physicians. The *Principles of Medical Ethics* are intended to discourage abusive practices that exploit patients and the public and interfere with freedom in making an informed choice of physicians and free competition among physicians. . . .

Competition—Some competitive practices accepted in ordinary commercial and industrial enterprises—where profit-making is the primary objective—are inappropriate among physicians. Commercial enterprises, for example, are free to solicit business by paying commissions. They have no duty to lower prices to the poor. Commercial enterprises are generally free to engage in advertising "puffery," to be boldly self-laudatory in making claims of superiority, and to emphasize favorable features without disclosing unfavorable information.

Physicians, by contrast, have an ethical duty to subordinate financial reward to social responsibility. A physician should not engage in practices for pecuniary gain that interfere with his medical judgment and skill or cause a deterioration of the quality of medical care. Ability to pay should be considered in reducing fees, and excessive fees are unethical.

Physicians should not pay commissions or rebates or give kickbacks for the referral of patients. Likewise, they should not make extravagant claims or proclaim extraordinary skills. Such practices, however common they may be in the commercial world, are unethical in the practice of medicine because they are injurious to the public.

Freedom of choice of physician and free competition among physicians are prerequisites of optimal medical care. The *Principles of Medical Ethics* are intended to curtail abusive practices that impinge on these freedoms and exploit patients and the public. . . .

VIRGINIA STATE BOARD OF PHARMACY V. VIRGINIA CITIZENS CONSUMER COUNCIL, INC. *

U.S. Supreme Court (1976)

MR. JUSTICE BLACKMUN delivered the opinion of the Court.

The plaintiff-appellees in this case attack, as violative of the First and Fourteenth Amendments, . . . that portion . . . of Va. Code Ann. . . . which provides that a pharmacist licensed in Virginia is guilty of unprofessional conduct if he " . . . publishes, advertises or promotes, directly or indirectly, in any manner whatsoever, any amount, price, fee, premium, discount, rebate or credit terms . . . for any drugs which may be dispensed only by prescription." . . .

The appellants contend that the advertisement of prescription drug prices is outside the protection of the First Amendment because it is "commercial speech." . . . Our pharmacist does not wish to editorialize on any subject, cultural, philosophical, or political. He does not wish to report any particularly newsworthy fact, or to make generalized observations even about commercial matters.

*425 U.S. 748

The "idea" he wishes to communicate is simply this: "I will sell you the X prescription drug at the Y price." . . .

Our question is whether speech which does "no more than propose a commercial transaction," *Pittsburgh Press Co.* v. *Human Relations Comm'n*, . . . is so removed from any "exposition of ideas," *Chaplinsky* v. *New Hampshire*, . . . and from " 'truth, science, morality, and arts in general, in its diffusion of liberal sentiments on the administration of Government,' " *Roth* v. *United States*, . . . that it lacks all protection. Our answer is that it is not. . . . Advertising, however tasteless and excessive it sometimes may seem, is nonetheless dissemination of information as to who is producing and selling what product, for what reason, and at what price. So long as we preserve a predominantly free enterprise economy, the allocation of our resources in large measure will be made through numerous private economic decisions. It is a matter of public interest that those decisions, in the aggregate, be intelligent and well informed. To this end, the free flow of commerical information is indispensable. . . . And if it is indispensable to the proper allocation of resources in a free enterprise system, it is also indispensable to the formation of intelligent opinions as to how that system ought to be regulated or altered. Therefore, even if the First Amendment were thought to be primarily an instrument to enlighten public decisionmaking in a democracy, . . . we could not say that the free flow of information does not serve that goal. . . .

Arrayed against these substantial individual and societal interests are a number of justifications for the advertising ban. These have to do principally with maintaining a high degree of professionalism on the part of licensed pharmacists. . . . Indisputably, the State has a strong interest in maintaining that professionalism. It is exercised in a number of ways for the consumer's benefit. There is the clinical skill involved in the compounding of drugs, although, as has been noted, these now make up only a small percentage of the prescriptions filled. Yet, even with respect to manufacturer-prepared compounds, there is room for the pharmacist to serve his customer well or badly. Drugs kept too long on the shelf may lose their efficacy or become adulterated. They can be packaged for the user in such a way that the same results occur. The expertise of the pharmacist may supplement that of the prescribing physician, if the latter has not specified the amount to be dispensed or the directions that are to appear on the label. The pharmacist, a specialist in the potencies and dangers of drugs, may even be consulted by the physician as to what to prescribe. He may know of a particular antagonism between the prescribed drug and another that the customer is or might be taking, or with an allergy the customer may suffer. The pharmacist himself may have supplied the other drug or treated the allergy. Some pharmacists, concededly not a large number, "monitor" the health problems and drug consumptions of customers who come to them repeatedly. . . . A pharmacist who has a continuous relationship with his customer is in the best position, of course, to exert professional skill for the customer's protection.

Price advertising, it is argued, will place in jeopardy the pharmacist's expertise and, with it, the customer's health. It is claimed that the aggressive price competition that will result from unlimited advertising will make it impossible for the pharmacist to supply professional services in the compounding, handling, and dispensing of prescription drugs. Such services are time consuming and expensive; if competitors who economize by eliminating them are permitted to advertise their resulting lower prices, the more painstaking and conscientious pharmacist will be forced either to follow suit or to go out of business. It is also claimed that prices might not necessarily fall as a result of advertising. If one pharmacist advertises, others must, and the resulting expense will inflate the cost of drugs. It is further claimed that advertising will lead people to shop for their prescription drugs among the various pharmacists who offer the lowest prices, and the loss of stable pharmacist-customer relationships will make individual attention—and certainly the practice of monitoring—impossible. Finally, it is argued that damage will be done to the professional image of the pharmacist. This image, that of a skilled and specialized craftsman, attracts talent to the profession and reinforces the better habits of those who are in it. Price advertising, it is said, will reduce the pharmacist's status to that of a mere retailer. . . .

The strength of these proffered justifications is greatly undermined by the fact that high professional standards, to a substantial extent, are guaranteed by the close regulation to which pharmacists in Virginia are subject. And this case concerns the retail sale by the pharmacist more than it does his professional standards. Surely, any pharmacist guilty of professional dereliction that actually endangers his customer will promptly lose his license. . . .

. . . The advertising ban does not directly affect professional standards one way or the other. It affects them only through the reactions it is assumed people will have to the free flow of drug price information. There is no claim that the advertising ban in any way prevents the cutting of corners by the pharmacist who is so inclined. That pharmacist is likely to cut corners in any event. The only effect the advertising ban has on him is to insulate him from price competition and to open the way for him to make a substantial, and perhaps even excessive, profit in addition to providing an inferior service. The more painstaking pharmacist is also protected but, again, it is a protection based in large part on public ignorance.

It appears to be feared that if the pharmacist who wishes to provide low-cost, and assertedly low-quality, services is permitted to advertise, he will be taken up on his offer by too many unwitting customers. They will choose the low-cost, low-quality service and drive the "professional" pharmacist out of business. They will respond only to costly and excessive advertising, and end up paying the price. They will go from one pharmacist to another, following the discount, and destroy the pharmacist-customer relationship. They will lose respect for the profession because it advertises. All this is not in their best interests, and all this can be avoided if they are not permitted to know who is charging what.

There is, of course, an alternative to this highly paternalistic approach. That alternative is to assume that this information is not in itself harmful, that people will perceive their own best interests if only they are well enough informed, and that the best means to that end is to open the channels of communication rather than to close them. If they are truly open, nothing prevents the "professional" pharmacist from marketing his own assertedly superior product, and contrasting it with that of the low-cost, high-volume prescription drug retailer. But the choice among these alternative approaches is not ours to make or the Virginia General Assembly's. It is precisely this kind of choice, between the dangers of suppressing information, and the dangers of its misuse if it is freely available, that the First Amendment makes for us. Virginia is free to require whatever professional standards it wishes of its pharmacists; it may subsidize them or protect them from competition in other ways. . . . But it may not do so by keeping the public in ignorance of the entirely lawful terms that competing pharmacists are offering. In this sense, the justifications Virginia has offered for suppressing the flow of prescription drug price information, far from persuading us that the flow is not protected by the First Amendment, have reinforced our view that it is. We so hold.

MR. JUSTICE REHNQUIST, dissenting. . . .

In the case of "our" hypothetical pharmacist, he may now presumably advertise not only the prices of prescription drugs, but may attempt to energetically promote their sale so long as he does so truthfully. Quite consistently with Virginia law requiring prescription drugs to be available only through a physician, "our" pharmacist might run any of the following representative advertisements in a local newspaper:

> "Pain getting you down? Insist that your physician prescribe Demerol. You pay a little more than for aspirin, but you get a lot more relief."

> "Can't shake the flu? Get a prescription for Tetracycline from your doctor today."

> "Don't spend another sleepless night. Ask your doctor to prescribe Seconal without delay."

Unless the State can show that these advertisements are either actually untruthful or misleading, it presumably is not free to restrict in any way commercial efforts on the part of those who profit from the sale of prescription drugs to put them in the widest possible circulation. But such a line simply makes no allowance whatever for what appears to have been a considered legislative judgment in most States that while prescription drugs are a necessary and vital part of medical care and treatment, there are sufficient dangers attending their widespread use that they simply may not be promoted in the same manner as hair creams, deodrants, and toothpaste. The very real dangers that general advertising for such drugs might create in terms of encouraging, even though not sanctioning, illicit use of them by individuals for whom they have not been prescribed, or by generating patient pressure upon physicians to prescribe them, are simply not dealt with in the Court's opinion. If prescription drugs may be advertised, they may be advertised on television during family viewing time.

Nothing we know about the acquisitive instincts of those who inhabit every business and profession to a greater or lesser extent gives any reason to think that such persons will not do everything they can to generate demand for these products in much the same manner and to much the same degree as demand for other commodities has been generated. . . .

Here the rights of the appellees seem to me to be marginal at best. There is no ideological content to the information which they seek and it is freely available to them—they may even publish it if they so desire. The only persons directly affected by this statute are not parties to this lawsuit. On the other hand, the societal interest against the promotion of drug use for every ill, real or imaginary, seems to me extremely strong. I do not believe that the First Amendment mandates the Court's "open door policy" toward such commercial advertising. . . .

HELLING V. CAREY*

Supreme Court of Washington (1974)

HUNTER, Associate Justice.

This case arises from a malpractice action instituted by the plaintiff (petitioner), Barbara Helling.

The plaintiff suffers from primary open angle glaucoma. Primary open angle glaucoma is essentially a condition of the eye in which there is an interference in the ease with which the nourishing fluids can flow out of the eye. Such a condition results in pressure gradually rising above the normal level to such an extent that damage is produced to the optic nerve and its fibers with resultant loss in vision. The first loss usually occurs in the periphery of the field of vision. The disease usually has few symptoms and, in the absence of a pressure test, is often undetected until the damage has become extensive and irreversible.

The defendants (respondents), Dr. Thomas F. Carey and Dr. Robert C. Laughlin, are partners who practice the medical specialty of ophthalmology. Ophthalmology involves the diagnosis and treatment of defects and diseases of the eye.

The plaintiff first consulted the defendants for myopia, nearsightedness, in 1959. At that time she was fitted with contact lenses. She next consulted the defendants in September, 1963, concerning irritation caused by the contact lenses. Additional consultations occurred in October, 1963; February, 1967; September, 1967; October, 1967; May, 1968, July, 1968; August, 1968; September, 1968; and October, 1968. Until the October 1968 consultation, the defendants considered the plaintiff's visual problems to be related solely to complications associated

*519 P. 2d 981

with her contact lenses. On that occasion, the defendant, Dr. Carey, tested the plaintiff's eye pressure and field of vision for the first time. This test indicated that the plaintiff had glaucoma. The plaintiff, who was then 32 years of age, had essentially lost her peripheral vision and her central vision was reduced to approximately 5 degrees vertical by 10 degrees horizontal.

Thereafter, in August of 1969, after consulting other physicians, the plaintiff filed a complaint against the defendants alleging, among other things, that she sustained severe and permanent damage to her eyes as a proximate result of the defendants' negligence. During trial, the testimony of the medical experts for both the plaintiff and the defendants established that the standards of the profession for that specialty in the same or similar circumstances do not require routine pressure tests for glaucoma upon patients under 40 years of age. The reason the pressure test for glaucoma is not given as a regular practice to patients under the age of 40 is that the disease rarely occurs in this age group. Testimony indicated, however, that the standards of the profession do require pressure tests if the patient's complaints and symptoms reveal to the physician that glaucoma should be suspected. . . .

We find this to be a unique case. The testimony of the medical experts is undisputed concerning the standards of the profession for the specialty of ophthalmology. It is not a question in this case of the defendants having any greater special ability, knowledge and information than other ophthalmologists which would require the defendants to comply with a higher duty of care than that "degree of care and skill which is expected of the average practitioner in the class to which he belongs, acting in the same or similar circumstances." *Pederson* v. *Dumouchel* . . . .

The issue is whether the defendants' compliance with the standard of the profession of ophthalmology, which does not require the giving of a routine pressure test to persons under 40 years of age, should insulate them from liability under the facts in this case where the plaintiff has lost a substantial amount of her vision due to the failure of the defendants to timely give the pressure test to the plaintiff.

The defendants argue that the standard of the profession, which does not require the giving of a routine pressure test to persons under the age of 40, is adequate to insulate the defendants from liability for negligence because the risk of glaucoma is so rare in this age group. The testimony of the defendant, Dr. Carey, however, is revealing as follows:

Q. Now, when was it, actually, the first time any complaint was made to you by her of any field or visual field problem?
A. Really, the first time that she really complained of a visual field problem was the August 30th date. [1968]
Q. And how soon before the diagnosis was that?
A. That was 30 days. We made it on October 1st.
Q. And in your opinion, . . . how long had she had this glaucoma?
A. I would think she probably had it ten years or longer.

Q. Now, Doctor, there's been some reference to the matter of taking pressure checks of persons over 40. What is the incidence of glaucoma, the statistics, with persons under 40?

A. In the instance of glaucoma under the age of 40, is less than 100 to one per cent. The younger you get, the less the incidence. It is thought to be in the neighborhood of one in 25,000 people or less.

Q. How about the incidence of glaucoma in people over 40?

A. Incidence of glaucoma over 40 gets into the two to three per cent category, and hence, that's where there is this great big difference and that's why the standards around the world has been to check pressures from 40 on.

The incidence of glaucoma in one out of 25,000 persons under the age of 40 may appear quite minimal. However, that one person, the plaintiff in this instance, is entitled to the same protection, as afforded persons over 40, essential for timely detection of the evidence of glaucoma where it can be arrested to avoid the grave and devasting result of this disease. The test is a simple pressure test, relatively inexpensive. There is no judgment factor involved, and there is no doubt that by giving the test the evidence of glaucoma can be detected. The giving of the test is harmless if the physical condition of the eye permits. The testimony indicates that although the condition of the plaintiff's eyes might have at times prevented the defendants from administering the pressure test, there is an absence of evidence in the record that the test could not have been timely given.

Justice Holmes stated in *Texas & Pac. Ry.* v. *Behymer* . . .

What usually is done may be evidence of what ought to be done, but what ought to be done is fixed by a standard of reasonable prudence, whether it usually is complied with or not.

In *The T. J. Hooper* . . . Justice Hand stated:

[I]n most cases reasonable prudence is in fact common prudence; but strictly it is never its measure; a whole calling may have unduly lagged in the adoption of new and available devices. It never may set its own tests, however persuasive be its usages. *Courts must in the end say what is required; there are precautions so imperative that even their universal disregard will not excuse their omission.* (Italics ours.)

Under the facts of this case reasonable prudence required the timely giving of the pressure test to this plaintiff. The precaution of giving this test to detect the incidence of glaucoma to patients under 40 years of age is so imperative that irrespective of its disregard by the standards of the opthlmology profession, it is the duty of the courts to say what is required to protect patients under 40 from the damaging results of glaucoma.

We therefore hold, as a matter of law, that the reasonable standard that should have been followed under the undisputed facts of this case was the timely giving of this simple, harmless pressure test to this plaintiff and that, in failing to do so, the defendants were negligent, which proximately resulted in the blindness sustained by the plaintiff for which the defendants are liable. . . .

7

PUBLIC HEALTH
AND SAFETY

We live in a dangerous world replete with microbes, noxious chemicals, and threats as varied as noise and radiation. Governments choose not to stand idly by as these forces work their worst on society. The following cases concern the state's efforts to alleviate the dangers without crushing personal rights and commerce.

In *Gasper* v. *Louisiana Stadium and Exposition District*, we look to the matter of "indoor pollution." Kenneth Gasper and his nonsmoking comrades object to the smoky environment of the New Orleans Superdome. Judge Gordon holds that while the U.S. Constitution offers them no relief, it does not prevent a legislature from acting on their behalf.

A similar case has arisen over noise pollution in the form of loud music on municipal buses. It's based on the same conviction that citizens should enjoy an inoffensive environment in public buildings.

How serious is the indoor concentration of tobacco smoke? Is it harmful or merely annoying? At what level of offense should the state intervene?

The pollution is of the outdoor variety in *Crowther* v. *Seaborg*. In that controversy, the Atomic Energy Commission is confident that radioactive gas from a nuclear experiment will not harm the populace. Richard Crowther, a Colorado citizen, does not share the Commission's confidence.

Judge Arraj describes two theories of biological danger, the "linear" and the "threshold." Finding that there is no conclusive support for either theory, he favors the latter and permits the release of radionuclides. Assuming that there is the promise of benefit, he prefers the attitude "We cannot demonstrate that it's hazardous, so let's go ahead" to "We cannot demonstrate that it's harmless, so let's not go ahead." He does not, however, run roughshod over the opposition, for he notes that the actual safety margin will exceed that which the plantiff requests.

Has he acted responsibly in this case? Is he a good model for other judges facing environmental hazard decisions?

We move to consumer product safety in *Crotty* v. *Shartenberg's–New Haven, Inc.* Jacqueline Crotty insists that the store which sold her some hair remover should compensate her for the damage it did. Is her demand unreasonable? Must the manufacturer and retailer accommodate sensitive people, or should sensitive people look out for themselves? Is the standard of harmfulness to an "appreciable class" workable?

Grossman v. *Baumgartner* shows a city's drastic response to a trade. It is one thing to police an industry or profession. It is another thing to eliminate one.

New York has imposed a citywide ban on tatoo establishments because the spread of hepatitis has been linked with the practice. Fred Grossman objects that his own procedures are sanitary and that his establishment is not dangerous. Nevertheless, Judge Steuer upholds the ban.

Is it fair for Grossman to suffer for the carelessness of others in the business? Should the law stick to situations where actual offense or danger occurs, or may it operate in this more sweeping fashion? Does Judge Rabin's dissenting opinion make more sense?

It's understandable when a business or agency objects to efforts to police it in the interest of public health. But why would a citizen object to the state's public health efforts on his or her behalf? *Dowell* v. *City of Tulsa* shows us one such instance of citizen ire. Dowell objects to fluoridation of the city water on several grounds. He acknowledges the importance of public health measures to ward off infectious diseases, but he sees no justification for the attack on tooth decay. Of course, tooth decay is bad, but there's no danger of an epidemic. So, he reasons, the city errs in forcing this chemical on its people.

Others have opposed what even Dowell accepts, vaccination. Some point to the risks involved, to the statistically slight but undeniable cases of damage through innoculation. Others resist on religious grounds.

Do only cranks and misguided zealots fight these programs? Or is there a moral case to be made? Are those who evade and frustrate mass treatment libertarian heroes? Are they dangerous criminals?

The last case, *State* v. *Lankford*, seems a small squabble, a problem for one family. But the broader implications for public health are significant.

Harry Lankford gave syphilis to his wife, Alice. Judge Boyce calls it assault and battery, assuming that Harry knew he had the disease.

The case raises the interesting prospect of suits for other infections. What if the flu you negligently give me undermines my performance at a crucial job interview? Do you owe me compensation for my loss? And if a friend is given herpes by one aware of the danger, should someone call the police?

Is the moral case for this hard line compelling? Would it make for workable law?

GASPER V. LOUISIANA STADIUM AND EXPOSITION DISTRICT*

U.S. District Court for the Eastern District of Louisiana (1976)

JACK M. GORDON, District Judge.

This action is brought . . . in an attempt by the named plaintiffs to enjoin the Louisiana Stadium and Exposition District from continuing to allow tobacco-smoking in the Louisiana Superdome during events staged therein. The Louisiana Superdome is an enclosed arena located in New Orleans, Louisiana, owned and maintained by a political subdivision of the State of Louisiana known as the Louisiana Stadium and Exposition District (hereinafter referred to as "LSED"). The building is a public, multipurpose facility, and, since its completion, has been used for many events ranging from concerts to Mardi Gras parades. . . .

The plaintiffs, Kenneth O. Gasper, Allen C. Gasper, Beverly Guhl, Dorothy L. Smira, Edward Smira, Albert E. Patent, and David A. Patent, individually and as representatives of other nonsmokers who have attended, or who will attend, such functions in the Louisiana Superdome, challenge LSED's permissive attitude toward smoking as being constitutionally violative of their right to breathe smoke-free air while in a State building. In support of their complaint, the plaintiffs aver that by allowing patrons to smoke in the Louisiana Superdome, LSED is causing other nonsmokers involuntarily to consume hazardous tobacco smoke, thereby causing physical harm and discomfort to those nonsmokers, as well as interfering with their enjoyment of events for which they have paid the price of admission, all in violation of the First, Fifth, Ninth and Fourteenth Amendments to the United States Constitution. . . .

. . . The nonsmokers argue that the existence of tobacco smoke in the Superdome creates a chilling effect upon the exercise of their First Amendment rights, since they must breathe that harmful smoke as a precondition to enjoying events in the Superdome. . . .

To say that allowing smoking in the Louisiana Superdome creates a chilling effect upon the exercise of one's First Amendment rights has no more merit than an argument alleging that admission fees charged at such events have a chilling effect upon the exercise of such rights, or that the selling of beer violates First Amendment rights of those who refuse to attend events where alcoholic beverages

*418 F. Supp. 716

are sold. This Court is of the opinion that the State's permissive attitude toward smoking in the Louisiana Superdome adequately preserves the delicate balance of individual rights without yielding to the temptation to intervene in purely private affairs. Hence, this Court finds no violation of the First Amendment to the United States Constitution. . . .

. . . the courts have never seriously considered the right to a clean environment to be constitutionally protected under the Fifth and Fourteenth Amendments. It is well established that the Constitution does not provide judicial remedies for every social and economic ill. *Lindsey* v. *Normet*, . . . Accordingly, if this Court were to recognize that the Fifth and Fourteenth Amendments provided the judicial means to prohibit smoking, it would be creating a legal avenue, heretofore unavailable, through which an individual could attempt to regulate the social habits of his neighbor. . . .

The Ninth Amendment renaissance began with *Griswold* v. *State of Connecticut, supra*, wherein the Court recognized that the right of privacy in a marital relationship is a fundamental right protected by the Constitution. The plaintiffs herein contend that the right to be free from hazardous smoke fumes caused by the smoking of tobacco is as fundamental as the right of privacy recognized in the *Griswold* decision. This Court does not agree. To hold that the First, Fifth, Ninth or Fourteenth Amendments recognize as fundamental the right to be free from cigaret smoke would be to mock the lofty purposes of such amendments and broaden their penumbral protections to unheard-of boundaries. . . .

. . . this Court is satisfied that the plaintiffs herein have failed to allege a deprivation of any right secured by the United States Constitution and, hence, have failed to state a claim upon which relief could be granted. . . . It is worth repeating that the United States Constitution does not provide judicial remedies for every social and economic ill. For the Constitution to be read to protect nonsmokers from inhaling tobacco smoke would be to broaden the rights of the Constitution to limits heretofore unheard of, and to engage in that type of adjustment of individual liberties better left to the people acting through legislative processes. . . .

CROWTHER V. SEABORG*

U.S. District Court for the District of Colorado (1970)

ARRAJ, Chief Judge. . . .

Project Rulison is a joint experiment sponsored by the Atomic Energy Commission (AEC), the Department of Interior and Austral Oil Company, Inc., (Austral). The program manger is CER Geonulcear Corporation (CER). Rulison is a

*312 F. Supp. 1205

part of the Plowshare Program of the AEC, which is designed to develop peaceful use of nuclear exposive technology. The specific purpose of the project is to study the economic and technical feasibility of nuclear stimulation of the low permeability gas bearing Mesaverde sandstone formation in the Rulison Field of Colorado. "Nuclear stimulation" is the detonation of a nuclear device in the formation which will create a cavity and attendant fracture system that will stimulate the production of natural gas from the formation. The Mesaverde formation, because of its low permeability, does not produce natural gas in commercial quantities, although it does contain a significant gas reserve.

The nuclear device was detonated at a depth of 8,431 feet at the Rulison site near Rulison, Colorado, on September 10, 1969. . . .

The ultimate issue of fact presented by these cases is whether the proposed flaring of gas from the Rulison cavity will endanger life, health and property of the plaintiffs or any other similarly situated, in contravention of the mandate of the Atomic Energy Act. . . .

Dr. Victor Bond, a medical doctor with a Ph.D. in medical physics, who is the Associate Director of Brookhaven National Laboratory in charge of Live Sciences and Chemistry, testified as to the properties of tritium and krypton 85 and the dose to be expected from the release of these radionuclides in the flaring. He testified that a dose of radiation from tritium is the same as a dose of radiation from X rays. He stated that the quality factor of tritium is to be revised downward from 1.7 to 1.0, meaning tritium has a lesser ability to damage living cells than was previously thought. In conventional terms, tritium does not concentrate in the human body.

Dr. Bond stated that the discharge of 1,000 curies of krypton 85 into the atmosphere in the Rulison area will not constitute a medical hazard. He stated that if 2,000 curies of tritium are released at the Rulison site over a one-year period (as the flaring plans contemplate), and this amount is deposited in the environment at a rate and in concentrations consonant with the normal precipitation pattern, the maximum dose any person will receive will be 0.0025 rem.

In order to place this dose in perspective, he gave the dose received from common sources of radiation. A chest X ray exposes a man to 50 milliroentgens, which is about twenty-five times the maximum predicted dose from Rulison. A round trip between New York and Denver in a jet airplane at high altitude will expose a man to a dose equal to that predicted from Rulison. The 0.0025 rem dose from Rulison is equal to the dose from solar radiation a person would receive by spending two weeks at a high altitude ski resort in Colorado. A person who lives in a concrete house rather than a wooden house will receive 100 millirads more of a radiation dose, which is fifty times the upper limit of the dose from the Rulison flaring. In his opinion, 0.0025 rem dose would not constitute a health hazard.

. . . We find that the AEC and FRC standards for radiation exposure is 0.5 rem per year for individuals whose dose can be measured and 0.17 for an average dose to an exposed population. We also find from the uncontroverted testimony of

Dr. Bond that there is no reasonable possibility for a dose to the population exposed to the gas flared from the Rulison cavity to exceed 0.0025 rem. We therefore conclude that the dose to the population in and about the Rulison site resulting from the flaring is thus well within the standards of the AEC and FRC. . . .

. . . The radionuclide production of the Rulison device has been contained within the cavity for six months, thus providing time for all radionuclides with a short half-life to deteriorate. The controlled release of the Rulison gas and its constituent radionuclides will be monitored and an excessive concentration will dictate the cessation of operations.

These standards are based on the conservative assumption that there is a linear relation between the dose received and the damage to living cells, the assumption that for every fraction of a rem exposure there is some injury, although perhaps too minute to be detected. "Dose," as explained above, is the amount of radiation received and must be distinguished from "dose rate," which is the speed at which a given amount of radiation is received. If a given amount is received very rapidly, in a second for instance, it is received at a higher dose rate than if it is received over a time span of several minutes or hours. The "linear assumption" ignores dose rate, the significance of which will be discussed later, and assumes that there is some injury at low dose levels regardless of dose rate, although no evidence was produced to validate the assumption. We find that the adoption of this assumption constitutes a conservative approach by the standards setters and does not constitute a recognition of the scientific validity of the linear theory.

There has been a history of disagreement with the established radiation protection standards on the part of some members of the scientific community. The basis for this disagreement has often been the fact that science has been unable to fully discover the biological effects and costs of ionizing radiation. This lack of knowledge is not the product of insufficient scientific inquiry, but rather of the complexity of the problem presented. This ignorance makes it impossible to assess fully the risks attendant to exposure to ionizing radiation. Disagreement with the standards is thus often a manifestation of a value judgment that it is wrong to set a standard which may in fact turn out in the future to have been wrong. It appears to us that the "scientific" disagreement in such cases, where there is no evidence of biological effects from radiation at levels below the standards, may in reality be a disagreement with the value judgment that utilization of materials and processes which produce radiation should proceed even though all risks may not be known. . . .

The plaintiffs sought to prove that the present standards are too high and should be lowered by a factor of ten. We find that they failed to establish this proposition with competent evidence. They claimed that "new evidence" of the effects of ionizing radiation, "hard evidence," indicates the necessity of such a lowering of the acceptable exposure levels. Plaintiffs offered, through the testimony of Dr. Puck, evidence of a correlation between chromosomal aberrations and irradiation of chromosomes, which evidence has developed since the present standards for population exposure were established in 1957. Dr. Puck testified that these chromosmal aberrations cause serious congenital abnormalities, and although there is no direct evidence that aberrations causing such defects are caused by irradiation of the chromosomes, these aberrations can be mimicked in the laboratory by irradiation of the chromosomes. Evidence was also offered of the expansion of knowledge in the field of human genetics, which may have illuminated effects of ionizing radiation unknown in 1957. Dr. Puck stated that this evidence provided reason to be cautious, and in his opinion dictated a review of the exposure standards. We agree that these standards should be continually reviewed and revised when the scientific and medical knowledge suggests such revision.

However, although the plaintiffs did introduce impressive evidence of new developments in the field of radiation biology, they failed to prove that these developments show the necessity of lowering the standards. The failure of proof has two elements. First, they did not establish an adequate correlation between this information and radiation exposure at low dose levels. Second, they did not refute equally new and impressive evidence of repair of the biological damage from radiation at low dose rates and levels.

The first element can itself be divided into two distinct problems. One is the methodology utilized in arriving at the conclusion that the standards should be lowered by a factor of ten, and the other is that there is no evidence of biological effects from radiation at low dose levels. First, the evidence shows that Dr. Tamplin and his associate Dr. Gofman used data of radiation exposure at high dose levels, utilized the linear assumption, and extrapolated to arrive at the conclusion that cancers are induced by radiation at low dose levels. This method has been reviewed, according to Dr. Storer, and disagreed with by members of the scientific community. The use by Tamplin and Gofman of the "doubling dose" in predicting the incidence of cancer is also questioned, since this concept has primary applicability in the study of genetic effects of radiation and the mutations produced thereby.

Dr. Tamplin stated that his conclusions were *not* based on evidence of radiation effects at low dose levels. Nor did the plaintiffs produce any evidence of a causal relation between radiation exposure at low dose levels and chromosomal aberrations. Thus, although the plaintiffs claim that their demand for a lowering of the standards is supported by "hard evidence," they have failed to produce in this Court any "hard evidence" of radiation effects at or below the low dose levels of the radiation protection standards.

A substantial amount of uncontradicted evidence of recovery from the effects of radiation was introduced in this case. Recovery is the ability of a biological mechanism exposed to radiation to repair the damage done by the radiation. Dr. Puck testified that the essence of the radiation damage to living systems is a random disorganization of the complex order of the system. It is this order which makes the molecular structure a living organism. Dr. Evans and Dr. Upton both testified that their experimental work has produced data which suggest that at the low dose levels of the protection standards living cells are able to repair the damage done by radiation. Dr. Evans' research deals with human beings who have received dosage from radium, and Dr. Upton's deals with research done on mice. Their data reveal that the ability of the repair mechanism to function depends upon dose rate. Repair of damage is more complete when radiation is received at low dose rates.

This evidence of repair and recovery from radiation damage has been characterized as evidence which supports a theory of a "threshold" or a "practial threshold." The *threshold* assumption is that below certain levels of dose or dose rate the repair mechanism keeps abreast of the insult, and the exposed organism suffers no permanent damage. The *practical threshold* theory postulates that at certain higher levels of dose or dose rate the repair mechanism cannot keep abreast of the damage to the cells from radiation, but that the cumulative damage to the body is not sufficient to manifest itself during the lifetime of the exposed person. Thus, if in fact the cumulative damage would cause cancer, the time that would be required for a tumor to appear would exceed the lifespan.

We find that the evidence of repair provides support for the theories of threshold and practical threshold and has not been controverted. . . . Thus, although we do not accept evidence of repair as conclusively establishing the scientific validity of the threshold theories, we do accept it as satisfactory rebuttal of plaintiffs' evidence for lowering of the standards, since the standards as established are more conservative than this evidence would indicate they need be.

. . . The field of radiation protection is constantly changing with the appearance of new scientific knowledge on the biological effects of ionizing radiation. Careful decisions must be made in the context of contemporaneous knowledge. Such decisions cannot be indefinitely postponed if the potentials of atomic energy are to be fully realized. All that is required to establish reasonableness of the decision setting a standard under the statutory directive to protect the public health and safety is that it be made carefully in light of the best of available scientific knowledge. Absolute certainty is neither required nor possible. . . . We therefore find that the plaintiffs have failed to establish that the FRC and AEC radiation protection standards are not reasonably adequate to protect life, health and safety. We note that our previous findings in this opinion permitted the avoidance of this issue completely, for the uncontroverted evidence is that the dose to be expected from the Rulison flaring is 0.0025 rem. The FRC and AEC standards are sixty-eight times greater than this dose. If the standard was lowed by a factor of ten as urged by plaintiffs, the revised standard would still be six and eight-tenths times greater than the dose to be expected from the Rulison flaring. . . .

CROTTY V. SHARTENBERG'S–NEW HAVEN, INC.*

Supreme Court of Errors of Connecticut (1960)

SHEA, Associate Justice. . . .
. . . The plaintiff asked the salesgirl at the cosmetic counter in the defendant's store for a good hair remover, without specifying any brand. The clerk sold her a hair remover called Nudit, a preparation contained in a tube which was packed, together with a tube of finishing cream, in a cardboard box. Under the directions on the box and on the tube of Nudit, the user whose skin was supersensitive was, on the first occasion, to make a test in accordance with instructions in a booklet enclosed in the box. The plaintiff read these instructions and made the test as directed. When no reaction was observed, she applied the hair remover to her upper lip. A few hours later she suffered an allergic reaction. Her condition was disagnosed as contagious impetigo secondary to an allergic dermatitis. She gave notice to the defendant of a claimed breach of warranty within a few days after she sustained her injuries. In the opinion of her physician, they were caused by the application of Nudit. Previously, the plaintiff had used other hair removers without harmful effect. Nudit and these other hair removers contain a chemical known as calcium thioglycolate. Some persons are allergic to this substance. It is not an intrinsically unhealthy ingredient. The plaintiff is one of a group of persons who develop sensitivity from its use. Skin tests are given as an aid to diagnosis, but sometimes such a test does not demonstrate sensitivity even though it is known to be present. . . .
. . . Authorities agree that a buyer who, having a unique or peculiar sensitivity, suffers injury from some innocent substance should not be entitled to recover damages from the seller. There is a divergence of opinion, however, as to the rights of persons whose susceptibility is not peculiar to them alone. The medical profession has made an extensive study of allergies. It has found that the human body may become sensitized to a substance so that, upon exposure to it, there is a bodily reaction which results in one or another of the allergic disturbances. It is common knowledge that eggs, strawberries, fish, and other products in common use, as well as the pollen of certain flowering plants or shrubs, will produce allergic reactions in some people. The sale of an article or product in its natural state may cause an allergic reaction, but the seller should not be held liable under the law of implied warranty unless there is some inherent defect in the product sold. A warranty of reasonable fitness must be construed in the light of common knowledge with reference to the nature of the article or product sold. *Silverman v. Swift & Co.* . . . A warranty of this kind does not mean that the goods can be used with absolute safety or that they are perfectly adapted to the intended use, but only that they shall be reasonably fit therefor. *Cavanagh v. F. W. Woolworth Co.* . . .

*162 A. 2d 513

. . . When a chemical or other substance is used in the manufacture of a product for human use, a different situation is presented. Here the chemical or the ingredient which the manufacturer puts into the product may be harmful to humans. The term "reasonable fitness" under the law, must, of necessity, be considered one of degree. . . . The term must be related to the subject of the sale. The determination of the question whether goods are reasonably fitted for the purpose for which they are required cannot be fixed arbitrarily in advance by limiting the application of the term "reasonable fitness" to a predetermined class or group of buyers designated as normal persons. To establish a breach of the warranty, the plaintiff must show (1) that the product contains a substance or ingredient which has a tendency to affect injuriously an appreciable number of people, though fewer in number than the number of normal buyers, and (2) that he has, in fact, been injured or harmed by the use of the product. *Bianchi* v. *Denholm & McKay Co.* . . . The burden is on the plaintiff to establish these facts. Proof of the harmful propensities of the substance and that it can affect injuriously an appreciable number of persons is essential to his case. . . . If a buyer has knowledge, either actual or constructive, that he is allergic to a particular substance and purchases a product which he knows or reasonably should know contains that substance, he cannot recover damages for breach of an implied warranty. Nor can he recover if he suffers harm by reason of his own improper use of the article warranted. *Silverman* v. *Swift & Co.* . . .

. . . In the present case, the court, in directing the verdict, adopted the rule that if an article sold under an implied warranty can be used by a normal person without injury, there is no breach of the implied warranty of reasonable fitness. When a manufacturer puts into a product to be sold for human use a substance which has deleterious qualities and a tendency to harm an appreciable number of its users, the manufacturer, and not the user, should shoulder the risk of injurious consequences. The same risk should be borne by the retailer who sells the article to a prospective user who, relying on the retailer, is entitled to believe that the article is reasonably fit for the purpose for which it is sold. When the plaintiff bought Nudit, she had no opportunity to examine or inspect it. Directions for its use made it known to the purchaser that it could injuriously affect one who might be allergic to some substance or ingredient contained in it. A skin test to determine possible reaction was recommended. The test suggested is not always efficacious. The plaintiff made the test but suffered no reaction from it. She later applied Nudit to her upper lip. The injuries appeared soon after in the exact area where it had been applied. There were facts from which the jury could have found that Nudit contained an ingredient which had a tendency to product an injurious reaction in persons allergic to it, that the plaintiff was one of an appreciable number of persons who could be injuriously affected by its use, and that her injuries were caused by a breach of implied warranty.

There is error, the judgment is set aside and a new trial is ordered. . . .

GROSSMAN V. BAUMGARTNER, AS COMMISSIONER OF THE DEPT. OF HEALTH*

New York Supreme Court, Appellate Division (1964)

STEURER, Justice.

This action, brought by two operators of tattooing establishments, seeks a declaratory judgment declaring section 181.15 of the New York Cith Health Code unconstitutional and enjoining respondents, the Board of Health and the Department of Health, from enforcing it. The section makes it unlawful for any person to tattoo a human being. An exception is made for physicians acting for medical purposes. . . .

. . . Of the many other points raised at Special Term and on this appeal, we find but two worthy of mention. It is of no significance that the two proprietors who are the plaintiffs are able and willing to meet the sanitary standards that would provide a reasonable expectation of immunity from infection. It is not they who are on trial but the trade they are engaged in. And as it is the practices of the trade that endanger the community, they must suffer the same fate despite their ability to rise above their fellow practitioners. The test has always been whether the statute "has at least in fact some relation to the public health, that the public health is the end actually aimed at, and that it is appropriate and adapted to that end." (See *Matter of Application of Jacobs* . . .)

If the statute meets that test, individual exceptions cannot prevail against it. The goal of the common welfare as the test of constitutionality of police power regulation has not changed, though the concept of what is reasonably necessary or appropriate has. . . .

. . . The record shows, to our minds conclusively, that the prohibition of lay tattooing was an advisable procedure for the security of life and health. It was established that hepatitis, a serious disease of the blood for which there is no known cure, is caused by a virus. This virus, which lives in the blood of infected persons, is transmitted to the healthy by injection into their blood or tissue of the blood or blood products of the infected. Such transmissions occur to persons who have been tattooed seven times more frequently than they occur in persons who have not been tattooed. Concededly, restricting the spread of hepatitis is a proper subject of Health Code regulations. And it would appear to be uncontradictable that tattooing is a source of the spread of this dread disease. It would therefore follow indisputably that the control of tattooing comes well within the field of securing the health of the community. . . .

RABIN, Justice (dissenting). . . .

*254 N.Y.S. 2d 335

The use of the police power of the State may be exercised to correct a practice that presents a danger to public health. There is no question about that. How far the State may go in the exercise of that power presents a problem quite different. We deal with that problem in this appeal. . . .

I have no quarrel with the validity and unassailability of the finding that the practice of tattooing as presently conducted is a hazard to public health and that the hazard must be eliminated. However, the testimony of the defendants' medical experts indicates that the practice of tattooing can be safe, if properly conducted in accordance with appropriate principles of asepsis. That being so, I am of the opinion that the outright prohibition of the practice of tattooing is an unwarranted extension of the police power and therefore is invalid.

It might well be that tattooing serves a minimal social or economic purpose. But, today it is tattooing that is being prohibited, tomorrow it may be some other pursuit with a conceded social and economic usefulness. While it is unlikely that businesses such as barber shops, electrolysis or beauty salons would be outlawed— rather than regulated if possible—if they generally became a danger to the health of the community yet, holding as the majority does in this case establishes the power of an Administrative Agency to do so. Such power should not be sanctioned. "The Legislature may not validly make it a crime to do something which is innocent in itself merely because it is sometimes done improperly. . . ." (*People* v. *Bunis* . . .). . . .

In conclusion, I am of the opinion that in the circumstances, the defendants' attempt to prohibit what was heretofore, and for many years, a lawful pursuit, constitutes an excessive use of necessary police power and thereby is violative of the fundamental rights of these plaintiffs protected and guaranteed by the Constitution.

DOWELL V. *CITY OF TULSA**

Supreme Court of Oklahoma (1954)

BLACKBIRD, Justice.

Plaintiffs . . . commenced the present action . . . to enjoin the defendants . . . from enforcing and/or complying with Ordinance No. 6565, passed by the Board of Commissioners of the City of Tulsa, on March 3, 1953, authorizing fluoridation of said city's water supply by its Water Department and Commissioner of Water-works and Sewerage. The purpose of such fluoridation, as indicated in the ordinance, was "to aid in the control of dental caries" (tooth decay). . . .

*273 p. 2d 859

Plaintiffs are individual taxpayers of the city. Their effort to enjoin the enforcement of the Ordinance was based upon the alleged ground that it is invalid. The only alleged reasons for such invalidity which they apparently urged are that (1) the ordinance constitutes an "unwarranted exercise of police power"in violation of the Fourteenth Amendment of the U.S. Constitution; (2) that it is an exercise of power beyond that delegated to the city by the State Legislature; (3) it violates the U.S. Constitution's First Amendment concerning freedom of religion; and (4) it violates Title 63 O.S. . . . forbidding the manufacture and sale of "food" to which "fluorine compounds" have been added as the term "food" is defined in Section 183 to include "articles of food, meat, drink . . . beverage. . . ." . . .

With apparent reference to (1) and (3) above, plaintiffs contend under the first two propositions formulated in their briefs that our State Legislature has never established a policy of attempting to regulate or control any disease except those that are "contagious, infectious or dangerous"; and that it could not constitutionally do so. In denying the first part of this contention, defendants point to various statutes enacted by the Oklahoma Legislature . . . which they say plainly show that its policy in matters of public health and welfare has never been confined to seeking control, regulation and prevention of contagious, infectious, or dangerous diseases. Among these are provisions for safeguards pertaining to bedding and the germicidal treatment of secondhand materials, . . . provisions requiring the injection of "nitrate of silver or other proven antiseptic" into the eyes of newborn infants, for their protection against "Inflammation of the eyes . . ." (ophthalma neonatorum), . . . those pertaining to the regulation of milk production and marketing, . . . and of hotels, etc. . . . to the regulation of bakeries and other foodstuff factories, . . . to the regulation of bottling works, . . . to the Section, 296.2, specifying the vitamin and mineral requirement for flour; and to the statutes creating the State Board of Health, . . . and creating in the State Health Department a division to be known as the " 'Division of Preventive Dentistry.' " . . .

. . . In view of the broad terms in which our Legislature has spoken on the subject, we cannot believe that it has intended to restrict its enactment of measures designed to promote the public health and welfare to those designed to prevent the spread of infectious, contagious or dangerous diseases. We think the mere reading of the statutes herein cited and others enacted by our Legislature is sufficient to show that it has not so restricted its policy, and that it has chosen to make many minimum requirements with reference to food, lodging and a myriad of subjects connected with the public health and/or welfare that have no direct connection with or relation to infectious, contagious or dangerous diseases.

The next question then is: Recognizing that such a thing is not against public policy as declared by our Legislature, can the police power delegated to a city by the Legislature be exercised to the extent of what in practical analysis amounts to a compulsory measure requiring people of the city to use or pay for water that is fluoridated in order to control a physical characteristic or weakness which is not an infectious, contagious or dangerous disease? Plaintiffs say that it cannot—that under the guarantees of freedom contained in the 1st and 14th Amendments to the U.S. Constitution the citizens of Tulsa have a right to be furnished city water not "medicated" or treated with fluorides. We do not agree. . . .

. . . Plaintiffs concede, as they must, that municipalites may chlorinate their water supply, *Commonwealth* v. *Town of Hudson* . . . and though they contend, under one proposition, that a city's treatment of its water supply with fluorides is the unlicensed practice of medicine, dentistry and pharmacy under our Statutes, they here argue that such treatment must be distinguished from treatments with chlorides, because the latter will kill germs, purify water and accordingly aid in the prevention and spread of disease, whereas florides will not. We think that if the putting of chlorides in public water supplies will in fact promote the public health, the distinction sought to be drawn by plaintiffs is immaterial. To us it seems ridiculous and of no consequence in considering the public health phase of the case that the substance to be added to the water may be classed as a mineral rather than a drug, antiseptic or germ killer; just as it is of little, if any, consequence whether fluoridation accomplishes its beneficial result to the public health by killing germs in the water, or by hardening the teeth or building up immunity in them to the bacteria that causes caries or tooth decay. If the latter, there can be no distinction on principle between it and compulsory vaccination or inoculation, which, for many years, has been well-established as a valid exercise of police power. . . .

. . . While the evidence in the present case did not purport to establish fluoridation as a remedy or prevention for any specific contagious disease, it did show, without contradiction, that it will materially reduce the incidence of caries in youth. The relation of dental hygiene to the health of the body generally is now so well recognized as to warrant judicial notice. Accordingly, we hold that in establishing the fluoridation prescribed by Ordinance 6565, as effective to reduce dental caries, the evidence also sufficiently established it as a health measure to be a proper subject for exercise of the police power possessed by the City of Tulsa.

We now come to plaintiffs' argument that fluoridation of Tulsa's water supply cannot be justified as a *public* health measure because the evidence went no further than establishing it as an aid to the prevention of caries in persons under sixteen years of age, and tended to show that consumption of such water is of no benefit to older persons. The evidence did not reveal what proportion of Tulsa's population is under sixteen years of age, but under our view this was not necessary. When it is borne in mind that the children and youth of today are the adult citizens of tomorrow, and that this one segment of the population unquestionably benefitted by the drinking of flouridated water now, will in a few years comprise all or a very large percentage of Tulsa's population; and it is further realized that reducing the incidence of dental caries in children will also benefit their parents, the fallacy of plaintiffs' argument is manifest.

We think the uncontradicted testimony of Dr. Paul Haney, Superintendent of Health for the City and County of Tulsa, who was the only witness used at the trial, is sufficient answer to plaintiffs' claim that on the basis of the evidence, the same benefits to be obtained from fluoridation of said city's water supply could be obtained by leaving individuals to fluoridate their own water on a voluntary basis. Dr. Haney's testimony shows not only that the treatment of drinking water by individuals not directly under the supervision of health authorities or as prescribed by a private physician (whose services many families would be financially unable to employ) may be dangerous, but also that it is necessary that all or nearly all of the water consumed by children in the age group involved be fluoridated over a period of years in order for them to obtain the benefits of such process. He explained that such total consumption would not be likely to occur in children of school age, if the fluoridation was left to be done individually or in their homes, because they are at school or away from home much of the time. . . .

. . . Plaintiffs do not elaborate on their contention that Ordinance 6565 is in violation of the "free exercise" of religion, which, in the First Amendment of the United States Constitution, Congress is forbidden to prohibit, but we assume this is based on the hypothesis that the fluoridation prescribed in the Ordinance is a form of "medication" or "medical treatment" forbidden by the tenets of one or more well-known churches or religious sects. This argument is closely allied to one phase of the plaintiffs' "Proposition 4" to the effect that fluoridiation is treatment of a disease and therefore that the Ordinance constitutes the unlicensed practice of medicine as defined and forbidden in Title 59 O.S. . . . To what was said concerning a similar argument in *De Aryan* v. *Butler, supra*, which we hereby approve and adopt, we wish to add our opinion that in the contemplated water fluoridation, the City of Tulsa is no more practicing medicine or dentistry or manufacturing, preparing, compounding or selling a drug, than a mother would be who furnishes her children a well-balanced diet, including foods containing vitamin D and calcium to harden bones and prevent rickets, or lean meat and milk to prevent pellagra. No one would contend that this is practicing medicine or administering drugs. . . .

STATE V. *LANKFORD**

Court of General Sessions of Delaware (1917)

Harry S. Lankford was indicted for an assault upon Alice M. Lankford, his wife. Verdict guilty.

At the trial, the wife testified that she and the accused were married June 10th, 1916; that about the first of March following, she began suffering in her private parts, and asked her husband what ailed her; that he told her she had ulcers, and he got some medicine for her but she could not take it. He told her she

*102 A. 63

would get well, if she waited awhile, which she did, but her ailment grew worse; that the latter part of the month or the first of April she consulted a physician and learned that she had syphilis; that from the time of her marriage until she learned that she was infected she had lived with her husband and that he had continued to have sexual relations with her until March after their marriage. A physician testified for the state that he had been consulted by the accused, the latter part of November or the first of December, 1916, and that, on finding he had syphilis, he informed the accused of the nature of his malady.

The husband admitted that his wife contracted syphilis from him and that he did not tell her that he was suffering with the disease until she had learned that she was suffering with it; but contended that he had contracted the disease about nine months before his marriage, at which time he supposed himself to have been cured; that some time in October, following his marriage, he consulted a physician and became aware that he still had the disease; and that from that time he did not have sexual intercourse with his wife.

The court was requested on behalf of the state, to instruct the jury that if they should believe that the accused, knowing that he was infected with a venereal disease, syphilis, and without informing his wife of the fact had sexual intercourse with her after such knowledge had been communicated to him, and thereby infected her with the disease, he would be guilty of assault. The fraud practiced upon the wife would abrogate any consent she might give for sexual intercourse, as it cannot be supposed that a wife would consent to sexual intercourse with her husband if she knew that he was infected with a disease such as syphilis. . . .

For the accused the court was requested to instruct the jury, first defining an assault, that if the evidence fails to show the alleged act of assault unjustifiable, or leaves that question in doubt, the criminal act is not proved, and the defendant is entitled to an acquittal; that the intent to injure is the essential element of the offense charged, and before the jury can find the accused guilty they must find that he had an intention to injure his wife; that if the accused had syphilis prior to his marriage to the prosecutrix and believed that he had been cured of the disease before his marriage, and that as soon thereafter as he learned that he still had the disease, he ceased to have, and has not since had, sexual intercourse with his wife, though the jury should believe that the wife contracted the disease from him, the verdict should be not guilty.

BOYCE, J., charging the jury, in part: It is admitted that the accused and the prosecuting witness were married on the tenth day of June, 1916, and that the former communicated syphilis to his wife. . . .

1. A husband may commit an assault and battery upon his wife, notwithstanding the marriage relation. *State* v. *Buckley.* . . .

2. A wife in confiding her person to her husband does not consent to cruel treatment, or to infection with a loathsome disease. A husband, therefore, knowing that he has such a disease, and concealing the fact from his wife, by accepting her consent, and

communicating the infection to her, inflicts on her physical abuse, and injury, resulting in great bodily harm; and he becomes, notwithstanding his marital rights, guilty of an assault, and indeed, a completed battery. . . .

If the accused knew he was infected with syphilis, and his infection was unknown to his wife, the intent to communicate the disease to her by having sexual intercourse with her, may be inferred from the actual results.

If the jury should find the evidence that the accused, knowing that he was infected with a venereal disease, and, without informing his wife of the fact, had sexual intercourse with her after such knowledge had been communicated to him, and thereby infected her with the disease, their verdict should be guilty.

If the jury should find that the accused, during the period he had sexual relations with his wife, did not know that he was infected with a venereal disease, and that he did not communicate with his wife after being informed that he was infected, their verdict should be not guilty.

Verdict, guilty.

8

GENETICS

Diamond v. *Chakrabarty* reflects a new technology whose prospects are at once particularly promising and particularly horrible. Corporations have sprung up to take advantage of microbiological research as it unfolds. As yet, this is more the stuff of dreams than substance, but the heavy investment shows strong confidence in payoff. Although the expression "playing God" is overworked, it seems to retain some of its cutting edge in this context. Work with genes is so fundamental to the form and quality of subsequent life that many find it impious.

Today, we're dickering with bacteria. Tomorrow, we may go to work on human cells. Do we know what we're getting into?

Chakrabarty, a microbiologist, has developed a bacterium which shows promise for combatting oil spills. The U.S. Patent Office has refused him a patent on the organism. In its judgment, a bacterium is not the sort of thing a person can commercially control. Furthermore, it finds Chakrabarty's work dangerous and doesn't want to encourage it.

Do you share the Patent Office's scruples? Is there something improper about owning the rights to a species or variety of organism? Would the same thing go for a new type of rose or hybrid corn as for a bacterium? Is it presumptuous of humanity to try to add to Creation, or is it simply a stewardly handling of resources?

Those involved in the World War II Manhattan Project did not know for sure what would happen when they initiated the nuclear reaction under the University of Chicago football stadium. They believed the event would be under control, but some sort of holocaust was possible. Many feel that the uncertainty of microbiologists is as dangerous as that of these early nuclear physicists. Can we afford to have this sort of high-risk research in our midst?

Although Chicago did not vaporize as a result of that first reactor run, nuclear energy has caused its share of terror and ruin. Might the research in genetic engineering be safe, but the technological applications regrettable? What evils may be mixed with the blessings?

The next two cases are merely suggestive of the issues that will arise as genetic technology matures. Carl Ray Millard of *Millard* v. *State* has forty-seven rather than forty-six chromosomes in each of his cells. He claims that the extra Y-chromosome causes aggressive insanity, and that he was therefore a "driven man" when he committed armed robbery. The judge is not impressed.

Millard does indeed have a genetic abnormality, but is it the sort that geneticists should work to prevent? Not all abnormalities are undesirable. Gifted people are abnormal in a happy sense. How shall we determine which unusual genetic properties need our corrective care?

If we have any doubt that geneticists will find themselves in stormy waters, we need only to read *Hobson* v. *Hansen*. Julius Hobson objects to public school policy which places students on different educational "tracks" on the basis of aptitude tests. He contends that the tests are unsound and they unfairly stigmatize and "sidetrack" black students. The "nature or nurture" issue figures prominently in this lengthy court opinion.

One of the nastiest controversies in recent times concerns race and IQ. The names Jensen and Shockley arouse widespread contempt because they've claimed a rough connection between the two. Judge Wright joins those who find this claim insupportable. He locates the causes for racially distinctive test performance in the environment. And he resists those who would accept low scores by blacks as simply a genetic fact of life. Is his reasoning persuasive? Is the opposite view so outrageous that it does not deserve a hearing? And even if it is true, so what?

Buck v. *Bell* confronts the question, What might we do if and when a genetic problem is identified? In this famous decision Justice Holmes reasons that "three generations of imbeciles are enough." In his view, the state has a right to protect itself from the consequences of sexual relations among the "feeble minded."

It has recently come to light that Carrie Buck and her sister, both sterilized, went on to live satisfactory married lives in society. And so there is the problem of tragic mistake. But even if the incompetency and unhappy genetic consequences were certain, would so drastic a step as sterilization be warranted?

Here the court approved one stringent form of genetic screening. There are other possible methods. For example, a society might require genetic testing before granting a permit to marry. Could such testing and the subsequent ban on certain marriages pass moral muster?

DIAMOND, COMMISSIONER OF PATENTS AND TRADEMARKS V. CHAKRABARTY*

U.S. Supreme Court (1980)

MR. CHIEF JUSTICE BURGER delivered the opinion of the Court.

In 1972, respondent Chakrabarty, a microbiologist, filed a patent application, assigned to the General Electric Co. The application asserted 36 claims related to Chakrabarty's invention of "a bacterium from the genus *Pseudomonas* containing therein at least two stable energy-generating plasmids, each of said plasmids providing a separate hydrocarbon degradative pathway."[1] This human-made, genetically engineered bacterium is capable of breaking down multiple components of crude oil. Because of this property, which is possessed by no naturally occurring bacteria, Chakrabarty's invention is believed to have significant value for the treatment of oil spills.[2]

Chakrabarty's patent claims were of three types: first, process claims for the method of producing the bacteria; second, claims for an inoculum comprised of a carrier material floating on water, such as straw, and the new bacteria; and third, claims to the bacteria themselves. The patent examiner allowed the claims falling into the first two categories, but rejected claims for the bacteria. His decision rested on two grounds: (1) that micro-organisms are "products of nature," and (2) that as living things they are not patentable subject matter. . . .

. . . The Patent Act of 1793, authored by Thomas Jefferson, defined statutory subject matter as "any new and useful art, machine, manufacture, or composition of matter, or any new or useful improvement [thereof]." . . . The Act embodied Jefferson's philosophy that "ingenuity should receive a liberal encouragement." . . .

. . . The laws of nature, physical phenomena, and abstract ideas have been held not patentable. *Funk Brothers Seed Co.* v. *Kalo Inoculant Co.* . . .

. . . Thus, a new mineral discovered in the earth or a new plant found in the wild is not patentable subject matter. Likewise, Einstein could not patent his

---

*447 U.S. 303

[1] Plasmids are hereditary units physically separate from the chromosomes of the cell. In prior research, Chakrabarty and an associate discovered that plasmids control the oil degradation abilities of certain bacteria. In particular, the two researchers discovered plasmids capable of degrading camphor and octane, two components of crude oil. In the work represented by the patent application at issue here, Chakrabarty discovered a process by which four different plasmids, capable of degrading four different oil components, could be transferred to and maintained stably in a single *Pseudomonas* bacterium, which itself has no capacity for degrading oil.

[2] At present, biological control of oil spills requires the use of a mixture of naturally occurring bacteria, each capable of degrading one component of the oil complex. In this way, oil is decomposed into simpler substances which can serve as food for aquatic life. However, for various reasons, only a portion of any such mixed culture survives to attack the oil spill. By breaking down multiple components of oil, Chakrabarty's microorganism promises more efficient and rapid oil-spill control.

celebrated law that $E = mc^2$; nor could Newton have patented the law of gravity. Such discoveries are "manifestations of . . . nature, free to all men and reserved exclusively to none." *Funk* . . .

Judged in this light, respondent's micro-organism plainly qualifies as patentable subject matter. His claim is not to a hitherto unknown natural phenomenon, but to a nonnaturally occurring manufacture or composition of matter—a product of human ingenuity "having a distinctive name, character [and] use." *Hartranft* v. *Wiegmann.* . . . The point is underscored dramatically by comparison of the invention here with that in *Funk*. There, the patentee had discovered that there existed in nature certain species of root-nodule bacteria which did not exert a mutually inhibitive effect on each other. He used that discovery to produce a mixed culture capable of inoculating the seeds of leguminous plants. Concluding that the patentee had discovered "only some of the handiwork of nature," the Court ruled the product nonpatentable:

> Each of the species of root-nodule bacteria contained in the package infects the same group of leguminous plants which it always infected. No species acquires a different use. The combination of species produces no new bacteria, no change in the six species of bacteria, and no enlargement of the range of their utility. Each species has the same effect it always had. The bacteria perform in their natural way. Their use in combination does not improve in any way their natural functioning. They serve the ends nature originally provided and act quite independently of any effort of the patentee. . . .

Here, by contrast, the patentee has produced a new bacterium with markedly different characteristics from any found in nature and one having the potential for significant utility. His discovery is not nature's handiwork, but his own; accordingly it is patentable subject matter. . . .

The petitioner's second argument is that micro-organisms cannot qualify as patentable subject matter until Congress expressly authorizes such protection. His position rests on the fact that genetic technology was unforeseen. . . . From this it is argued that resolution of the patentability of inventions such as respondent's should be left to Congress. The legislative process, the petitioner argues, is best equipped to weigh the competing economic, social, and scientific considerations involved, and to determine whether living organisms produced by genetic engineering should receive patent protection. . . .

. . . A rule that unanticipated inventions are without protection would conflict with the core concept of the patent law that anticipation undermines patentability. . . . Mr. Justice Douglas reminded that the inventions most benefiting mankind are those that "push back the frontiers of chemistry, physics, and the like." *Great A. & P. Tea Co.* v. *Supermarket Corp.*[3] . . . (concurring opinion). Congress

---

[3]Even an abbreviated list of patented inventions underscores the point: telegraph (Morse, No. 1,647); telephone (Bell, No. 174,465); electric lamp (Edison, No. 223,898); airplane (the Wrights, No. 821,393); transistor (Bardeen & Brattain, No. 2,524,035); neutronic reactor (Fermi & Szilard, No. 2,706,656); laser (Schawlow & Townes, No. 2,929,922). . . .

employed broad general language . . . precisely because such inventions are often unforeseeable. . . .

To buttress his argument, the petitioner, with the support of *amicus*, points to grave risks that may be generated by research endeavors such as respondent's. The briefs present a gruesome parade of horribles. Scientists, among them Nobel laureates, are quoted suggesting that genetic research may pose a serious threat to the human race, or, at the very least, that the dangers are far too substantial to permit such research to proceed apace at this time. We are told that genetic research and related technological developments may spread pollution and disease, that it may result in a loss of genetic diversity, and that its practice may tend to depreciate the value of human life. These arguments are forcefully, even passionately, presented; they remind us that, at times, human ingenuity seems unable to control fully the forces it creates—that, with Hamlet, it is sometimes better "to bear those ills we have then fly to others that we know not of."

It is argued that this Court should weigh these potential hazards in considering whether respondent's invention is patentable subject matter. . . . We disagree. The grant or denial of patents on micro-organisms is not likely to put an end to genetic research or to its attendant risks. The large amount of research that has already occurred when no researcher had sure knowledge that patent protection would be available suggests that legislative or judicial fiat as to patentability will not deter the scientific mind from probing into the unknown any more than Canute could command the tides. Whether respondent's claims are patentable may determine whether research efforts are accelerated by the hope of reward or slowed by want of incentives, but that is all.

What is more important is that we are without competence to entertain these arguments—either to brush them aside as fantasies generated by fear of the unknown, or to act on them. The choice we are urged to make is a matter of high policy for resolution within the legislative process after the kind of investigation, examination, and study that legislative bodies can provide and courts cannot. That process involves the balancing of competing values and interests, which in our democratic system is the business of elected representatives. Whatever their validity, the contentions now pressed on us should be addressed to the political branches of the Government, the Congress and the Executive, and not to the courts.[4]

---

[4]We are not to be understood as suggesting that the political branches have been laggard in the consideration of the problems related to genetic research and technology. They have already taken action. In 1976, for example, the National Institutes of Health released guidelines for NIH-sponsored genetic research which established conditions under which such research could be performed. . . . In 1978 those guidelines were revised and relaxed.

MILLARD V. STATE*

Court of Special Appeals of Maryland (1970)

MURPHY, Chief Judge.

Charged with the offense of robbery with a deadly weapon, appellant filed a written plea that he was insane at the time of the commission of the crime under Maryland Code, Article 59, Section 9(a), which provides:

> A defendant is not responsible for criminal conduct and shall be found insane at the time of the commission of the alleged crime if, at the time of such conduct as a result of mental disease or defect, he lacks substantial capacity either to appreciate the criminality of his conduct or to conform his conduct to the requirements of law. As used in this section, the terms 'mental disease or defect' do not include an abnormality manifested only by repeated criminal or otherwise antisocial conduct."

The basis for appellant's insanity plea, as later unfolded at the trial, was that he had an extra Y chromosome in the brain and other cells of his body which constituted . . . a mental defect resulting in his lacking substantial capacity either to appreciate the criminality of his conduct or to conform his conduct to the requirements of law. . . .

Dr. Cecil Jacobson, the appellant's only medical witness, testified that he was an Assistant Professor in the Department of Obstetrics and Gynecology and Chief of the Reproduction Genetics Unit of the George Washington University School of Medicine; that he had obtained a degree in genetics from the University of Utah in 1960 and was "a research teacher teaching the full-time faculty" at the University; that he had published 42 articles in the field of genetics, had conducted extensive research in the field, supervised a number of genetics laboratories, and was a consultant in genetics to the Federal Government. He stated that in 1964 he also obtained a medical degree and was licensed to practice medicine in Maryland, Virginia and the District of Columbia; that he had interned for one year in 1964–1965 but did not serve a residency in medicine but "went directly into the academic program [at George Washington University] because he had an active teaching responsibility as a medical student." He testified that while he received formal training in psychiatry as a medical student, and had received clinical experience in the psychiatric wards during his medical internship, he was not a psychiatrist, had received no post-graduate training in psychiatry, was neither Board eligible nor Board certified, and had "no competence" in the field of psychiatry beyond that possessed by "the conventional physician." He testified that he was in the active practice of "academic medicine" but only as a consultant to other physicians; that he had participated in a number of research protocols in mental illness; that a considerable portion of his practice in genetics fell within the

*261 A. 2d 227

area of mental illness, "especially mental retardation"; that he had acquired intimate experience counselling patients who sought therapeutic abortions to realize the "psychological implications of the miscarriage"; and that a considerable part of his genetics practice involved "counselling the recurrence significant of birth defects"—an area which he said fell within "the realm of psychiatric practice."

Dr. Jacobson testified that genetics was "a sub-speciality biology" having "quite a bit of inference in medicine," involving a specific diagnostic technique dealing with the "very basis of human development, the chromosome material"; that "chromosomes [in the cells of the body] are the way that all genetic machinery is passed from one generation to another"; that "all things that are passed on from parent to child must go through chromosomes"; and that 46 chromosomes constituted the normal complement per cell and a person who possessed 47 chromosomes was genetically abnormal.

Dr. Jacobson testified that on December 16, 1968, appellant was examined and his body cells found to contain an extra Y chromosome (XYY); that the presence of this extra chromosome constituted a "basic defect in the genetic complement of the cell" affecting not only the way the cells grow in the body, but also the physical growth of the body itself; that the presence of the extra Y chromosome caused "marked physical and mental problems" affecting the manner in which persons possessing the extra Y chromosome "will react to certain stimulus; certain physiological problems; certain behavioral characteristics." Dr. Jacobson then told of approximately 40 published reports indicating that persons possessed of an extra Y chromosome tended to be very tall, with limbs disproportionate to their body; that such persons had marked antisocial, aggressive and schizoid reactions and were in continual conflict with the law.

Dr. Jacobson stated that he had never previously testified in court. Asked whether he was familiar with the Maryland test of insanity, as defined in Section 9(a), he said that he had never read it, but believed it contained two parts—"One, whether there was a basic defect involved, and, secondly, whether or not the person is competent for his act." Section 9(a) was then read to Dr. Jacobson, and he was then asked whether appellant was insane. Dr. Jacobson responded with a professional narrative of appellant's genetic make-up, after which he concluded that "if the definition of insanity has a mental defect, the answer is yes, he has a mental defect based upon his abnormal [chromosome] test." Asked whether the "defect" was such as to cause appellant to lack "substantial capacity either to appreciate the criminality of his conduct or to conform his conduct to the requirements of law," Dr. Jacobson answered:

"I cannot say that because I have not examined him as a psychiatrist. I have no competence in that area."

Appellant's counsel then told the court that he intended to show through "case histories" that individuals having the extra Y chromosome have extremely aggressive personalities, "to the extent that most of them end up in jail for one reason or another because of their aggressive reactions." Dr. Jacobson was then asked to examine appellant's arms to determine whether the cuts thereon were "suicidal or merely attention cuts." Dr. Jacobson did so briefly and stated that based on his experience as a medical doctor, he believed the cuts constituted an actual attempt at suicide; that based on this fact, and his brief questioning of appellant during a five-minute court recess, he felt appellant's "reactions" were not normal; that appellant had a fear of "forceful activity with an attempt at extension of this regression and a lack of adequately controlling this"; that although he was "greatly restricted" by not knowing the "developmental history" of appellant, he believed, based upon the testimony of the jail lieutenant concerning appellant's conduct while in confinement, including the suicide attempts, coupled with appellant's genetic defect, that "this does not fall within the realm of sanity, as I understand it." Dr. Jacobson then testified that the extra Y chromosome in appellant's genetic make-up affected his behavioral patterns, as reported in other cases of persons similarly possessed of the extra Y chromosome. He conceded that persons having the extra Y chromosome may differ among themselves depending upon "what other physical effects are found in the body of the XYY," environment also being a factor accounting for differences between XYY individuals.

Under further questioning by the trial judge, the prosecutor, and defense counsel, Dr. Jacobson stated that appellant's genetic defect—which he characterized as a mental defect—influenced "his competence or ability to recognize the area of his crime"; that appellant had a "propensity" toward crime because of his genetic abnormality; that based upon the medical literature, the appellant's conduct and behavioral patterns, and his genetic defect, he was insane and not even competent to stand trial. The doctor defined insanity in terms of the "ability to comprehend reality" or the "inability to judge one's action as far as consequence." Dr. Jacobson next testified that he had "insufficient evidence" upon which to base a conclusion whether appellant appreciated the consequences of his action, but that because he had attempted to commit suicide, such an act constituted "an inability to comprehend the consequences of his act, the act of suicide, being death"; and that appellant's actions were "not consistent with sanity."

At the conclusion of Dr. Jacobson's testimony, the trial judge indicated that he believed appellant had adduced sufficient evidence to rebut the presumption of sanity and permit the case to go to the jury. The prosecutor urged that the court withold its ruling until it heard from the State's psychiatrist, Dr. Robert Sauer. There being no objection by appellant to this procedure, Dr. Sauer then testified that after extensive psychiatric examination of appellant, he had concluded, as did five other State psychiatrists, that appellant was not insane within the test prescribed in Section 9(a). He diagnosed appellant's condition as antisocial personality, severe, with schizoid trends, which indicated the likelihood of psychotic episodes in the future. Dr. Sauer testified that while he was aware of the literature pertaining to the extra Y chromosome, he made no study of appellant in this connection since be believed that if such genetic defect existed, it was not a "mental defect" within the contemplation of Section 9(a), but a physical defect, not affecting the mental functioning of the brain.

At the conclusion of Dr. Sauer's testimony, the trial judge ruled that he was not persuaded that reasonable minds could differ as to appellant's sanity; that the appellant's defect was physical and not mental; and that Dr. Jacobson's testimony did not, with reasonable medical certainty, overcome the presumption that appellant was sane. The trial judge thus declined to submit the issue of appellant's sanity to the jury. The jury subsequently found appellant guilty of robbery with a deadly weapon and he was sentenced to eighteen years under the jurisdiction of the Department of Correction. . . .

. . . The mere fact then that appellant had a genetic abnormality which Dr. Jacobson characterized as "a mental defect" would not, of itself, suffice to show that, under Section 9(a), he lacked, because of such defect, "substantial capacity either to appreciate the criminality of his conduct or to conform his conduct to the requirements of law." And to simply state that persons having the extra Y chromosome are prone to aggressiveness, are antisocial, and continually run afoul of the criminal laws, is hardly sufficient to rebut the presumption of sanity and show the requisite lack of "substantial capacity" under Section 9(a). Moreover, we think it entirely plain from the record that in testifying that appellant had a "mental defect," Dr. Jacobson did so only in a most general sense, without full appreciation for the meaning of the term as used in Section 9(a), and particularly without an understanding that such term expressly excludes "an abnormality manifested only by repeated criminal or otherwise antisocial conduct." But even if it were accepted that appellant had a "mental defect" within the contemplation of Section 9(a), Dr. Jacobson, by his own testimony, indicated an inability to meaningfully relate the effect of such defect to the "substantial capacity" requirements of the subsection. Not only did Dr. Jacobson candidly admit that he had "no competence" in the field of psychiatry, but he demonstrated that fact by showing that he had not theretofore familiarized himself with the substance of Section 9(a); indeed, his conception of the test of criminal responsibility in Maryland was shallow at best, at least until the test was read to him during his testimony. While Dr. Jacobson did ultimately testify in conclusory fashion that he thought appellant insane and even incompetent to stand trial, his testimony in this connection was obviously predicated on a definition of "insanity" different than that prescribed under Section 9(a)—a definition so general as to encompass as insane a person who would attempt suicide. At one point in his testimony Dr. Jacobson conceded that he had "insufficient evidence" upon which to conclude whether appellant appreciated the "consequences of his actions." Whether this concession was due to the fact that Dr. Jacobson had never subjected appellant to a psychiatric examination is unclear; what is clear is that Dr. Jacobson's testimony was too generalized and lacking in specifics to form the basis for an opinion, with reasonable medical certainty, that appellant was insane under Section 9(a). In so concluding, we do not intend to hold, as a matter of law, that a defense of insanity based upon the so-called XYY genetic defect is beyond the pale of proof under Section 9(a). . . . We only conclude that on the record before us the trial judge properly declined to permit the case to go to the jury—a determination which, contrary to appellant's further contention, is not violative of any of his constitutional rights, state or federal. . . .

That Dr. Jacobson was a well qualified geneticist was clear beyond question. Equally clear is the fact that he was not a practicing physician, and his experience in mental illness was related essentially to his practice in the field of genetics. He conceded a lack of competence in the field of psychiatry, admitted having no prior familiarity with the provisions of Section 9(a), had not subjected appellant to any psychiatric examination, and defined "insanity" in terms different than those prescribed by the applicable law. As we said in *Greenleaf* v. *State* . . . to constitute proof of insanity sufficient to raise a doubt in the minds of reasonable men, competent medical evidence must be adduced to the positive effect that the accused, as a result of mental disease or defect, lacked substantial capacity either to appreciate the criminality of his conduct or to conform his conduct to the requirements of law; and evidence of some undefined mental disorder or instability is insufficient proof to overcome the presumption of sanity. On the record before us, we think Dr. Jacobson's opinion as to appellant's sanity under Section 9(a) was not competent in that it was not based on reasonable medical certainty, and that the trial judge, had he so concluded, would not have been in error. . . .

*HOBSON V. HANSEN**

U.S. District Court for the District of Columbia (1967)

J. SKELLY WRIGHT, Circuit Judge. . . .

. . . The basic question presented is whether the defendants, the Superintendent of Schools and the members of the Board of Education, in the operation of the public school system here, unconstitutionally deprive the District's Negro and poor public school children of their right to equal educational opportunity with the District's white and more affluent public school children. This court concludes that they do.

In support of this conclusion the court makes the following principal findings of fact: . . . .

. . . The track system as used in the District's public school is a form of ability grouping in which students are divided in separate, self-contained curricula or tracks ranging from "Basic" for the slow student to "Honors" for the gifted.

*269 F. Supp. 401

... The aptitude tests used to assign children to the various tracks are standardized primarily on white middle class children. Since these tests do not relate to the Negro and disadvantaged child, track assignment based on such tests relegates Negro and disadvantaged children to the lower tracks from which, because of the reduced curricula and the absence of adequate remedial and compensatory education, as well as continued inappropriate testing, the chance of escape is remote.

... Education in the lower tracks is geared to what Dr. Hansen, the creator of the track system, calls the "blue collar" student. Thus such children, so stigmatized by inappropriate aptitude testing procedures, are denied equal opportunity to obtain the white collar education available to the white and more affluent children. ...

... PLACEMENT AND TESTING.

What emerges as the most important single aspect of the track system is the process by which the school system goes about sorting students into the different tracks. This importance stems from the fact that the fundamental premise of the sorting process is the keystone of the whole track system: that school personnel can with reasonable accuracy ascertain the maximum potential of each student and fix the content and pace of his education accordingly. If this premise proves false, the theory of the track system collapses, and with it any justification for consigning the disadvantaged student to a second-best education. ...

... CAUSES OF LOW TEST SCORES.

A low aptitude test score may mean that a student is innately limited in intellectual ability. On the other hand, there may be other explanations possible that have nothing to do with native intelligence. ...

... HANDICAPS TO LEARNING.

Disadvantaged children typically are saddled with tremendous handicaps when it comes to competing in the ethnocentric academic society of public schools. That society, mirroring American society generally, is strongly influenced by white and middle class experiences and values. While there is nothing necessarily wrong about this orientation, it does raise certain barriers for lower class and Negro children—barriers that are to be found in most aptitude tests as well.

1. Environmental factors. The chief handicap of the disadvantaged child where verbal tests are concerned is in his limited exposure to people having command of standard English. Communication within the lower class environment, although it may rise to a very complex and sophisticated level, typically assumes a language form alien to that tested by aptitude tests. Slang expressions predominate; diction is poor; and there may be ethnically based language forms. The language spoken by Negro children in the ghetto has been classified as a dialect. . . .

Other circumstances interact with and reinforce the language handicap. Verbalization tends to occur less frequently and often less intensively. Because of crowded living conditions, the noise level in the home may be quite high with the result that the child's auditory perception—his ability to discriminate among word sounds—can be retarded. There tends to be less exposure to books or other serious reading material—either for lack of interest or for lack of money.

The disadvantaged child has little or no opportunity to range beyond the boundaries of his immediate neighborhood. He is unfamiliar, therefore, with concepts that will expand both his range of experiences and his vocabulary. He has less exposure to new things that he can reduce to verbal terms. For example, one defense witness, a principal of a low-income Negro elementary school, told of how most of the children had never been more than a few blocks from home; they had never been downtown, although some had been to a Sears department store; they did not know what an escalator was, had not seen a department-store Santa Claus, had not been to a zoo. These experiences, common in the subject matter of tests and textbooks, were alien to the lives of these children.

The way in which environmental factors affect the development of non-verbal skills is not quite as clear. There is evidence that such factors are less of a handicap to scoring well on a non-verbal aptitude test than they are to scoring well on a verbal test. . . . Nonetheless, the child's environment remains very much a factor in the development of nonverbal skills. Defendant's expert, Dr. Dailey, was of the opinion that a nonlanguage test of abstract reasoning tests the same intellectual process required to read a paragraph and answer questions about it. Thus the skill a child develops in the process of reducing life experiences to verbal terms is really but another aspect of the process by which a child reasons abstractly about geometric symbols in nonlanguage terms. The less a child is exposed to situations in which he has the stimulation or the opportunity to deal with complex experiences or concepts, the more retarded both his verbal and nonverbal development will be—although the retarding effect may be greater in the case of verbal skills. . . .

2. Psychological factors.   Although any student taking a test may be subject to psychological influences of various sorts, there is a good deal of evidence that disadvantaged children and Negro children are more likely than others to suffer from influences that have a depressing effect on test scores. The problem can generally be described as one of low self-esteem, or lack of self-confidence.

i. Socio-economic causes.   There is evidence that disadvantaged children, black or white, are those most likely to lack self-confidence in the school situation. This is due to a complex of causes, many of them directly related to the environmental factors already discussed. The disadvantaged child is made profoundly aware of this academic shortcoming as soon as he enters school. There is a great risk of his losing confidence in his ability to compete in school with children who are "better off." A frequent manifestation of this is for the child to become a discipline problem, as he goes through the process of rejecting a situation in which he feels inadequate. All of this can have a direct and significant effect on test performance as much as on scholastic performance.

ii. Racial causes. Apart from factors related to socio-economic status, there is striking evidence that Negro children undergo a special kind of psychological stress that can have a debilitating effect on academic and test performance. . . . Because of their race and the ever present reminders of being "different," Negro chidren generally are subject to very serious problems of self-identification. By the time the Negro child is about to enter school he has become very much racially self-conscious, which causes considerable psychological turmoil as he attempts to come to terms with his status as a Negro. He tends to be imbued with a sense of worthlessness, of inferiority, of fear and despair which is transmitted to him primarily through his parents.

In this state of turmoil, many Negro children approach school with the feeling they are entering a strange and alien place that is the property of a white school system or of white society, even though the school may be all-Negro. And when the school *is* all-Negro or predominantly so, this simply reinforces the impressions implanted in the child's mind by his parents, for the school experience is then but a perpetuation of the segregation he has come to expect in life generally. Evidence of turmoil can be found in the ability of many Negro pre-schoolers and first graders to draw themselves as colored, or other than in an animal-like or caricature-like fashion. This general psychological phenomenon is not confined to the South but is common to Negroes throughout the country. . . .

When economically based deprivation is combined with the traumas suffered simply because of being Negro, the psychological impact can be crushing.

iii. Manifestations of low self-esteem: anxiety and apathy. When a child lacks confidence in himself or is self-degrading, he is likely to manifest this during the test-taking experience. One reaction that has been identified has been called "test anxiety." The child, apprehensive about his ability to score well and fearful about what others—especially his teacher or principal—might see in the test score, reacts in a self-defeating manner: He becomes highly nervous, even "wildly rampant"; or he withdraws. Either reaction lowers his test score. . . .

Aside from anxiety-caused withdrawal, a child may be apathetic about a test simply because he does not see it as important. Children who come from backgrounds lacking in parental and environmental support for academic achievement will be more prone to be apathetic about testing; and disadvantaged children are those most likely to have nonsupportive backgrounds. . . .

Plaintiffs' expert, Dr. Cline, has concluded that one of the most important influences on both academic achievement and aptitude test scores inheres in the teacher-pupil relationship, a syndrome Dr. Cline has termed "teacher expectation." Studies have found that a teacher will commonly tend to underestimate the abilities of disadvantaged chldren and will treat them accordingly—in the daily classroom routine, in grading, and in evaluating these students' likelihood of achieving in the future. The horrible consequence of a teacher's low expectation is that it tends to be a self-fulfilling prophecy. The unfortunate students, treated as if they were subnormal, come to accept as a fact that they *are* subnormal. They act out in their school behavior and in the testing situation what they have been conditioned to believe is their true status in life; and in conforming to expectations, they "confirm" the original judgment. A noted expert, Professor Kenneth Clark, has summed up the problem thusly:

> ... When a child from a deprived background is treated as if he is uneducable because he has a low test score, he becomes uneducable and the low test score is thereby reinforced. If a child scores low on an intelligence test because he cannot read and then is not taught to read because he has a low test score, then such a child is being imprisoned in an iron circle and becomes the victim of an educational self-fulfilling prophecy....

... perhaps the most ideal circumstance for making an accurate estimate of innate ability from comparing test scores would be in the case of twins. If the twins were given the same test and one scored significantly higher than the other, a reasonable inference would be that the higher scoring twin had the superior innate ability; both children presumably would have had the same opportunity to learn the tested skills and both would probably have been subject to similar psychological influences.

Transferring this principle to standard aptitude tests in general, the best circumstance for making accurate estimates of ability is when the tested student is most like the typical norming student: white and middle class. Because the white middle class student predominates in the norming sample, it is possible to say the average student in that group will have had roughly the same opportunities to develop standard verbal and nonverbal skills as the rest of the group and will probably be psychologically similar as well. Thus the national median or norm is a reasonably accurate statistical statement of what the average American student ought to have learned in the way of verbal and nonverbal skills by a certain age and what can therefore be considered average intelligence or ability to learn. For this reason, standard aptitude tests are most precise and accurate in their measurements of innate ability when given to white middle class students.

When standard aptitude tests are given to low income Negro children, or disadvantaged children, however, the tests are less precise and less accurate—so much so that test scores become practically meaningless. Because of the impoverished circumstances that characterize the disadvantaged child, it is virtually impossible to tell whether the test score reflects lack of ability—or simply lack of opportunity. Moreover, the probability that test scores of the Negro child or the disadvantaged child will be depressed because of somewhat unique psychological influences further compounds the risk of inaccuracy.

Lorton study.   Striking evidence of the inaccuracy of standard tests is revealed in a study made in 1965 at the Lorton Youth Center, a penal institution set up under the Federal Youth Corrections Act and serving the District of Columbia. Inmates range in age from 18 to 26 years; 90% are dropouts from the District schools; and 95% of these are Negroes. Sixty-nine inmates enrolled in the Youth Center School pursuing a course of study leading to a high-school-equivalent diploma were examined as a follow-up to an earlier study to determine these inmates' educational progress under "ideal" educational circumstances. In the earlier study several factors had been identified as causing these inmates to underachieve in school and eventually to drop out; the second study was designed to measure achievement once those factors had been removed. A summary of the study is quoted in the margin . . . ; the major points of interest are these:

1. Two types of aptitude tests were used to measure ability, the Otis test used in District schools, a verbal test; and the Revised Beta Examination, which is nonverbal. The IQ ranges for the two tests differed markedly. For the whole group of 69 inmates the range of IQ's obtained by using the Otis test was from 50 to 110; the average was 78, substantially below normal. Scores on the nonverbal Beta test, however, were higher, ranging from 71 to 118; the average was 98–20 points higher than the Otis average, and a level considered to indicate average intelligence.

Twenty-four of the 69 inmates scored at 75 or below on the Otis test, the IQ's ranging from 50 to 75; the average was 62. . . . Yet on the Beta test the range was from 71 to 112, the average being 91–or 29 points higher than the Otis average.

2. Gains in achievement in reading and arithmetic over a one-year period were measured using the Stanford Achievement Tests, one of the series used in the District schools. The expected gain for a student of average intelligence, according to Stanford norms, is 1.0 (*i. e.,* a progress equivalent to one grade level in one year).

Reading.   The average gain for all 69 inmates was 1.3 years, increasing from an average grade level equivalent of 6.9 (ninth month of the sixth grade) to 8.2 (second month of the eighth grade). For the 24 inmates in the 75 or below range (Otis), the average gain also was 1.3 yers, increasing from a grade level equivalent of 3.9 to 5.2.

Arithmetic.   The average gain for all inmates was 1.8 years, increasing from 5.6 to 7.4. For the 24 low-scoring inmates the average gain was 1.8, increasing from 4.2 to 6.0.

This study reveals in hard fact that a disadvantaged Negro student with a supposedly low IQ can, given the opportunity, far surpass what might be expected of a truly "subnormal" student. It illustrates the principle that a standard verbal aptitude test—in this case the Otis test—can be a faulty predictor of actual achievement for disadvantaged students, and confirms Dr. Clines assessment of the disabilities of such tests in making accurate inferences about inmate ability. . . .

Conclusion. In light of the above evidence regarding the accuracy of aptitude test measurements, the court makes the following findings. First, there is substantial evidence that defendants presently lack the techniques and the facilities for ascertaining the inmate learning abilities of a majority of District schoolchildren. Second, lacking these techniques and facilities, defendants cannot justify the placement and retention of these children in lower tracks on the supposition that they could do no better, given the opportunity to do so. . . .

None of this is to suggest either that a student should be sheltered from the truth about his academic deficiencies or that instruction cannot take account of varying levels of ability. It is to say that a system that presumes to tell a student what his ability is and what he can successfully learn incurs an obligation to take account of the psychological damage that can come from such an encounter between the student and the school; and to be certain that it is in a position to decide whether the student's deficiencies are true, or only apparent. The District of Columbia school system has not shown that it is in such a position. . . .

BUCK V. *BELL*, SUPERINTENDENT*

U.S. Supreme Court (1927)

MR. JUSTICE HOLMES delivered the opinion of the Court. . . .

. . . Carrie Buck is a feeble minded white woman who was committed to the State Colony . . . in due form. She is the daughter of a feeble-minded mother in the same institution, and the mother of an illegitimate feeble-minded child. She was eighteen years old at the time of the trial of her case in the Circuit Court, in the latter part of 1924. An Act of Virginia, approved March 20, 1924, recites that the health of the patient and the welfare of society may be promoted in certain cases by the sterilization of mental defectives, under the careful safeguard, &c.; that the sterilization may be effected in males by vasectomy and in females by salpingectomy, without serious pain or substantial danger to life; that the Commonwealth is supporting in various institutions many defective persons who if now discharged would become a menace but if incapable of procreating might be discharged with safety and become self-supporting with benefit to themselves and to society; and that experience has shown that heredity plays an important part in the transmis-

*274 U.S. 200

sion of insanity, imbecility, &c. The statute then enacts that whenever the superintendent of certain institutions including the above named State Colony shall be of
opinion that it is for the best interests of the patients and of society that an inmate
under his care should be sexually sterilized, he may have the operation performed
upon any patient afflicted with hereditary forms of insanity, imbecility, &c., on
complying with the very careful provisions by which the act protects the patients
from possible abuse. . . .

    . . . We have seen more than once that the public welfare may call upon the
best citizens for their lives. It would be strange if it could not call upon those who
already sap the strength of the State for these lesser sacrifices, often not felt to be
such by those concerned, in order to prevent our being swamped with incompe-
tence. It is better for all the world, if instead of waiting to execute degenerate
offspring for crime, or to let them strave for their imbecility, society can prevent
those who are manifestly unfit from continuing their kind. . . . Three generations
of imbeciles are enough. . . .

9

BIOLOGY AND ETHICS: OTHER ISSUES

When an ethical issue turns upon some biological or physiological understanding, we may say that the issue is bioethical. This chapter presents a potpourri of such matters.

Tennessee Valley Authority v. *Hill* is the famous snail-darter case, concerning the completion and use of the Tellico Dam on the Little Tennessee River. The standoff is striking. On one side is an enormous structure and project into which tens of millions of dollars have already been sunk. On the other is a small variety of perch. Why in the world should we look after this small, tannish-colored fish?

There is an interesting tension here. Darwin has taught us that there is superfluity in nature, that organisms fall by the wayside in the course of evolutionary history. On this model, the disappearance of a species need not be tragic. Of course, humanity's intervention queers the natural processes he described. Nevertheless, it is difficult to make out a Darwinian argument for the indispensibility of each species.

There does seem to be some sense of natural design at work in the minds of those who framed this law: "We may not know why this organism has been put here, but we're not going to jeopardize its existence. There must be some good reason for its presence, some role it's meant to play."

There is, of course, an empirical argument for caution. Who would have guessed that the plant mentioned in the case would have medical value? We repeatedly find uses for things thought useless.

And we've found nature full of elaborate interlinkage, as in food chains. It's hard to say what diastrous ecological reaction we might set in motion by eliminating some species.

Are we obliged to protect every type of living thing? Should we really waste all that money for the snail darter? Should the protection extend to rats, mosquitoes, flies, and infectious bacteria if they need it? Do the same arguments for the preservation of the snail darter apply to staphylococcus and poison ivy?

Lovato v. *Irvin* concerns moral responsibility. Jamie Lynn Irvin is guilty of "felony assault" on her homosexual companion, Betty Ann Lovato, whom she must compensate for injury. She blames impending menstruation for the attack, and so asks to be relieved of the duty to pay damages.

Irvin's history of violence in all seasons is enough to ruin her case. But might there be other women for which this excuse could fit? Could PMS (premenstrual syndrome) count as "the straw that broke the camel's back" for those whose restraint is tenuous? What other physical conditions might excuse someone from responsibility for wrongful actions?

In Re Kemmler leads us to consider whether execution can be humane.

What exactly happens to the electrocuted prisoner? What is felt? How long is the suffering? How long does life go on? How does the electric chair compare with the firing squad, gas chamber, gallows, or syringe?

Execution technicians feel obliged to take into account several criteria. Minimal suffering is valued, so the guillotine seems good. But we have an aversion to such mutilation, so the search continues elsewhere. The use of lethal drugs is a late arrival. The prisoner is dealt a succession of drugs intravenously. Before the poison comes, there is a sleep inducer. Pain, mutilation, and horror at the moment of death are absent or negligible. Have we gotten it right?

Doctors are squeamish about assisting in this procedure. Should they be any more reluctant than the average citizen to insert the needle in the prisoner's vein? Would they thereby violate some professional principle?

In *Ingraham* v. *Wright*, we view another sort of punishment. The use of the paddle in Miami's Charles R. Drew Jr. High School was alarming. Judge Rives recognizes a place for the corporal punishment of school youth, but he finds the punishment at this school unacceptable. His decision is based in large measure on the medical reports of harm done to the young people.

Setting aside for a moment the haphazard and impulsive way in which the decisions to punish were made, what shall we say about the severity? Is it ever permissible to cause young teenagers this much pain? What level of damage is acceptable? Is a bruise forbidden?

What if the parents do the spanking? When must they stop? Are there different standards for different ages, one for three-year-olds, another for six-year-olds, and so on? When does the punishment of children turn into child abuse? Is permanence of damage the key?

Darrin v. *Gould* is a sex discrimination case. Carol and Delores Darrin were holding their own with the boys in high school football practice. But as the first game neared, they were told they could not play on account of a ruling by the Washington Interscholastic Activities Association. Here they contest the standards and assumptions of the WIAA.

Does biology teach us that there are certain activities women shouldn't attempt? If so, may the state forbid them to do so?

Murgia v. *Commonwealth of Massachusetts Board of Retirement*, an age discrimination case, closes out the chapter. State policeman Robert Murgia objects to his forced retirement at age fifty after twenty years of service. He claims that he is fit for the job and that his retirement is arbitrary. Judge Aldrich agrees since he sees no clear connection between the age of fifty and significant loss of powers. He believes that some age limit might be set, but insists that it must have a rational basis.

He cites the airline pilots' case, with its limit of age sixty. Was that a just ruling? And if fifty is not right for the Massachusetts State Police, what age, if any, is? Should there be different compulsory retirement ages for different professions, one for teachers, another for bus drivers, and yet another for judges? Is the aging process so predictable as to make such generalizations possible and moral?

*TENNESSEE VALLEY AUTHORITY V. HILL**

U.S. Supreme Court (1978)

MR. CHIEF JUSTICE BURGER delivered the opinion of the Court. . . .
The Little Tennessee River originates in the mountains of northern Georgia and flows through the national forest lands of North Carolina into Tennessee, where it converges with the Big Tennessee River near Knoxville. The lower 33 miles of the Little Tennessee takes the river's clear, free-flowing waters through an area of great natural beauty. Among other environmental amenities, this stretch of river is said to contain abundant trout. Considerable historical importance attaches to the areas immediately adjacent to this portion of the Little Tennessee's banks. To the south of the river's edge lies Fort

*437 U.S. 153

Loudon, established in 1756 as England's southwestern outpost in the French and Indian War. Nearby are also the ancient sites of several native American villages, the archeological stores of which are to a large extent unexplored. . . . These include the Cherokee towns of Echota and Tennase, the former being the sacred capital of the Cherokee Nation as early as the 16th century and the latter providing the linguistic basis from which the State of Tennessee derives its name. . . .

In this area of the Little Tennessee River the Tennessee Valley Authority, a wholly owned public corporation of the United States, began constructing the Tellico Dam and Reservoir Project in 1967, shortly after Congress appropriated initial funds for its development. . . . Tellico is a multipurpose regional development project designed principally to stimulate shoreline development, generate sufficient electric current to heat 20,000 homes . . . and provide flatwater recreation and flood control, as well as improve economic conditions in "an area characterized by underutilization of human resources and outmigration of young people." . . . Of particular relevance to this case is one aspect of the project, a dam which TVA determined to place on the Little Tennessee, a short distance from where the river's waters meet with the Big Tennessee. When fully operational, the dam would impound water covering some 16,500 acres—much of which represents valuable and productive farmland—thereby converting the river's shallow, fast-flowing waters into a deep reservoir over 30 miles in length.

The Tellico Dam has never opened, however, despite the fact that construction has been virtually completed and the dam is essentially ready for operation. Although Congress has appropriated monies for Tellico every year since 1967, progress was delayed, and ultimately stopped, by a tangle of lawsuits and administrative proceedings. . . .

. . . Exploring the area around Coytee Springs, which is about seven miles from the mouth of the river, a University of Tennessee ichthyologist, Dr. David A. Etnier, found a previously unknown species of perch, the snail darter, or *Percina (Imostoma) tanasi.* . . . This three-inch, tannish-colored fish, whose numbers are estimated to be in the range of 10,000 to 15,000, would soon engage the attention of environmentalists, the TVA, the Department of the Interior, the Congress of the United States, and ultimately the federal courts, as a new and additional basis to halt construction of the dam.

Until recently the finding of a new species of animal life would hardly generate a cause célèbre. This is particularly so in the case of darters, of which there are approximately 130 known species, 8 to 10 of these having been identified only in the last five years.[1] The moving force behind the snail darter's sudden fame came some four months after its discovery, when the Congress passed the Endan-

---

[1]In Tennessee alone there are 85 to 90 species of darters, . . . of which upward to 45 live in the Tennessee River system. . . . New species of darters are being constantly discovered and classified—at

gered Species Act of 1973. . . . This legislation, among other things, authorizes the Secretary of the Interior to declare species of animal life "endangered"[2] and to identify the "critical habitat"[3] of these creatures. When a species or its habitat is so listed, the following portion of the Act—relevant here—becomes effective:

> The Secretary [of the Interior] shall review other programs administered by him and utilize such programs in futherance of the purposes of this chapter. All other Federal departments and agencies shall, in consultation with and with the assistance of the Secretary, utilize their authorities in furtherance of the purposes of this chapter by carrying out programs for the conservation of endangered species and threatened species listed pursuant to section 1533 of this title and *by taking such action necessary to insure that actions authorized, funded, or carried out by them do not jeopardize the continued existence of such endangered species and threatened species or result in the destruction or modification of habitat of such species* which is determined by the Secretary, after consultation as appropriate with the affected States, to be critical. . . .

. . . After receiving comments from various interested parties, including TVA and the State of Tennessee, the Secretary formally listed the snail darter as an endangered species on October 8, 1975. . . . In so acting, it was noted that "the snail darter is a living entity which is genetically distinct and reproductively isolated from other fishes." . . . More important for the purposes of this case, the Secretary determined that the snail darter apparently lives only in that portion of the Little Tennessee River which would be completely inundated by the reservoir created as a consequence of the Tellico Dam's completion.[4] . . . The

---

the rate of about one per year. . . . This is a difficult task for even trained ichthyologists since species of darters are often hard to differentiate from one another. . . .

[2]An "endangered species" is defined by the Act to mean "any species which is in danger of extinction throughout all or a significant portion of its range other than a species of the Class Insecta determined by the Secretary to constitute a pest whose protection under the provisions of this chapter would present an overwhelming and overriding risk to man." . . .

" 'The act covers every animal and plant species, subspecies, and population in the world needing protection. There are approximately 1.4 million full species of animals and 600,000 full species of plants in the world. Various authorities calculate as many as 10% of them—some 200,000—may need to be listed as Endangered or Threatened. When one counts in subspecies, not to mention individual populations, the total could increase to three to five times that number.' " Keith Shreiner, Associate Director and Endangered Species Program Manager of the U. S. Fish and Wildlife Service. . . .

[3]The Act does not define "critical habitat," but the Secretary of the Interior has administratively construed the term:

> " 'Critical habitat' means any air, land, or water area (exclusive of those existing man-made structures or settlements which are not necessary to the survival and recovery of a listed species) and constituent elements thereof, the loss of which would appreciably decrease the likelihood of the survival and recovery of a listed species or a distinct segment of its population. The constituent elements of critical habitat include, but are not limited to: physical structures and topography, biota, climate, human activity, and the quality and chemical content of land, water, and air. Critical habitat may represent any portion of the present habitat of a listed species and may include additional areas for reasonable population expansion."

[4]Searches by TVA in more than 60 watercourses have failed to find other populations of snail darters. . . . The Secretary has noted that "more than 1,000 collections in recent years and addi-

Secretary went on to explain the significance of the dam to the habitat of the snail darter:

[T]he snail darter occurs only in the swifter portions of shoals over clean gravel substrate in cool, low-turbidity water. Food of the snail darter is almost exclusively snails which require a clean gravel substrate for their survival. *The proposed impoundment of water behind the proposed Tellico Dam would result in total destruction of the snail darter's habitat....* (emphasis added).

Subsequent to this determination, the Secretary declared the area of the Little Tennessee which would be affected by the Tellico Dam to be the "critical habitat" of the snail darter.

. . . Using these determinations as a predicate, and notwithstanding the near completion of the dam, the Secretary declared that . . . "all Federal agencies must take such action as is necessary to insure that actions authorized, funded, or carried out by them do not result in the destruction or modification of this critical habitat area." . . . This notice, of course, was pointedly directed at TVA and clearly aimed at halting completion or operation of the dam.

During the pendency of these administrative actions, other developments of relevance to the snail darter issue were transpiring. Communication was occurring between the Department of the Interior's Fish and Wildlife Service and TVA with a view toward settling the issue informally. These negotiations were to no avail, however, since TVA consistently took the position that the only available alternative was to attempt relocating the snail darter population to another suitable location. To this end, TVA conducted a search of alternative sites which might sustain the fish, culminating in the experimental transplantation of a number of snail darters to the nearby Hiwassee River. However, Secretary of the Interior was not satisfied with the results of these efforts, finding that TVA had presented "little evidence that they have carefully studied the Hiwassee to determine whether or not" there were "biological and other factors in this river that [would] negate a successful transplant."[5] . . .

. . . the House Committee on Appropriations, in its June 20, 1975, Report, stated the following in the course of recommending that an additional $29 million be appropriated for Tellico:

tional earlier collections from central and east Tennessee have not revealed the presence of the snail darter outside the Little Tennessee River." . . . It is estimated, however, that the snail darter's range once extended throughout the upper main Tennessee River and the lower portions of its major tributaries above Chattanooga—all of which are now the sites of dam impoundments. . . .

[5]The Fish and Wildlife Service and Dr. Etnier have stated that it may take from 5 to 15 years for scientists to determine whether the snail darter can successfully survive and reproduce in this new environment. . . . In expressing doubt over the long-term future of the Hiwassee transplant, the Secretary noted: "That the snail darter does not already inhabit the Hiwassee River, despite the fact that the fish has had access to it in the past, is a strong indication that there may be biological and other factors in this river that negate a successful transplant."

'The *Committee* directs that the project, for which an environmental impact statement has been completed and provided the Committee, should be completed as promptly as possible. . . .'

Congress then approved the TVA general budget, which contained funds for continued construction of the Tellico Project. . . . In December 1975, one month after the snail darter was declared an endangered species, the President signed the bill into law. . . . In February 1976, pursuant to . . . the Endangered Species Act, . . . respondents filed the case now under review, seeking to enjoin completion of the dam and impoundment of the reservoir on the ground that those actions would violate the Act by directly causing the extinction of the species *Percina (Imostoma) tanasi.* The District Court denied respondents' request for a preliminary injunction and set the matter for trial. Shortly thereafter the House and Senate held appropriations hearings which would include discussions of the Tellico budget. . . .

At these hearings, TVA Chairman Wagner reiterated the agency's position that the Act did not apply to a project which was over 50% finished by the time the Act became effective and some 70% to 80% complete when the snail darter was officially listed as endangered. It also notified the Committees of the recently filed lawsuit's status and reported that TVA's efforts to transplant the snail darter had "been very encouraging." . . .

. . . The District Court found that closure of the dam and the consequent impoundment of the reservoir would "result in the adverse modification, if not complete destruction, of the snail darter's critical habitat,"[6] making it "highly probable" that "the continued existence of the snail darter" would be "jeopardize[d]." . . . Despite these findings, the District Court declined to embrace the plaintiffs' position. . . .

In reaching this result, the District Court stressed that the entire project was then about 80% complete and, based on available evidence, "there [were] no alternatives to impoundment of the reservoir, short of scrapping the entire project." . . . The District Court also found that if the Tellico Project was permanently enjoined, "some $53 million would be lost in nonrecoverable obligations," . . . meaning that a large portion of the $78 million already expended would be

[6]The District Court made the following findings with respect to the dam's effect on the ecology of the snail darter:

"The evidence introduced at trial showed that the snail darter requires for its survival a clear, gravel substrate, in a large-to-medium, flowing river. The snail darter has a fairly high requirement for oxygen and since it tends to exist in the bottom of the river, the flowing water provides the necessary oxygen at greater depths. Reservoirs, unlike flowing rivers, tend to have a low oxygen content at greater depths.

"Reservoirs also tend to have more silt on the bottom than flowing rivers, and this factor, combined with the lower oxygen content, would make it highly probable that snail darter eggs would smother in such an environment. Furthermore, the adult snail darters would probably find this type of reservoir environment unsuitable for spawning.

"Another factor that would tend to make a reservoir habitat unsuitable for snail darters is that their primary source of food, snails, probably would not survive in such an environment."

wasted. The court also noted that the Endangered Species Act of 1973 was passed some seven years after construction on the dam commenced and that Congress had continued appropriations for Tellico, with full awareness of the snail darter problem. Assessing these various factors, the District Court concluded:

> At some point in time a federal project becomes so near completion and so incapable of modification that a court of equity should not apply a statute enacted long after inception of the project to produce an unreasonable result. . . . Where there has been an irreversible and irretrievable commitment of resources by Congress to a project over a span of almost a decade, the Court should proceed with a great deal of circumspection.

To accept the plaintiff's position, the District Court argued, would inexorably lead to what is characterized as the absurd result of requiring "a court to halt impoundment of water behind a fully completed dam if an endangered species were discovered in the river on the day before such impoundment was scheduled to take place. We cannot conceive that Congress intended such a result." . . . On June 29, 1976, both Houses of Congress passed TVA's general budget, which included funds for Tellico; the President signed the bill on July 12, 1976. . . .

Thereafter, in the Court of Appeals, respondents argued that the District Court had abused its discretion by not issuing an injunction in the face of "a blatant statutory violation." . . . The Court of Appeals agreed, and on January 31, 1977, it reversed, remanding "with instructions that a permanent injunction issue halting all activities incident to the Tellico Project which may destroy or modify the critical habitat of the snail darter." . . . The Court of Appeals directed that the injunction "remain in effect until Congress, by appropriate legislation, exempts Tellico from compliance with the Act or the snail darter has been deleted from the list of endangered species or its critical habitat materially redefined." . . .

. . . the court stated:

> Current project status cannot be translated into a workable standard of judicial review. Whether a dam is 50% or 90% completed is irrelevant in calculating the social and scientific costs attributable to the disappearance of a unique form of life. Courts are ill-equipped to calculate how many dollars must be invested before the value of a dam exceeds that of the endangered species. Our responsibility . . . is merely to preserve the status quo where endangered species are threatened, thereby guaranteeing the legislative or executive branches sufficient opportunity to grapple with the alternatives. . . .

. . . While recognizing the irretrievable loss of millions of dollars of public funds which would accompany injunctive relief, the court nonetheless decided that the Act explicitly commanded precisely that result:

> It is conceivable that the welfare of an endangered species may weigh more heavily upon the public conscience, as expressed by the final will of Congress, than the writeoff of those millions of dollars already expended for Tellico in excess of its present salvageable value. . . .

As a solution to the problem, the House Committee advised that TVA should cooperate with the Department of the Interior "to relocate the endangered species to another suitable habitat so as to permit the project to proceed as rapidly as possible." . . . Toward this end, the Committee recommended a special appropriation of $2 million to facilitate relocation of the snail darter and other endangered species which threatened to delay or stop TVA projects. Much the same occurred on the Senate side, with its Appropriations Committee recommending both the amount requested to complete Tellico and the special appropriation for transplantation of endangered species. . . .

TVA's budget, including funds for completion of Tellico and relocation of the snail darter, passed both Houses of Congress and was signed into law on August 7, 1977. . . .

It may seem curious to some that the survival of a relatively small number of three-inch fish among all the countless millions of species extant would require the permanent halting of a virtually completed dam for which Congress has expended more than $100 million. The paradox is not minimized by the fact that Congress continued to appropriate large sums of public money for the project, even after congressional Appropriations Committees were apprised of its apparent impact upon the survival of the snail darter. We conclude, however, that the explicit provisions of the Endangered Species Act require precisely that result.

One would be hard pressed to find a statutory provision whose terms were any plainer than those in . . . the Endangered Species Act. Its very words, affirmatively command all federal agencies "to *insure* that actions *authorized, funded,* or *carried out* by them do not *jeopardize* the continued existence" of an endangered species or "*result*" in the destruction or modification of habitat of such species. . . ." . . . . (Emphasis added.) This language admits of no exception. Nonetheless, petitioner urges, as do the dissenters, that the Act cannot reasonably be interpreted as applying to a federal project which was well under way when Congress passed the Endangered Species Act of 1973. To sustain that position, however, we would be forced to ignore the ordinary meaning of plain language. It has not been shown, for example, how TVA can close the gates of the Tellico Dam without "carrying out" an action that has been "authorized" and "funded" by a federal agency. Nor can we understand how such action will "*insure*" that the snail darter's habitat is not disrupted. . . . Accepting the Secretary's determinations, as we must, it is clear that TVA's proposed operation of the dam will have precisely the opposite effect, namely the *eradication* of an endangered species.

Concededly, this view of the Act will produce results requiring the sacrifice of the anticipated benefits of the project and of many millions of dollars in public funds.[7] But examination of the language, history, and structure of the legislation

---

[7]The District Court determined that failure to complete the Tellico Dam would result in the loss of some $53 million in nonrecovrable obligations. . . . Respondents dispute this figure, and point to a recent study by the General Accounting Office, which suggests that the figure could be considerably less. . . . The GAO study also concludes that TVA and Congress should explore alternatives to

under review here indicates beyond doubt that Congress intended endangered species to be afforded the highest of priorities. . . .

The legislative proceedings in 1973 are . . . replete with expressions of concern over the risk that might lie in the loss of *any* endangered species.[8] Typifying these sentiments is the Report of the House Committee on Merchant Marine and Fisheries on H. R. 37, a bill which contained the essential features of the subsequently enacted Act of 1973; in explaining the need for the legislation, the Report stated:

> As we homogenize the habitats in which these plants and animals evolved, and as we increase the pressure for products that they are in a position to supply (usually unwillingly) we threaten their—and our own—genetic heritage.
>
> *The value of this genetic heritage is, quite literally, incalculable. . . .*
>
> From the most narrow possible point of view, *it is in the best interests of mankind to minimize the losses of genetic variations.* The reason is simple: they are potential resources. They are keys to puzzles which we cannot solve, and may provide answers to questions which we have not yet learned to ask.
>
> To take a homely, but apt, example: one of the critical chemicals in the regulation of ovulations in humans was found in a common plant. Once discovered, and analyzed, humans could duplicate it synthetically, but had it never existed—or had it been driven out of existence before we knew its potentialities—we would never have tried to synthesize it in the first place. ·
>
> Who knows, or can say, what potential cures for cancer or other scourges, present or future, may lie locked up in the structures of plants which may yet be undiscovered, much less analyzed? . . . Sheer self-interest impels us to be cautious.
>
> *The institutionalization of that caution* lies at the heart of H. R. 37. . . .
>
> (Emphasis added.)

As the examples cited here demonstrate, Congress was concerned about the *unknown* uses that endangered species might have and about the *unforeseeable* place such creatures may have in the chain of life on this planet.

In shaping legislation to deal with the problem thus presented, Congress started from the finding that "[t]he two major causes of extinction are hunting and

impoundment of the reservoir, such as the creation of a regional development program based on a free-flowing river. None of these considerations are relevant to our decision, however; they are properly addressed to the Executive and Congress.

[8] . . . One statement, made by the Assistant Secretary of the Interior, particularly deserves notice:

"I have watched in my lifetime a vast array of mollusks in southern streams totally disappear as a result of damming, channelization, and pollution. It is often asked of me, 'what is the importance of the mollusks for example in Alabama.' I do not know, and I do not know whether any of us will ever have the insight to know exactly why these mollusks evolved over millions of years or what their importance is in the total ecosystem. However, I have great trouble being party to their destruction without ever having gained such knowledge." . . . . One member of the mollusk family existing in these southern rivers is the snail, . . . which ironically enough provides the principal food for snail darters.

destruction of natural habitat." . . . . Of these twin threats, Congress was informed that the greatest was destruction of natural habitats. . . .

. . . we are urged to view the Endangered Species Act "reasonably," and hence shape a remedy "that accords with some modicum of common sense and the public weal." . . . But is that our function? We have no expert knowledge on the subject of endangered species, much less do we have a mandate from the people to strike a balance of equities on the side of the Tellico Dam. Congress has spoken in the plainest of words, making it abundantly clear that the balance has been struck in favor of affording endangered species the highest of priorities, thereby adopting a policy which it described as "institutionalized caution."

Our individual appraisal of the wisdom or unwisdom of a particular course consciously selected by the Congress is to be put aside in the process of interpreting a statute. Once the meaning of an enactment is discerned and its constitutionality determined, the judicial process comes to an end. We do not sit as a committee of review, nor are we vested with the power of veto. The lines ascribed to Sir Thomas More by Robert Bolt are not without relevance here:

> "The law, Roper, the law. I know what's legal, not what's right. And I'll stick to what's legal. . . . I'm *not* God. The currents and eddies of right and wrong, which you find such plain-sailing, I can't navigate, I'm no voyager. But in the thickets of the law, oh there I'm a forester. . . . What would you do? Cut a great road through the law to get after the Devil? . . . And when the last law was down, and the Devil turned round on you—where would you hide, Roper, the laws all being flat? . . . This country's planted thick with laws from coast to coast—Man's laws, not God's—and if you cut them down . . . d'you really think you could stand upright in the winds that would blow them? . . . Yes, I'd give the Devil benefit of law, for my own safety's sake." R. Bolt, *A Man for All Seasons*, Act. I. . . .

We agree with the Court of Appeals that in our constitutional system the commitment to the separation of powers is too fundamental for us to pre-empt congressional action by judicially decreeing what accords with "common sense and the public weal." Our Constitution vests such responsibilities in the political branches. . . .

LOVATO V. *IRVIN**

U.S. District Court for the District of Colorado in Bankruptcy (1983)

By the Court: JAY L. GUECK, Judge. . . .

Plaintiff (hereinafter referred to as Lovato) and debtor-defendant (hereinafter referred to as Irvin) first met in 1977. They began living together in late 1977 for a period of several months. The relationship was a tempestuous one from the beginning, primarily centered around Irvin's jealousy over prior relationships of Lovato. There were at least three occasions into 1978 when Irvin threatened Lovato at knife point. Irvin testified that on those occasions that she was "irrational" and "out of control." This resulted in a brief termination of the relationship, but in the fall of 1978, the parties reconciled and traveled together in October to Pennsylvania. Shortly after their return to Colorado, Irvin became upset at the prospect of Lovato packing to move away again and kept Lovato at the premises at knife point. However, Lovato left while Irvin was taking a shower.

Later, in approximately January or February, 1979, Irvin broke into the home where Lovato was then living and hid under Lovato's bed with a tomahawk, a knife and other paraphernalia, waiting for Lovato to retire. After Lovato was asleep, Irvin attacked her with the knife and tomahawk actually cutting Lovato's hand. Nonetheless, Lovato moved back into residence with Irvin in March, 1979.

During the course of this relationship there were numerous other incidents of violence, threats of suicide as well as threats by Irvin to kill Lovato and actual overt acts and emotional outbursts on the part of Irvin. During this same period, Irvin admitted to Lovato that she had similarly attacked women from prior relationships, even to the extent of traveling to Germany where she attacked a former friend nearly severing that individual's arm. In short, the evidence indicates a long history of episodic violence leading to the incident in question.

The matter which gives rise to the controversy in this action occurred on April 27, 1979. The relationship between Lovato and Irvin had been understandably tense, and they were jointly seeking counselling. On that date, they jointly consulted with Dr. Dorothy LaFleur, a clinical psychologist. Dr. LaFleur had been treating Irvin since January, 1979. Together, Dr. LaFleur and Irvin had explored Irvin's history of violence and depression at the thought of abandonment. It had been discovered that much of the violence had been tied to Irvin's menstrual periods. Dr. LaFleur and Lovato both testifed that on the occasion of this joint consultation, April 27, 1979, Irvin's appearance was markedly different. She was quite distressed, appeared "irrational" and seemed quite anxious and depressed. She noted that she had just started menstruating. The parties had engaged in conversation earlier that day wherein Lovato had expressed a desire to join the National Guard, which Irvin interpreted as some

*Adversary Case No. 82M933

indication that Lovato might be leaving the area and "abandoning" Irvin once again.

On April 27, 1979, Dr. LaFleur suggested during the counselling session that the parties should remain separated from one another during the weekend. Irvin became very upset over this. Following the session, Irvin followed Lovato outside and insisted they continue their discussion in private. Lovato declined. Irvin then followed Lovato in her automobile and, after a bizarre auto chase, she forced the Lovato automobile over and then forced her way into the Lovato vehicle. Thereafter, Betty Lovato got out of her automobile and tried to run. Irvin followed her, caught up with her and began stabbing her in the back and across the chest with a steak knife. Lovato then incurred a severe laceration to her hands when she tried to grab the knife to protect herself. Lovato escaped and ran, with Irvin again in pursuit. When Irvin again caught Lovato, Irvin said she would take Lovato to the hospital. They got into the Lovato vehicle with Lovato bleeding profusely, feeling faint, and her clothes soaked with blood. Instead of driving to the hospital, Irvin drove past St. Anthony's Hospital and proceeded toward Louisville, Colorado, then drove past Rocky Flats, through a mountain canyon, to a motel. During this time, Lovato continued to plead to go to the hospital, while Irvin occupied herself in discussion about their relationship, past relationships, and her fears that Lovato would reveal to the authorities the attack that had just occurred.

After checking into a motel, Irvin assisted Lovato in washing her wounds in a tub of water and washed some of Lovato's clothes. They remained at the motel while Irvin continued to involve Lovato in further discussions about their relationship. During this time Lovato's hand would not stop bleeding and she testified that they could see "bone and ligaments." Finally, Irvin conceded that they needed to get to a hospital. However, even after they left the motel to take Lovato to the hospital, Irvin continued to wander around, finally driving to a sand pit while she made up a story for Lovato to tell to the hospital Personnel in an effort to avoid implicating Irvin in any assault. It was only after Lovato agreed not to reveal the truth about what had happened that Irvin finally took her to Denver General Hospital. This was approximately 1:30 A.M., over five or six hours after the incident. Upon entering the hospital, Lovato immediately sought protection and revealed what had happened. Irvin was then arrested and subsequently charged with aggravated assault. The criminal matter was resolved by virtue of the entry of a guilty plea to attempted felony assault. It is noted that one of the elements of felony assault is the intent to do bodily harm.

Important to the resolution of the issues herein is the fact that prior to and in preparation for the consulting session with Dr. LaFleur, Irvin took the knife from her kitchen drawer, concealed it in her sock and took it to the counselling session. This is the steak knife which was used during the course of the assault.

In addition to criminal charges, Lovato commenced a civil suit against Irvin in the Denver District Court, seeking compensation for her injuries. This matter was resolved by a stipulated settlement in the amount of $5,200.00. Shortly there-after, Irvin filed the Petition in Bankruptcy, wherein she seeks a discharge of all of her debts, including the Lovato judgment. . . .

. . . Irvin contends that her conduct was not willful and malicious, but was the result of uncontrollable conduct on her part, in that she was suffering from "premenstrual syndrome," (also referred to as "PMS").

Irvin testified that she had begun menstruating on April 27, 1979, that she was suffering from cramps and pain, was confused and frightened, that she couldn't think, and that as the events unfolded it was as if "someone else took over" her body. She stated that during the attack it was as if she were "outside of my body watching a dark-complected woman doing the stabbing." Irvin does not resemble this description and contends this conduct was the product of some irrational, uncontrollable behavior. Irvin indicates that within moments she returned to a rational state, but that she was still scared. She explains that she did not immediately proceed to the hospital because from her observations of Lovato's condition, it did not appear Lovato required immediate attention. Irvin bases this upon her medical experience as a veterinary technician. She attributes all of her bizarre conduct during the period surrounding April 27, 1979, to suffering from premenstrual syndrome.

Irvin explains she discovered as early as 1973 while serving in the Army, that some violent behavior appeared to be associated with her menstrual cycles. It is her contention that up to two weeks prior to her menstrual period she would show symptoms of depression and violence, often with an inability to control her conduct. However, she did not realize she suffered any dysfunction, but did explain this problem to therapists and psychiatrists when admitted to the VA hospital in Pittsburgh in approximately 1975. She was given prescriptions for valium, but little else was accomplished by way of therapy. Irvin testified she continued to seek therapy after leaving military service, and that she explained to various therapists and physicians that there seemed to be a correlation between her violent behavior and her menstrual problems. However, she indicates nothing was done by way of treatment until she sought the assistance of Dr. David Muller in the fall of 1979, after the incident in question. Dr. Muller referred her to Dr. John Farinholt, an OB-GYN. Treatment was initiated through progesterone injections. Finally, after suffering deleterious side effects from this treatment, a hysterectomy was performed in September, 1982. The testimony indicates that Irvin has suffered no further emotional difficulties since that surgery.

The record reflects numerous incidents of violence, apparently not associated with any menstrual cycle at all. One witness, who had been a roommate of Irvin's for one and one-half to two years, from 1976 through 1978, testified to several such occurrences. On one occasion, Irvin attacked this woman, breaking her jaw and loosening teeth. On another occasion, while Irvin was employed as a veterinary technician, Irvin attacked and overpowered this same witness, placed a tourniquet on her arm and threatened to inject her with euthanasia drugs. The witness succeeded in talking Irvin out of proceeding with this threat and actually continued to live with Irvin thereafter. Additionally, this same person was slammed against the wall by Irvin when Irvin exhibited a fit of anger after taking an overdose of drugs. On another occasion, Irvin was arrested for resistance. There were numerous incidents with knives, even to the extent of cutting the chest of this roommate after Irvin had forced her onto the bed. Another occurrence was noted when Irvin hid a knife under the seat of the automobile and used it in one of her threatening episodes. There were high-speed automobile incidents, wherein Irvin threatened to drive off the road or into a tree, killing herself and the occupant. This particular roommate testified that there were 20 to 25 events of various threats, occurring 3 or 4 times a week. There was no indication that these were in any way correlated with any cycle. Indeed, the testimony of this witness was that there were "no peak times, even with major incidents." Irvin did not refute this testimony.

It is also noted that this roommate indicated Irvin had stated she could control her actions "if she wanted to," and that she only acted-out when members of the public were not present.

Another roommate who had lived with Ms. Irvin for over one and one-half years, from early 1973 through mid-1974, indicated she knew by Irvin's comments as well as her own observations when Irvin was menstruating. This individual was the subject of the knife attack which nearly severed her arm, resulting in the loss of 50% of the use of her right arm. There were other episodes of jealous rages wherein knives were brandished amid accusations of "affairs." This individual indicated that in over one and one-half years, Irvin must have "pulled a knife a 100 times." She also stated that Irvin threatened or attacked her at least once a week over this period of time. On one occasion, Irvin held a shotgun to this roommate's head for approximately two hours in an effort to extract admissions of infidelity or intended abandonment. On another occasion, Irvin allegedly struck this lady in the eye, fracturing her eye orbit. Irvin also broke this witness' collar bone in a separate incident and bruised her ribs when she hit the woman with a fist, knocking her against the wall.

Finally, Irvin intentionally ruined this witness' military career by angrily revealing their homosexual relationship, knowing the Army would dismiss this individual from the military service. Irvin stated on numerous occasions, according to the testimony, that she could avoid responsibility for her actions by "telling the shrinks what they want to hear" and that she could "fake the shrinks out." There was no apparent correlation of these incidents with any menstrual cycle. In fact, on Irvin's second trip to Germany which resulted in disabling this woman's arm, there was a great deal of evidence of deliberation and planning. During this time, according to the testimony, the former roommate was experiencing her own menstrual period and recalled Irvin stating she had already had hers. This witness also indicated that during this period of one and one-half years, Irvin never stated to her that she felt any connection between psychological problems, violence and her menstrual period, although Irvin had testified she observed this as early as 1973.

One may well wonder why these witnesses continued to come back for more and persisted in their relationship with Irvin. However, this is a separate psychological phenomenon which need not be addressed in this opinion. Suffice it to say, the evidence seemed straightforward and overwhelming and generally not contradicted by Ms. Irvin. Indeed, most of the conduct was admitted by Irvin and was even the subject of some of her own testimony. . . .

The debtor contends that her actions were not deliberate or intentional and, thus, not "willful" because she was allegedly suffering from premenstrual syndrome. She argues that she was unable to exercise her will, and that she was not able to formulate any intent. As she testified, it was as if "someone else took over" her body. She would have the Court believe she was totally out of control as a result of her confusion, anxiety and hysteria. However, this is simply not borne out by the weight of the evidence.

The evidence indicated numerous other acts of violence disassociated from any cycle. The action in this case, as well as many prior acts, was planned and deliberated before it was committed. The knife used against the plaintiff was purposefully concealed in Irvin's sock and taken to the counselling session. There was testimony that Irvin was manipulative and had the ability to control herself even under stressful situations when in public. She also claimed the self-professed ability of using psychiatry to excuse her conduct. This individual demonstrated a long history of a generally violent nature regardless of any menstrual cycle. She tended to blame others for her conduct. It is sometimes difficult to tell when Irvin's acts are the result of impetuous anger or the result of planned jealous revenge. The act in this case has elements of planning and deliberation, both before and after the stabbing. Finally, perhaps the most dispositive evidence is the lack of credible medical opinion stating that, to a reasonable degree of medical certainty, Irvin's acts were the product of her impaired ability resulting from premenstrual syndrome.

Dr. LaFleur testified that the theory of PMS is very new in the medical profession, it is highly controversial and there is little literature on the subject. Dr. Muller, the psychiatrist, admitted that the DSM III, relied upon by psychiatrists in the diagnosis of psychiatric disorders, doesn't even recognize PMS as a mental problem. He also pointed out that the psychiatric profession is still in disagreement regarding many aspects of PMS. Based upon a rather sketchy history of Irvin, Dr. Muller could only state that Irvin suffered an impaired ability, to the extent of about 25 to 30% of normal, to think out and form logical decisions. He did not state that her conduct was the probable result of premenstrual syndrome. He did not state that Irvin was unable to control her actions on the occasion in question.

Dr. Farinholt, the OB-GYN, felt that "almost every lady who menstruates," suffers to one degree or another from premenstrual syndrome. However, except in the rarest cases, it is not disabling. No expert in this trial opined that PMS is an excuse for violence.

The scientific evidence relating to PMS and its application here is too sketchy, inconclusive, and unreliable to be accepted as an explanation for otherwise willful and malicious conduct. Application of premenstrual syndrome as a defense would require two things. First, the premise upon which any such scientific theory is based must have achieved general acceptance in the medical community; and secondly, there must be evidence that, to a reasonable degree of medical certainty, the conduct was proximately caused by this medical disorder.

In *U.S.* v. *Brown* . . . the court was called upon to decide if ion microprobic analysis (hair comparison) should be accepted as a valid scientific theory. In rejecting testimony relating to that theory, the court stated as follows:

> A necessary predicate to the admission of scientific evidence is that the principle upon which it is based "must be sufficiently established to have gained general acceptance in the particular field to which it belongs." . . .

The court then equated general acceptance in the scientific community with a showing that scientific principles and the procedures upon which expert testimony was based is reliable and sufficiently accurate, without requiring absolute certainty. The court declined to accept the testimony, noting that research had failed to disclose a single reported case where such testimony had been held to be admissible, and the parties could provide no cases, reported or unreported, where the court had admitted evidence based on ion microprobic analysis. There was nothing in the record which indicated the analysis may achieve a reliable and meaningful result and there was no published scientific authority advocating the merits of the theory. In conclusion, the *Brown* . . . court stated: "While it is a truism that every useful new development must have its first day in court, . . . expert testimony on a critical fact relating to guilt or innocence is not admissible unless the principle upon which it is based has attained general acceptance in the scientific community and is not mere speculation or conjecture." . . .

No evidence was presented to indicate that the theory of premenstrual syndrome has ever been admitted as a defense to criminal conduct or an intentional tort in a United States Court before. It has never been accepted as a mitigating factor in a reported criminal case in this country.

None of the witnesses in this action offered much in support of or in opposition to any of the available literature or current research on PMS. Thus, the record is devoid of authority in this regard. However, defendant has submitted a brief containing citations to much of the research, and has provided the Court with a bibliography of current material on the subject of PMS and its affect on female behavior. . . . This was received over the plaintiff's objection. These authorities confirm that the subject is still controversial and not yet developed to the point where the information is considered reliable enough to be generally accepted in the psychiatric profession.

The medical profession apparently first began to recognize premenstrual syndrome as a specific psycho-physiological disorder in about 1953. Suarez Murias, *The Psychophysiologic Syndrome of Premenstrual Tension With Emphasis On The*

Psychiatric Aspect. . . . It has been found that the physical symptoms of PMS may cause psychological symptoms resulting in obvious personality alterations, such as recurrent frenzy, catatonic-like depression, schizophrenia, hallucinations and epileptiform seizures. Wallach & Rubin, *Premenstrual Syndrome and Criminal Responsibility.* . . . See, also, *Once A Month*, by Katharina Dalton. . . .

Dr. Katharina Dalton, of the premenstrual clinic, University College Hospital in London, England, is a frequently cited authority in the diagnosis and treatment of premenstrual syndrome. Dalton's books and articles have included considerable discussion about the relationship between PMS and criminal responsibility in women. . . . In her book, *Once A Month*, . . . she states, at page 12: " 'The Premenstrual Syndrome' is used to embrace any symptoms or complaints which regularly come just before or during menstruation but are absent at other times of the cycle." The evidence in this action indicates many incidents of violence occurring at various irregular times in the cycle, apparently having nothing to do with menstruation.

Another authority cited by the defendant is Ried and Yen, *Premenstrual Syndrome*, 139 *Am. Journal of Obstetrics & Gynecology*, 85 (1981). This article specifically notes that "although the pathogenesis of this disorder remains speculative, the weight of evidence supports the premise that PMS is related to an aberration in the cyclic function of the hypothalmic pituitary-ovarian axis." Thus, although it is recognized that there is much evidence to connect PMS to aberrant conduct, its pathogenic analysis remains speculative.

Given the present knowledge of PMS, it is not surprising that it has not yet been accepted in the U.S. as a defense to criminal conduct or intentional torts. However, Dr. Dalton's testimony in two criminal trials in England did result in reduced sentences for two women defendants, who were PMS sufferers, convicted of assault and homicide. . . . It is important to note that PMS was accepted in mitigation of punishment, not in defense of the substantive crime.

An article appearing in the Journal of the American Medical Association, entitled *Premenstrual Syndrome: An Ancient Woe Deserving of Modern Scrutiny*, . . . by Elizabeth Rasche Gonzalez, cites to the work of Katharina Dalton, and states: "Another reason Dalton's work has been ignored or discounted is that it has never been subjected to controlled studies. She herself has not conducted such studies, and other investigators have not shown interest in doing so."

This article then notes that even Dalton cautions that there may be many misdiagnoses of PMS. "It is clear that many scientific questions remain regarding PMS." *Premenstrual Syndrome: An Ancient Woe Deserving of Modern Scrutiny.* . . .

The evidence and testimony in the instant case establishes that the conduct of the debtor-defendant, Jamie Irvin, was willful and malicious. There is insufficient evidence presented in the within action to establish that premenstrual syndrome is sufficiently defined and accepted in the medical community to be an acceptable defense. Further, this debtor's history of violent conduct is not fully explained by premenstrual syndrome and there was no competent evidence to establish that her conduct on the occasion in question was proximately caused by this disorder.

There may well be a circumstance in the future where sufficient expertise and background establishes premenstrual syndrome as a legitimate defense to criminal or tortious conduct committed by an unfortunate sufferer from this medical difficulty. However, this is not that circumstance. . . .

> *Based upon the foregoing analysis and the testimony and evidence in the within action, it is my determination that the plaintiff has established by clear and convincing evidence that the judgment obtained by the plaintiff against the debtor-defendant in the State Court in the amount of $5,200.00, together with interest at the legal rate thereon, is non-dischargeable. . . .*

IN RE KEMMLER*

Cayuga County (N.Y.) Court (1889)

DAY, J. At a court . . . held at Buffalo, N.Y., on the 10th day of May, 1889, in a criminal action wherein the people of the state of New York were plaintiffs, and William Kemmler, otherwise called John Hort, was defendant, he was convicted of murder in the first degree, in that, on or about March 29th of that year, in that city, he killed Matilda Ziegler, *alias* Matilda Hort, from a deliberate and premeditated design to effect her death, and on the 14th day of May aforesaid he was, for his crime, sentenced by said court to suffer death, to be inflicted by the application of electricity, in the Auburn state-prison, or in the yard or inclosure thereto adjoining, on some day in the week commencing June 4, 1889. . . .

. . . the defendant, by his counsel, offered to prove "that the infliction of the death penalty named in the sentence, that is to say, the passing of an electrical current through the body of the said William Kemmler, is a cruel and unusual punishment within the meaning of the constitution, and that it cannot, therefore, be lawfully inflicted. . . .

. . . our own state fundamental law is so benignant that not even he who cruelly murders can be cruelly punished. Section 505 of the Code of Criminal Procedure, in force prior to the enactment of 1888, provided that the punishment of death should in every case be inflicted by hanging the convict by the neck until dead. . . .

. . . that section of the Code of Criminal Procedure was amended so as to read as follows: "The punishment of death must, in every case, be inflicted by causing to pass through the body of the convict a current of electricity of sufficient intensity to cause death; and the application of such current must be continued until such convict is dead." And it is this attempted change in the mode of

*7 N.Y.S. 145

inflicting the death penalty as punishment for crime that provokes the present controversy, and it is in these circumstances that I am asked to discharge the prisoner from his present detention; it being contended in his behalf that the legislative enactment under consideration provides punishment both cruel and unusual, the infliction whereof may well result in subjecting its unfortunate victim to the most extreme and protracted vigor and subtility of cruelty and torture; while, on the other hand, it is insisted that the act is one promotive of reform, a step forward and in keeping with the scientific progress of the age; that the application of electricity as proposed will result in the immediate and painless death of the culprit, so that the unsightly and horrifying spectacles which now not infrequently attend executions by hanging will effectually be prevented; that the question is not whether any particular engine provided or to be provided for use in the attempted enforcement of the law will prove successful in operation, whether the continuous or alternating current is better for the purpose, or whether any certain quantity or force of electricity will kill the condemned, except as that force or quantity is limited by ability to generate it. Paradoxical as it may seem, both of these positions are professedly based on grounds of mercy and humanity. . . .

. . . it is noteworthy that the questionable chapter became law after much more than ordinary consideration and deliberation. The executive had called the attention of the legislature to the subject of the infliction of the death penalty by hanging, suggesting the question of change, and by an act passed in 1886, and amended in 1887, a commission, consisting of gentlemen of recognized standing, ability, and learning, had been appointed to investigate and report the most humane and practical method known to modern science of carrying into effect the sentence of death in capital cases; and, after having made the subject their special care and study, they made report of their proceedings, and the act whose provisions are now criticised was the outcome of their labors and judgment, and met legislative favor and executive approval. And it is against all this that I am now asked to interpose and hold null that result as counter to the constitution. . . .

Although the phrase "cruel and unusual punishments" has a history of 200 years, it is not an easy task to define it. It was said in *Wilkerson* v. *Utah* . . . that "difficulty would attend the effort to define with exactness the extent of the constitutional provision." Courts have rarely been called upon to construe it. Nor is it now at all needful, in the view which I entertain of the present case, and of my duty in regard to it, to attempt any accurate and comprehensive definition. Beyond doubt, many of the methods used for the infliction of the death penalty in other times and countries would to-day and in our land be held illegal. As among these may be mentioned crucifixion, boiling in water, oil, or lead, blowing from cannon's mouth, burning, breaking on the wheel, dismemberment, burying alive. But not death itself is a cruel and unusual punishment, nor is death by gunshot or by hanging, though there seems to be an element of cruelty inseparable from any taking of human life as punishment for crime; but it is clearly not against this that the constitutional prohibition is directed. It was held by the supreme court of the United States in the *Wilkerson Case* above cited, that a sentence to death by shooting was not illegal in Utah. Death was the penalty for murder at the common law, and of its infliction, Blackstone said: "If upon judgment to be hanged by the neck till he is dead the criminal be not thoroughly killed, but revives, the sheriff must hang him again; for the former hanging was no execution of the sentence. . . .

. . . no question was made as to the legality of death by hanging. That statute but changed the means whereby to produce death. And can it be said that in this case it has been plainly and beyond doubt established that electricity as a death-dealing agent is likely to prove less quick and sure in operation than the rope? I believe not. . . .

INGRAHAM V. WRIGHT*

U.S. Court of Appeals, Fifth Circuit (1974)

RIVES, Senior Circuit Judge:
More than a century ago, a member of the Supreme Court of Indiana made the following observation:

> The husband can no longer moderately chastise his wife; nor, according to the more recent authorities, the master his servant or apprentice. Even the degrading cruelties of the naval service have been arrested. Why the person of the schoolboy, 'with his shining morning face,' should be less sacred in the eye of the law that that of the apprentice or the sailor, is not easily explained. . . .

. . . In the present case, we consider constitutional issues related to corporal punishment in the public school system of Dade County, Florida. . . .

Dade County School Board Policy 5144 expressly authorizes the use of corporal punishment, and prescribes the procedures to be followed where a teacher feels that corporal punishment is necessary. . . . During the 1970–71 school year, Policy 5144 provided, among other things, that the punishment be administered "in kindness and in the presence of another adult" and that "no instrument shall be used that will produce physical injury to the student, and no part of the body above the waist or below the knees may be struck."

The evidence shows that corporal punishment in Dade County during the relevant period consisted primarily, if not entirely, of "paddling." . . . Paddling involves striking the student with a flat wooden instrument . . . usually on the buttocks.

In at least 16 of the 231 Dade County schools, corporal punishment was not utilized in the 1970–71 school year. . . . The evidence suggests that in most of those schools which did use corporal punishment, the punishment was normally limited

*498 F.2d 248

to one or two licks, or sometimes as many as five, with no apparent physical injury to the children who were punished. Quoting from the district court's findings of fact, "The instances of punishment which could be characterized as severe . . . took place in one junior high school." This school was Charles R. Drew Junior High School, and the occurrences there merit description.

The experiences of individual students at Drew reveal the nature of the system of corporal punishment utilized at this educational institution. On October 6, 1970, a number of students, including fourteen-year-old James Ingraham, a named plaintiff, were slow in leaving the stage of the school auditorium when asked to do so by a teacher. A number of boys and girls involved in this incident were taken to the principal's office and paddled. James protested, claiming he was innocent, and refused to be paddled. Willie J. Wright, I, the principal called for the assistance of Lemmie Deliford, the assistant principal in charge of administration, and Solomon Barnes, an assistant to the principal. Barnes and Deliford held James by his arms and legs and placed him, struggling, face down across a table. Wright administered at least twenty licks. . . . After the paddling, Wright told James to wait outside his office—"he said if I move he was going to bust me on the side of my head"— . . . but James went home anyway.

At home, James examined his injuries; according to him, his backside was "black and purple and it was tight and hot." . . . James' mother took him to a local hospital. The examining doctor diagnosed the cause of James' pain to be a "hematoma." "The area of pain was tender and large in size, and . . . the temperature of the skin area of the hematoma was above normal which is a sign of inflammation often associated with hematoma." . . . The doctor prescribed pain pills, a laxative, sleeping pills and ice packs, and advised James to stay at home for at least a week. . . . A different doctor examined James on October 9, when he returned to the hospital for treatment, and on October 14. This doctor described James' injury as follows; "The patient's subjective [sic] signs of injury included a hematoma approximately six inches in diameter which was swollen, tender and purplish in color. Additionally, there was serousness or fluid oozing from the hematoma." . . . On October 14, eight days after the paddling, this doctor indicated that James should rest at home "for next 72 hours." . . . James testified that it was painful even to lie on his back in the days following the paddling, and that he could not sit comfortably for about three weeks. . . .

Roosevelt Andrews, the other named plaintiff, testified that he was paddled about ten times in one year at Drew. . . . He was paddled a number of times by his physical education teachers for being late or for not "dressing out." . . .

On one occasion, a teacher stopped Roosevelt, told him he could not possibly get to his next class in time and then took him to Barnes. Barnes told Roosevelt to go into a bathroom with a number of other boys. Barnes allegedly lined about 15 boys up against the urinals and paddled them. According to Roosevelt, the blows must have hurt, because some of the boys were "hollering, cry, prayed, and everything else" [sic]. . . . After the other boys left, Roosevelt told Barnes that he would have made it to class if the teacher had not stopped him. Barnes told

Roosevelt to bend over. Roosevelt refused. . . . Then, according to Roosevelt, Barnes

'pushed me against the urinate thing, the bowl, and then he snatched me around to it and that's when he hit me first. He first hit me on the backsides and then I stand up and he pushed me against the bathroom wall, them things—that part the bathroom, the wall. . . . Between the toilets, he pushed me against that and then he snatched me from the back there and that's when he hit me on my leg, then hit me on my arm, my back and then right across my neck, in the back here.'

. . . Incensed over his treatment, Roosevelt complained to Wright, but Wright seemed to support Barnes, his co-administrator.

At a later time, Wright paddled Roosevelt, apparently for the breakage of some glasses, in sheet metal class, although Roosevelt claimed it was not his fault. Roosevelt testified that during this paddling, his wrist was hit, and that painful swelling occurred. Roosevelt went to see a doctor about his wrist. The doctor gave him pain pills and advised him to keep something cold on his wrist. For about a week his wrist hurt, and he could not use his arm.

Donald Thomas testified that Barnes carried a paddle with him when he walked around the school and that Deliford carried brass knuckles. . . . Donald further testified to a scheme of punishment used in the auditorium. The seats were numbered and each student had an assigned seat. If a student misbehaved, his number was put on the board. Then Barnes would come into the auditorium and paddle the students whose numbers were listed, without asking who had done what. About five to eight students were paddled every day, generally receiving four or five licks or so each. Donald claimed he was paddled under these circumstances between 5 and 10 times. Another student, Nicky Williams, who was paddled under this system, complained that Barnes would not listen to any explanations.

Daniel Lee, who was paddled "lots of times," . . . at Drew, described how on one occasion Barnes had a number of students "in a line, holding onto the chair, already paddling them," and asked him to come over and "get a little piece of the board." . . . Daniel asked what he had done, and Barnes allegedly grabbed him and tried to throw him on the chair. In the ensuing confusion, Barnes hit Daniel on the hand four or five times. . . . The hand swelled and hurt "and the bone was—it seems like the bone was going to come out" . . . so Daniel's mother took him to the hospital for an X-ray. According to Daniel, a bone in his right hand was fractured. The Court, observing Daniel's hand, stated that "It seems to me to be disfigured, a portion of his right knuckle is enlarged to some degree." Daniel claimed that his hand still hurt, and swelled if he tried to use it.

Reginald Bloom testified that he was paddled at Drew about 15 times. One time Deliford paddled Reginald about fifty licks for allegedly making an obscene phone call to a teacher. Reginald claimed at the time that he had not made the call, and later another boy confessed to making it. Reginald testified on cross-examination that Deliford seemed to be hitting him as hard as he could, and that after the paddling was over, he had to go home because he couldn't sit down. A doctor examined Reginald's buttocks and prescribed ice packs. Reginald found it painful to sit down for about three weeks. Reginald's mother testified that her son's buttocks were "black and blue right across," swollen, and sore. She testified further that she applied ice packs to his buttocks for about three days or more after he was paddled. Another time Reginald and some other boys were called into the principal's office and accused of fighting on the way home from school. When the boys refused to be paddled, Deliford, Barnes and Wright allegedly manhandled one of the boys:

> Mr. Deliford grabbed him and Mr. Barnes and Mr. Deliford started jumping on him, throwing him around the room in the office.

> Then Mr. Wright, he got with Mr. Deliford and Mr. Barnes and started throwing the boy around the room, hitting him, throwing him on the table.

. . . The boy cried out that the men had broken his hand and two weeks later came back to school was a bandage on his hand. Reginald also testified that Barnes paddled boys for chewing gum and for not tucking in their shirttails.

Ray A. Jones and a boy named Carson were brought to the office at Drew by a policeman for "playing hooky." Deliford and Barnes gave each boy about fifty licks, causing both boys to cry. Two girls were present during this punishment and after the boys were paddled, the girls received about five licks each. Ray testified that he was unable to sit comfortably for about two weeks. Ray's grandmother stated that when she looked at Ray's buttocks, she saw "big swollen places."

Rodney Williams testified that because he wanted to wipe some foreign matter off his seat in the auditorium before sitting down, his number was put on the board and Barnes later took him to his office. Because he thought he was innocent, Rodney refused to "hook up." . . . Rodney testified that Barnes then hit him five or ten times on his head and back with a paddle, and then hit him with a belt. The side of Rodney's head swelled, and an operation proved necessary to remove a lump of some sort which had developed where Rodney had been struck. Rodney was out of school for about a week, and felt that the operation affected his memory and thinking. Another time, after Deliford had given him ten licks, Rodney's chest hurt and he threw up "blood and everything". . . . Perhaps because he had asthma and heart trouble of some sort, Rodney also reacted to this paddling by "shaking all over" and "trembling," and required treatment at a local hospital. On a later occasion, a paddling by Wright again caused Rodney to cough up blood. . . .

Larry Jones testifed that physical education teachers at Drew paddled him about ten times and that Deliford paddled him a "heap of times"—about ten. Several times Larry received ten licks. On one occasion, when Larry refused to be paddled, "he [Deliford, or perhaps Barnes] had to start hitting me with that stick, and he put two knots on my head". . . .

Janice Dean testified that, on her first day at Drew, she did not know about assigned seats in the auditorium and sat in the wrong place. As a result, Deliford gave her five licks. Another time, when Janice was sent to the office, Barnes administered fifteen licks, apparently without knowledge of the alleged misconduct, on a theory he allegedly explained as follows: "He said he knew we had done something wrong or we wouldn't have been there." . . .

Preston Sharpe testified that during four years at Drew, Deliford paddled him about ten times. One time Preston was paddled for having his shirttail hanging out. Another time, when he was supposed to receive ten licks, Preston received five extra licks for not reassuming a paddling position quickly enough after one of the licks, and three extra licks for allowing the chair to move and hit a door.

Nathaniel Evans testified that during one year at Drew, he was paddled four times. On one occasion, when the typing class was noisy, Barnes gave each of the fifteen students five licks. Another time, when Barnes was trying to find out who had been whistling, he took a class of 30–50 students and methodically began to paddle each student in an attempt to locate the one who had been whistling. After about half of the class had been paddled, some students told Barnes who had whistled, and the rest of the class was spared. Nathaniel received ten licks on another occasion when his name, along with six others, was written on the board in the auditorium. . . .

. . . Mild or moderate use of corporal punishment as a disciplinary measure in an elementary or secondary school normally will involve only transitory pain of a non-intense nature and will not cause intense or sustained suffering or permanent injury. For this reason, although many might object to corporal punishment for a variety of reasons, such punishment *per se* cannot presently be held to be "excessive" in a constitutional sense, . . . or so "degrading" to the "dignity" of school children as to violate the Eighth Amendment. . . . Although the scope of the Eighth Amendment admittedly is not "static" and must draw its meaning from "evolving standards of decency," *Trop* v. *Dulles* . . . it is significant that a large number of states continue to authorize the use of moderate corporal punishment, . . . and that corporal punishment apparently is still utilized in many school systems. Faced with this evidence of what is apparently considered appropriate by the American people, we would be loath to suggest that at this time corporal punishment is "unacceptable to contemporary society," *Furman* v. *Georgia* . . . or that it is "abhorred" by popular sentiment, *Furman* v. *Georgia*. . . .

Policy 5144 was revised extensively effective November 3, 1971. This revision imposes specific limits on the number of strokes—a maximum of five strokes for elementary school children and a maximum of seven strokes for junior and senior high school children. It requires the use of an instrument "calculated to eliminate possible physical injury." The punishment must be administered "posteriorly," and "under no circumstances shall a student be struck about the head or shoulders." The former provision as to students under psychological or medical treatment is retained. Emphasis upon consideration of the "nature of the misconduct" and the "seriousness of the offense," and the requirement of recording the "infraction of rules which caused the punishment," make it clear that the punishment is not to be inflicted arbitrarily or without cause. This revision is not obnoxious to the Eighth Amendment; it represents an effort to insure through specific guidelines that corporal punishment in Dade County will not go beyond "the moderate use of physical force or physical contact, as may be necessary to maintain discipline and to enforce school order and rules." . . .

From the evidence presented, it appears that Wright, the principal; Deliford, the assistant principal; and Barnes, an assistant to the principal, all agreed either explicitly or implicitly to impose a harsh regime upon the students at Drew. This is dramatically illustrated by their cooperation in administering corporal punishment to James Ingraham. It is further demonstrated by other instances where two or all three administrators were present during paddlings, or were aware of paddlings after they occurred. . . . Considering the evidence as a whole, it would be incredible to find that any one of these three individuals was unaware of the punishment policy pursued by the other two. Thus, the regime at Drew Junior High School was in fact a system of punishment established and imposed by those in authority. . . . The injuries sustained by various students at Drew demonstrate that the punishment meted out at this chool was often severe, and of a nature likely to cause serious physical and psychological damage. . . . The evidence of paddlings for relatively minor offenses, sometimes without any opportunity for the student to explain what happened, show that the punishment was sometimes arbitrary. The frequency of the use of corporal punishment suggests real oppressiveness. . . .

In the present case, children aged twelve through fifteen were punished for alleged misconduct at school. In most instances, this misconduct did not involve physical harm to any other individual or damage to property. Some students claim they never engaged in misconduct at all, but were not given an adequate opportunity to show their innocence or were ignored when they attempted to explain why they did not deserve punishment.

The system of punishment utilized at Drew resulted in a number of relatively serious injuries, and thus clearly involved a significant risk of physical damage to the child. Corporal punishment also creates a risk of psychological damage. Dr. Scott Kester, an assistant professor of educational psychology at the University of Miami, testified that corporal punishment could damage a child's development by engendering anxiety, frustration, and hostility, or by causing sheer pathological withdrawal or hatred of the school environment. He further commented that since children model their behavior after adults, a child who is corporally punished may learn from this that physical force is an appropriate way in which to handle conflicts. Dr. Kester emphasized that the child who is corporally punished often becomes more aggressive and more hostile than he was prior to his punishment. . . .

The evidence shows that corporal punishment is only one of a variety of measures available to school officials to punish students and to correct behavior. As found by the district court, "alternative measures in use range from parent and student conferences, the use of guidance counselors and psychologists, where available, to suspension and expulsion." . . .

Taking into consideration the age of the individuals, the nature of misconduct involved, the risk of physical and psychological damage, and the availability of alternative disciplinary measures, we conclude that the system of punishment at Drew was "excessive" in a constitutional sense. The severity of the paddlings and the system of paddling at Drew, generally, violated the Eighth Amendment requirement that punishment not be greatly disproportionate to the offenses charged. Our review of the evidence has further convinced us that the punishment administered at Drew was degrading to the children at that institution. . . .

*DARRIN V. GOULD**

Supreme Court of Washington (1975)

HOROWITZ, Associate Justice. . . .

The question is whether a school district operating a high school in this state may constitutionally deny two of its fully qualified high school students permission to play on the high school football team in interscholastic competition solely on the ground the students are girls. We hold the denial a prohibited discrimination based on sex. . . .

Carol and Delores Darrin were students at the Wishkah Valley High School in Grays Harbor County, Washington, during the fall of 1973. Carol was then a junior, 16 years of age, 5 feet 6 inches tall, weighing about 170 pounds. Delores was then a freshman, 14 years of age, 5 feet 9 inches tall, weighing about 212 pounds. The girls wished to play contact football. The high school had no girls' contact football team. The school did, however, have a high school football team eligible for interstate competition, all members of the team being boys. The high school football coach found both girls complied with all eligibility requirements and permitted them to play on the team in practice sessions. The girls passed the required physical examinations, met the medical insurance requirements and played the necessary number of practice sessions required by the rules of the Washington Interscholastic Activities Association (WIAA) for football players.

WIAA is an association of approximately 600 high school and junior high schools, comprising most, if not all, the high schools in the state. Through their elected representatives, the member schools have adopted rules and regulations governing sports and other activities. Wishkah Valley School District is a member of the association. Such membership, the court found, "is a practical necessity for any school which desires to participate in interscholastic sports."

*540 P. 2d 882

Just prior to the start of the football season, WIAA informed the football coach that WIAA regulations prohibited girls from participating in interscholastic contact football on boys' teams. For that reason only, the school board of the Wishkah Valley School District prohibited the Darrin girls from playing on the high school team. Indeed, the court found:

> According to their coach, both of the girls have in general been able to hold their own with the boys in practice sessions and would be allowed to play in interscholastic contests were it not for the W.I.A.A. regulation. . . .

Two basic questions arise:

> (1) Does the denial of permission to the Darrin girls to play on the boys' high school football team in interscholastic competition constitute a discrimination by state action based on sex per se or is the denial based on inability to play?
>
> (2) If the denial is a discrimination based on sex per se is it prohibited by law, constitutional, statutory, or both? . . .

In *Commonwealth* v. *Pennsylvania Interscholastic Athletic Ass'n.* . . . decided March 19, 1975, the court held invalid, as violative of Pennsylvania's ERA, the following bylaw of the Pennsylvania Interscholastic Athletic Association (PIAA):

> Girls shall not compete or practice against boys in any athletic contest.

PIAA is a voluntary unincorporated association whose members include every public senior high school in the Commonwealth, except for those in Philadelphia, some public junior high schools and some private schools. PIAA regulates interscholastic competition in some 17 sports including football. The court explained:

> There is no fundamental right to engage in interscholastic sports, but once the state decides to permit such participation, it must do so on a basis which does not discriminate in violation of the constitution.

The court refused to uphold the challenged bylaw on the basis that

> men generally possess a higher degree of athletic ability in the traditional sports offered by most schools and that because of this, girls are given greater opportunities for participation if they compete exclusively with members of their own sex.

The court stated:

> This attempted justification can obviously have no validity with respect to those sports for which only one team exists in a school and that team's membership is limited exclusively to boys. Presently a girl who wants to compete interscholastically in that sport is given absolutely no opportunity to do so under the challenged By-Law. Although she might be sufficiently skilled to earn a position on the team, she is presently denied that position solely because of her sex. Moreover, even

where separate teams are offered for boys and girls in the same sport, the most talented girls still may be denied the right to play at that level of competition which their ability might otherwise permit them. For a girl in that position, who has been relegated to the "girls' team," solely because of her sex, "equality under the law" has been denied.

Continuing, the court said:

> The notion that girls as a whole are weaker and thus more injury-prone, if they compete with boys, especially in contact sports, cannot justify the By-Law in light of the ERA. Nor can we consider the argument that boys are generally more skilled. *The existence of certain characteristics to a greater degree in one sex does not justify classification by sex rather than by the particular characteristic.* Wiegand v. Wiegand. . . . If any individual girl is too weak, injury-prone, or unskilled, she may, of course, be excluded from competition on that basis but she cannot be excluded solely because of her sex without regard to her relevant qualifications. We believe that this is what our Supreme Court meant when it said in . . . *Commonwealth* v. *Butler*, . . . that "sex may no longer by accepted as an exclusive classifying tool." . . .

The justification claimed for the challenged regulation is the *majority* of girls are "unable to compete with boys in contact football, and the potential risk of injury is great." . . . Furthermore, "allowing of girls to compete in contact sports with boys will result in boys competing on girls' teams resulting in disruption to the girls' athletic programs"; that therefore the challenged WIAA regulation "is reasonably calculated to accomplish a rational purpose." . . . There is no finding that what may be true for the majority of girls is true in the case of the Darrin girls . . . or girls like them. As for the risk of injury to the "average girl" the court found "the breasts could be adequately protected with proper equipment not currently available, and serious injury to the procreative organs is not a very substantial risk."[1] . . .

Boys as well as girls run the risk of physical injury in contact football games. The risk of injury to "the average boy" is not used as a reason for denying boys the opportunity to play on the team in interscholastic competition. Moreover, the fact that some boys cannot meet the team requirements is not used as a basis of disqualifying those boys that do meet such requirements. Instead, WIAA expressly permitted small, slightly built young boys, prone to injury, to play football without proper training to prevent injury. The very day the Darrin girls were denied permission to play, WIAA gave Wishkah Valley High School permission to permit one unqualified high school boy to play on its football team. No similar privilege was given to high school girls like the Darrin girls who, but for the fact they were girls, met the team requirements. Finding No. 6 . . . as to the ability to play of the "majority of

[1] In May 26, 1975 issue of TIME, it is stated at 41:
"Meanwhile *womenSports*, a new monthly dedicated to female athletics, reports that no fewer than seven women's pro football teams are now on the gridiron."

girls" or "average girl" is just as irrelevant as would a similar finding concerning the majority of boys or the "average boy" . . . in determining individual qualifications. . . .

Findings Nos. 9 and 10 dealing with the possible disruption of the girls' athletic programs if girls are permitted to play on boys contact football teams in interscholastic competition is based on opinion testimony necessarily conjectural in character as to what might happen. There is no such evidence based on experience of Wishkah Valley High School because that school has never had any girls contact football team. . . . Furthermore, the possibility of disruption has not prevented WIAA from approving boy-girl participation in noncontact sports. "[W]here there are mutual interests and comparative abilities," WIAA permits "girls and boys [to] compete with or against each other." . . . The opinion evidence on which defendants rely is the kind of evidence that has been elsewhere rejected as insufficient to validate sex discrimination in school athletic competition involving boys and girls. *Brenden* v. *Independent School Dist. No. 742. . . . Haas* v. *South Bend Community School Corp. . . .* Such conjectural evidence suffers from the infirmities of scintilla evidence which is insufficient to support a finding. . . .

. . . The WIAA rule forbidding qualified girls from playing on the high school football team in interscholastic competition cannot be used to deny the Darrin girls, and girls like them, the right to participate as members of that team. This is all the more so when the school provides no corresponding girls' football team on which girls may participate as players. . . .

MURGIA V. *COMMONWEALTH OF MASSACHUSETTS BOARD OF RETIREMENT**

U.S. District Court for the District of Massachusetts (1974)

ALDRICH, Senior Circuit Judge.

. . . plaintiff, a Lt. Colonel in the Uniformed Branch of the Massachusetts State Police, was involuntarily retired because, having completed over 20 years of service, he had reached age 50. He alleges that mandatory retirement at that age is a violation of his civil rights of due process and equal protection. He also alleges sex discrimination because under the law, although apparently not now in practice, women police officers may enlist after age 30, and thus automatically may serve beyond age 50. . . . We reach only one issue, that a classification based on age 50 alone lacks a rational basis in furthering any substantial state interest.

*376 F. Supp. 753

Until age 40 every officer is given a comprehensive physical examination every two years, and after age 40, every year. Failure to pass results in disability retirement unless the particular physical defect is waived by the Commissioner of Public Safety. . . . Plaintiff's standing is self-evident; the testimony is undisputed that at the time of his discharge he was in excellent physical health and capable of performing the duties of a state police officer, whether involving physical or psychological stress. At the same time, it is acknowledged that service in this branch is, or can be, arduous, . . . and that high versatility is required, with few, if any, backwaters available for the partially superannuated. Lest there be misunderstanding, we do not fault the service in this respect; the state is entitled to maintain rigorous job requirements; nor do we understand plaintiff to contend otherwise.

We dispose readily of certain of the state's contentions. Its argument that early retirement enhances the morale of the younger members, in a sense assumes the point. Of course, if there are only younger members, they are happier than the older members who are being eliminated. This does not add up on balance, but merely advances the time of ultimate unhappiness. . . . The same can be said with respect to the alleged desirability of rapid promotion; the attractiveness of quick promotion must be weighed against the unattractiveness of early retirement. Furthermore, to the extent that the purpose of early retirement is said to be to empty higher ranking positions after they have been occupied by one person for a reasonable time, the cut-off at 50 years is of questionable consequence since it is unrelated to the period of time the retiree has occupied his last position. . . . The alleged desirability of facilitating rapid promotion by early retirement, rather than a justification, will be seen on analysis to be age discrimination per se.

The only question requiring serious consideration is whether mandatory retirement at age 50 is rationally related to maintaining a vigorous, healthy personnel. Even plaintiff's experts concede that there is a general relationship between advancing age and decreasing physical ability to respond to the demands of the job. On the other hand, the state does not dispute their testimony that the relation between chronological age and functional age varies greatly from one individual to the next. Its response is that in matters of this sort it is administratively reasonable to select an arbitrary cut-off, and that irrationality is not established by the fact that certain individuals are disadvantaged thereby. . . .

We fully accept the necessity of choosing arbitrary standards in certain, and indeed in many, situations. For example, in dealing with the immeasurable changes relating to the onset of maturity, legislatures may require a specific age for voting, *Oregon* v. *Mitchell* . . . even though the particular age selected may seem indifferentiable from other ages in proximity to it. . . . *See also, e.g., United States* v. *Duncan* . . . (minimum age for jury service) . . . *Smith* v. *United States* . . . (selective service age limitations); *Scarangella* v. *Commissioner of Internal Revenue* . . . (classification of tax exemptions by age of dependent). But to say that a line may be drawn arbitrarily when there is no readily discernible breaking, or turning point, does not mean that the line can be drawn anywhere at all. To satisfy minimal standards of rationality the line must be drawn within a range where fairness, or some appreciable state interest, exists, even if no specific point within that range is preferable to any other.

In the voting and other cases above cited, the legislature was concerned with a broad spectrum of the population where it would not be practicable to make individual determinations. Under such circumstances an arbitrary standard is called for, if not inevitable, and the only question must be whether the one selected is, in the large, reasonable. In the case at bar the situation is exactly the reverse. Individual testing is not impracticable but, rather, is already the order of the day. There is no suggestion that it is more burdensome to examine an officer at age 50 than it was at age 49. We must look, therefore, in another direction for reasonableness—is there, for example, a greater risk at the higher age that the test, or, more exactly, the prognosis based upon testing, will be less reliable?

In this connection we note the case of *Air Line Pilots Ass'n, Int'l* v. *Quesada* . . . upholding as not "arbitrary and discriminatory and without relation to any requirement of safety" an administrative ruling disqualifying pilots from active duty upon reaching age 60. In so doing the court pointed out the comprehensive study conducted by the administrator, and the documented reasons for his conclusion that by age 60, in spite of medical testing, a critical area had been reached. . . . No such determination has been, or could be made, in the case at bar. So far as appears, no study has been conducted of any kind. While there has been a compilation of certain statistics, from defendants' standpoint they are counter-productive. Not only did no expert testify to any significance in age 50 in a group which, by hypothesis, had individually passed annual tests during the preceding decade, but statistics of actual experience forecast no imminent change. In the Uniformed Branch during the period November 1967 to December 1973 there were fifteen discharges of persons between the ages of 40 and 50 for non-injury disability, divided as follows.

Age 40–3	Age 45–1
41–3	46–3
42–1	47–2
43–1	48–1
44–0	49–0
8	7

The force of these figures is not offset by a growth curve of waivers in the place of disability retirements.[1] The statistics furnish no reason to suppose that age 50 is within, or even significantly approaching, a range where changes of conditions warrant a change of treatment. Rather, they contradict it. . . .

[1]Thus in the year 1973, ten waivers of partial, although permanent, non-injury disability were granted in the 40–50 age group. These divided as follows.

If, further, we turn from Massachusetts to national experience as disclosed by legislative response, plaintiff has furnished a list of statutes from which it appears that Massachusetts is the only state compulsorily retiring police officers before age 55.

On this record we find that mandatory retirement at age 50, where individualized medical screening is not only available but already required, is no more rational, and no more related to a protectable state interest, than the mandatory suspension or discharge of school teachers upon reaching their fourth or fifth month of pregnancy ... *Cleveland Board of Education* v. *LaFleur*. . . .

. . . Recognizing the public interest in protecting individuals' right to work, and against discrimination on account of age . . . we are compelled to strike down the present age distinction where plaintiff has established the absence of any factual basis therefor.[2] . . .

Age 40–0	Age 45–2
41–2	46–0
42–1	47–0
43–1	48–2
44–<u>2</u>	49–<u>0</u>
6	4

[2]Whether we would reach the same result if the statute selected a more customary retirement age is not before us. With great respect to Mr. Justice Rehnquist, dissenting in Cleveland Board of Education v. LaFleur, ante, we would anticipate the question of mandatory retirement at age 70 not to be the same as at age 50, but perhaps we say this because of the increasing difficulties that a plaintiff might have to show that at that greater age the state had not made out a factually rational argument.

GLOSSARY

acquittal: release from burden or charge
ad litem: for purposes of the law suit
amicus curiae: a "friend of the court"; a party interested but not involved in the case who offers advice to the judges in the form of a legal brief
appellant: one who brings a complaint to this court
appellee: one who must answer a complaint in this court
arms-length transactions: nonfiduciary transactions
aver: to declare
battery: wrongful physical violence or constraint inflicted on a human being without his or her consent
brief: an attorney's written argument concerning a case
canon law: the law handed down by church governing bodies
cause of action: ground for legal action
claimant: one who brings a complaint to this court
common law: the ancient, unwritten law of England, as reflected in court decisions rather than legislation
consistory court: a court of English bishops
counsel: attorney
court of equity: courts seeking fairness without appeal to strictly formulated rules
decedent: dead person
declaratory judgment: a court's statement of a party's rights and status
defendant: one who must answer a complaint in this court
directed verdict: a verdict which the judge tells the jury they must give in light of the evidence

dismissal: a court's refusal to grant a trial

enjoin: order or prohibit

fiduciary: based on trust

injunction: prohibition

in re: in the matter of; concerning

jurisprudence: the philosophy or study of law

litigation: a law suit

material risk: a risk of significant consequence

parens patriae: "parent of the country"; the role of the government in caring for its
   people

per curiam: opinion of the whole court, as distinct from that of a single judge

petitioner: one who brings a complaint to this court

plaintiff: one who brings a complaint to this court

pleading: formal allegation

prima facie: on the face of it

probate court: a court of wills, estates, and guardianship

proximate cause: the ruling cause

remand: send back

respondent: one who must answer a complaint in this court

reverse: revoke

scintilla: a spark; a least particle

statute: a legislative act or law

supra: above

tort: an injury or wrong for which compensation is sought; a wrong which is not strictly a
   matter of contract or criminal law violation

tort-feasor: a wrong-doer; one who commits a tort

trial court: the first court to face the law suit

writ of habeas corpus: an order that a person be brought before a court so that the
   restraint of his liberty might be reviewed

writ of mandamus: an order to a lower authority to act in accordance with some official
   duty